I0109387

Thiago Lima, Agostina Costantino (eds.)

Food Security and International Relations

Critical Perspectives From the Global South

CRITICAL STUDIES ON LATIN AMERICA
DEBATES AND ALTERNATIVES FOR SOCIAL CHANGE

Edited by Mariano Féliz

1   *Thiago Lima and Agostina Costantino (eds.)*
        Food Security and International Relations
        Critical Perspectives From the Global South
        ISBN 978-3-8382-1481-8

Thiago Lima, Agostina Costantino (eds.)

FOOD SECURITY AND
INTERNATIONAL RELATIONS

Critical Perspectives From the Global South

Editora
UFPB

ibidem
Verlag

Bibliographic information published by the Deutsche Nationalbibliothek
Die Deutsche Nationalbibliothek lists this publication in the Deutsche
Nationalbibliografie; detailed bibliographic data are available in the Internet at
http://dnb.d-nb.de.

Bibliografische Information der Deutschen Nationalbibliothek
Die Deutsche Nationalbibliothek verzeichnet diese Publikation in der Deutschen Nationalbibliografie;
detaillierte bibliografische Daten sind im Internet über http://dnb.d-nb.de abrufbar.

EU Editora
UFPB

ISBN-13: 978-3-8382-1481-8

© *ibidem*-Verlag, Stuttgart 2021

All rights reserved.

No part of this publication may be reproduced, stored in or introduced into a retrieval
system, or transmitted, in any form, or by any means (electronical, mechanical,
photocopying, recording or otherwise) without the prior written permission of the
publisher. Any person who does any unauthorized act in relation to this publication may
be liable to criminal prosecution and civil claims for damages.

Alle Rechte vorbehalten. Das Werk einschließlich aller seiner Teile ist urheberrechtlich geschützt. Jede Verwertung
außerhalb der engen Grenzen des Urheberrechtsgesetzes ist ohne Zustimmung des Verlages unzulässig und strafbar. Dies
gilt insbesondere für Vervielfältigungen, Übersetzungen, Mikroverfilmungen und elektronische Speicherformen sowie
die Einspeicherung und Verarbeitung in elektronischen Systemen.

Printed in the United States of America

About the Book series

'Critical Studies on Latin America.
Debates and Alternatives for Social Change'

This book series promotes the production and spread of original knowledge on Latin America from critical perspectives, mainly from the point of view of scholars working in Latin American setting. It includes analyses across all social science disciplines with an emphasis on the political economy, anthropology, and sociology.

While there is no shortage of critical research on Latin America, most studies tend to be produced by institutions and scholars from the Global North. Since the social context of production of knowledge is a key issue, we believe there is a need for Latin American scholars to be able to reach a wider audience. This will provide the global academic community of Latin American studies with a new, fresh perspective that is so far lacking, helping little known but highly relevant debates and researchers reach an international audience.

While books in the series may include contributions by non-Latin America based scholars, the series' main purpose is to provide rigorous research from scholars working in Latin American institutions.

Table of Contents

CHAPTER 1—INTRODUCTION. Food, Human Security and International Relations: Relations of Humanity?

Thiago Lima (UFPB); Agostina Costantino (IIESS, UNS-CONICET); Laís Forti Thomaz (UFG); Raquel Maria de Almeida Rocha (USP)

1 Introduction

The present Era on Earth has been named the Anthropocene. This era began in the late eighteenth century, when the industrial revolution, advances in agriculture and medicinal innovations allowed humanity to act and live on a scale that was entirely different from earlier eras. Producing and Reproducing[1]. The number of human beings has grown dramatically over the last two centuries; plotted on a Cartesian graph, it has been a veritable rocket launch. For this dizzying explosion of the species to occur, the amount of food produced also had to increase. We now know that there is an excess—rather than a lack—of food for humanity. The issue is how to distribute this food and which criteria should be used (ZIEGLER, 2013).

The Anthropocene means—nothing more, nothing less—that humanity is now able to affect the geophysical functioning of planet Earth. The magnitude of this is truly remarkable. Humanity's activities became so powerful that they unwittingly changed the climate of the globe. For those of us alive now, we are in a somewhat different situation, as we understand what is happening. It is distressing to realize that we may be forced to live with the consequences of our ancestors' decisions. It is reassuring, however, to think that something can be done to mitigate the consequences for the people still to come.

---

1   This reflection is based on DANOWSKI, D. and CASTRO, E. V. **Há mundo por vir? Ensaio sobre os medos e os fins**. Florianópolis, Instituto Socioambiental, 2014.

The concept of the Anthropocene did not arrive with a sense of celebration. It is not an award recognizing the progress of humanity. Rather, it is a warning that humanity may have produced and reproduced to such an extent that it unleashed factors capable of leading, if not to the end of the world, then at least to extremely serious ecological cataclysms that are likely to intensify conflicts around the world.

Conflict. A word that reminds us that the idea of "one Humanity" is—still?—illusory. Most of the social sciences were developed to address a fact inherent to the human being: people are divided into groups that conflict with one another. However, the groups themselves are a sign that conflict is not a solitary dynamic: it is possible to cooperate and to offer solidarity. But on what scale? Among nations? With our fellow citizens?

To think about the possibilities of cooperation and solidarity for the elimination of hunger, it is essential to refer to the report on "The State of Food Security and Nutrition in the World," organized annually by the Food and Agriculture Organization (FAO) of the United Nations (UN). The FAO (2018) indicates that over the last three years, the absolute number of undernourished people has increased to 821 million, or approximately 11% of the world's population. After several years of decline, the number is similar to that in 2010. However, if we go back to 2005, there were 945 million people facing chronic food shortages. The absolute number of undernourished people has thus been falling, but very slowly given the urgency of the problem, and unfortunately, this decline is not irreversible.

The global distribution of hunger is quite heterogeneous. The problem was virtually eliminated in North America and Europe, where it is reported that less than 2.5% of the population was experiencing hunger in 2017. In other regions, the scenario was as follows: Africa, 20.4%; Asia, 11.4%; Latin America and the Caribbean, 6.1%; and Oceania, 7%. Although the percentage of people in the world who are experiencing hunger has steadily declined in recent decades, we cannot overlook the fact that this rate has increased in recent years in all subregions of Africa, as well as parts of Asia, Oceania and South America. The intensification of social inequality in the United States may exacerbate the situation there. This reminds us once again that progress—which is being made extremely slowly—is not irreversible.

The leading causes of hunger today are adverse weather events, the prevalence of armed conflict and economic crises (FAO, 2018). Although there are some exceptions in the case of the first cause, the latter two are undoubtedly the result of human action. However, if we adopt the perspective of Amartya Sen (2008), even though not all hunger has human causes, it is possible to argue that since the mid-twentieth century, all hunger has been allowed by humans. In other words, if there is food and the technical means to deliver it to the hungry, there are only undernourished people because there is no policy for providing those people with food.

Politics and economics converge on this point: while economic growth is important, it does not guarantee any reduction in hunger, at least not on the possible scale. The intensifying concentration of wealth around the world, given the continued persistence of millions of hungry families, demonstrates that economic interests are not guided by humanity. In Brazil, 71 million people held 50% of the national income in 2015, while 1.4 million accounted for 28% of the country's wealth. The government failed to regulate that distribution and protect the country from the threat of returning to the Hunger Map in 2018. The number of people in extreme poverty in Brazil jumped from approximately 5.1 million in 2014 to approximately 10 million in 2016, and there is no reason to expect any improvement (RBA, 2018; G1, 2018). For our neighbor, Argentina, undernourishment and food exports have grown alongside each other in recent years, as analyzed by Costantino in Chapter 6.

The problem of food and nourishment no longer refers only to the lack of food. Undernourishment has become an increasingly notable problem on an international level. Strongly present in a number of developed countries, particularly in the US, a diet that leads to people becoming obese is spreading around the globe. Josué de Castro noted halfway through the last century that a large percentage of the poor suffered from hidden hunger, i.e., they were able to fill their stomachs, but they still lacked nutrients. The problem is now taking on another dimension: stomachs are becoming too full, leading to obesity and a host of nutritional disorders. There are currently 38.3 million overweight children in the world: 46% of them are in Asia, and 25% are in Africa. While childhood obesity has remained stable since 2012, adult obesity has increased since 1975. Today, 672 million people worldwide are obese (FAO, 2018). What many people still overlook is that our diets are not simply related to flavor and tradition. They are also the result of international dynamics driven by geopolitical factors, the trajectory of capitalism or other forces.

In the field of international relations, the issue of hunger still lacks prominence. Fortunately, the human security approach has helped bring it to the forefront, reverberating into discussions about rights, public policy and economic arrangements. The human security approach helps make it possible to understand the concept of food security. We will now take a critical look at this topic and the need for a multidimensional analysis of agrifood, as presented in the chapters of this collection.

2   Human Security: people first

The human security approach has a controversial origin. The international relations literature generally locates it within the debate on the expansion of international security studies, with an emphasis on the post-Cold War scenario. It originates, however, in debates among developmental economists. They thought about the humanization of the economy through the concerns raised by new threats to individuals (ROCHA, 2017). Some authors claim that human security was almost exclusively a contribution of the UN, while others argue that the organization was the birthplace of only some of the key insights (OWEN, 2008; MACFARLANE, KHONG, 2006).

In any case, the topic of human security emerges as both an instrument for advocacy and an intellectual device calling for the unification of protection, welfare and rights concerns inherent to individuals. At its core is the guarantee of "social security" (TADJBAKHSH, 2005). There is an attempt to identify threats and ways to mitigate them, focusing on the protection of people and communities, rather than the security of states, thus emphasizing the importance of human rights (KALDOR, 2007). People should be protected regardless of whether threats come from anthropogenic activities or natural events, whether they are within or outside the state, or whether they are direct or structural (THAKUR, 2004). For Thakur (2004), although this approach results in the loss of a certain analytical rigor, it is more important to be inclusive when defining threats (THAKUR, 2004)[2].

At the same time, poverty, natural disasters and epidemics are now being discussed as threats to international security itself, which ends up broadly influencing the debate on development and security, particularly as they are vocalized through the UN (ROCHA, 2017). In Brazil, for example, the threat of hunger is considered through the internalization of the human right to adequate food (HRAF) (LOPES, FEITOSA, Ch. 2).

Human security as a policy approach is defined for the first time in the 1994 Human Development Report (HDR) by the United Nations Development Program (UNDP) (UNDP, 1994). The term, however, had previously been used in the 1992 report, *An Agenda for Peace*, as well as being cited five times in the 1993 HDR, emphasizing the need for a "people-centered development" (UNDP, 1993)[3]. However, the 1994 HDR was responsible for making the idea more widespread. It sought to influence the debate, as well as international cooperation, on development and security actions among member states and other UN institutions. The report states that:

> Human security can be said to have two main aspects. It means, first, safety from such chronic threats as hunger, disease and repression. And second, it means protection from sudden and hurtful disruptions in the patterns of daily life—whether in homes, in jobs or in communities. Such threats can exist at all levels of national income and development. (UNDP, 1994, p. 23)

---

2   A narrower approach focuses on the human consequences of armed conflict and the dangers they present to individuals—primarily civilians—by repressive governments and situations of state failure. This approach has a greater influence on the security agenda and focuses on threats to physical integrity rather than incorporating issues related to human development and empowerment, as in the earlier approach. Modern conflicts reflect a high level of civil wars and state collapse, resulting in a high rate of civilian victimization and displacement, particularly for women and children (EVANS, 2004; KRAUSE, 2004; MACFARLANE & KHONG, 2006)

3   The HDR tracks and monitors the progress of humanity and ranks countries with its Human Development Index (HDI). The UNDP also produces Regional Reports, which propose actions that would enable each country to achieve human development (UNDP, 2015; UL HAQ, 1995).

The Report also states that there should be two components for understanding human security: (i) freedom from fear—freedom from threats that impede access to people's rights, security and guarantees to life; it is thus essential to be free from the fear of physical violence and fear more broadly; and (ii) freedom from want—individuals free from poverty, for example, through stable access to healthcare and the economy.

All the reports since 1990 have been based on the premise that a nation's wealth is its people and that it is necessary to broaden the possibilities for their personal fulfillment, rather than solely in terms of the nation's productivity. This premise is influenced by the conception of broadening the substantive freedoms of individuals (Sen, 2008). In other words, while an increase in income or GDP enables people to expand their freedoms as citizens, having access to healthcare, education or civil and political rights and freedom of expression, for example, are other determinants of freedoms that are equally important to human development. This means that human security can be underpinned by human development.

The HDR also establishes seven pillars for human security: (i) economic security: sufficient remuneration from labor activity or social welfare to guarantee the survival of the individual and their family; (ii) food security: guarantee of both economic and physical access to a basic diet that supplies the minimum daily intake of nutrients required by the individual; (iii) health security: guarantee to an environment free of chronic diseases and the availability of medical care; (iv) environmental security: absence of threats of environmental origin, as well as guarantees to drinking water, clean air and clean rivers, among others; (v) personal security: absence of bodily threats from physical violence, which may be political, ethnic, street, domestic, gender, child abuse, suicide or war, among others; (vi) community security: security guaranteed to people who are part of an ethnic group, for example; and (vii) political security: guarantee to fundamental human rights, such as freedom of political expression (UNDP, 1994). The Report demonstrates that human security should be a universal concern. Its components are interdependent, and the easiest way to guarantee it is through prevention.

The 1995 World Summit for Social Development in Copenhagen, however, did not adopt human security. States were skeptical, believing that the idea would lead to violations of state sovereignty. The most concrete step towards human security only occurs in 1997, with the signing of the Ottawa Convention, followed by the Rome Statute in 1998[4]. The Convention prohibits the use, stockpiling, production and transfer of anti-personnel landmines and requires their destruction (ACA, 2018), while the Statute creates the International Criminal Court (ICC), the first international court that judges individuals rather than states, i.e., the international community's first attempt to construct a punishment mechanism for individuals who commit crimes against humanity, in cases where the national court system is reluctant or unable to prosecute (ROCHA, 2011).

In 2000, at the initiative of Japan, the United Nations Human Security Fund (UNHSF) was created, which

> (..) [finances] projects related to peacebuilding, post-conflict restoration, and approaches to chronic poverty, disaster risk reduction, human trafficking and food security, seeking to translate them into operational activities that offer sustainable benefits to people and communities whose survival, dignity and livelihood are threatened as well as empower individuals to increase their resilience (ROCHA, 2017, p. 108).

Empowerment was included in the HDR as early as 1993, in the discussion on human development. This demonstrates that individual autonomy is essential to the state and the markets, not only for accessing civil and social rights but also because development is intended to help and support people, enabling them to have control over their own lives, whether it is within the context of physical or food security, for example.

---

4   Both instruments of international law were made possible by the Canadian-led coalition and the advocacy efforts of the Human Security Network (HRH), comprising Austria, Canada, Chile, Costa Rica, Greece, Ireland, Jordan, Mali, the Netherlands, Norway, Switzerland, Slovenia and Thailand, with South Africa as an observer. Japan was invited but declined to participate due to the emphasis on humanitarian intervention and the constitutional restriction on using force without authorization from the UN Security Council (TAKASU, 2015).

The UNHSF became operational with the approval of Resolution 66/290 by the UN General Assembly, which recognizes that human security has three pillars: development, human rights and peace and security. This is the most emblematic resolution in terms of human security. In addition to asking member states to use the approach, it defines human security in practical terms, to be applied across the UN system. It also alters the functioning of the UN system, as it was very difficult for the agencies to find ways to understand how human security should be incorporated into everyday life.

3   Food: threat, right and food sovereignty

As we have seen, food security is part of the human security approach. However, the FAO, which discusses the evolution of food security as an operational concept in public policy, indicates that over two hundred definitions have emerged since the 1970s. Since 2001, the official definition has been:

> Food security [is] a situation that exists when all people, at all times, have physical, social and economic access to sufficient, safe and nutritious food that meets their dietary needs and food preferences for an active and healthy life (FAO, 2003).

Burke and Lobell (2010, p.14) highlight the three components of the concept, in a conventional view: (1) food availability; (2) food accessibility; and (3) food utilization. Availability refers to the physical presence of food; accessibility refers to having the means to acquire food through production or purchase; and utilization refers to the food having an adequate nutritional content and to the body's ability to use it effectively.

However, other interpretations are more comprehensive. Treating food security as a right, Leão and Maluf (2012, p.7) characterize the right to food as a form of regular and permanent access to adequate food for all people, giving attention to the conditions under which it is produced and marketed. The authors explain that this right must be achieved without compromising other rights, such as housing, healthcare, education, income, environment, work, transportation, employment, leisure, freedom and land access and possession.

The divergence noted here is not trivial. It signals a clash of ideas that ultimately reverberates into domestic and international public policies. For example, in the streamlined view of Burke and Lobel (2010), there is no emphasis on the local specificities of food production and trade, which is present in Leão and Maluf (2012). We will not include a conceptual discussion in this introduction, as it can be found in the chapters. For example, in the chapter by Costantino, it is clear that the former view can coexist with increased undernourishment in Argentina, which would be unthinkable for the latter.

From the perspective of human security, food security is a foundation for peace, political stability and sustainability, as structural peace can only be achieved if there is food security. Food insecurity is thus a threat to people and the international system. It is even possible to state that we are not secure if we do not have guarantees to buy food nor the freedom to grow and store it.

It is also essential to understand that conflict damages crop cultivation, animal husbandry and harvesting. It also damages rural resources and disrupts food transportation and distribution systems. The impact that conflicts have on food security can last for long periods of time after the violence has ended; although destruction happens quickly, reconstruction requires time, effort and material, and human and financial resources.

McMichael (2004, p. 4) offers a distinction between the concepts of food security and food sovereignty. He argues that the concept of food security is better associated with the relationship between the nation-state and the international system. In turn, the concept of food sovereignty involves nonstate actors, which would be more closely tied to the political and economic rights of agricultural producers as a precondition for achieving food security. In a way, what McMichael (2004) argues is that each of these concepts represents a type of agricultural production, i.e., food security depends on the agribusiness model, and food sovereignty is based on agroecological relations.

For McMichael (2004), food sovereignty thus emerges as an alternative principle to productivist and quantitative measures of food security, which would be identified with monetary transactions in the capitalist system. Food sovereignty would be premised on an agriculture oriented towards the farmer, small producer and family farm, which for the author would be key to the relationships between environmental and social security and food security. It is important to understand the argument that food sovereignty should be a premise of food security, rather than its antithesis, as McMichael (2004) emphasizes.

To guarantee the food independence and sovereignty of all people, according to La Via Campesina (2001), food must be produced through diversified systems. The organization argues that people have the right to define their own agricultural and food policies, as well as protect and regulate agricultural production and domestic trade in order to achieve sustainability goals, and determine the extent to which they want to be self-sufficient and restrict product dumping on their markets. This requires trade policies and practices that serve people's rights to safe, healthy and ecologically sustainable production. The protectionist policies adopted primarily by developed countries make it difficult to act on a level playing field in commodities markets. However, there may be a need for protection precisely from the destructive potential of the international commodities market. The idea of food sovereignty therefore implies that communities have the autonomy to decide how to distribute and sell their food.

High commodities prices in 2007/2008 were emblematic of food insecurity caused by jolts in the international market. Ziegler (apud CHADE, 2009, p. 11), a former UN rapporteur on the right to food, emphasized that "in 2008, hunger killed more people than all the wars combined that year." Chade (2009) argues that the World Bank, the International Monetary Fund (IMF) and the UN itself stopped giving aid to small farmers in poor countries for approximately twenty years, which exacerbated problems when commodities prices increased. In truth, rather than abandonment, it may be possible to talk about a project making food sovereignty more vulnerable.

The idea of food sovereignty advocates for people's right to healthy and culturally appropriate food, produced ecologically and sustainably, while valuing the role of women. It implies that a community is able to define its own nutrition and agrifood systems, i.e., the effective right to choose what we should eat, where the food comes from and how it should be grown. However, it is important to avoid adopting a romantic approach to food sovereignty, which could hinder an open and creative reflection on the systemic challenges of eliminating hunger worldwide.

4 Agrifood relations: from a local to global capitalist system

Taking food as the central axis of human relations, the chapters in this collection raise and refocus the question of how to feed people in a world divided into nations, states and social classes. Indeed, one dimension common to all the texts is the international theme. This does not mean, however, that the analysis is restricted to the level of state relations. In contrast, the authors in this collection acknowledge that to address the topic of food, it is essential to remember that the biological constitution of the human being tethers us to the need to harvest from nature and eat in order to produce and reproduce. Every single day. How this occurs, however, is socially constructed, from relationships between neighbors to interactions among nations. Each chapter in this collection offers its own vision of how socially constructed aspects affect food and nourishment, never letting us forget that everything could be different. By identifying actors and examining relations, institutions and structures, we come to understand that agrifood relations are always in motion. Few would doubt that there is creative potential for devising a solution to food and nutrition insecurity. The challenge, however, is developing a solution that is politically achievable from the local to the global levels, passing through the international level.

The objective of this book is therefore to deepen the connection between international relations and food. While the texts share a common axis, the angle changes according to the chapters, giving the reader the opportunity to explore the subject through political economy, political science, law and international relations. The contents of the book's chapters are divided into three groups: i) the humanitarian and ethical importance of solving the problem of hunger; ii) the strategic relevance for states of achieving food security, including via food sovereignty; and iii) the nature of the food security problem in a world where production and distribution are guided by the rationalism of capitalism.

In this sense, the chapter of Praveen Jha, Santosh Verma, Manish Kumar is a great opportunity to start with the analytical chapters of the book, since it covers these dimensions. The authors relate the beginning and deepening of neoliberalism in India with the serious food problems that seem to be getting worse and worse in this country. In fact, they mention that the characteristics that development has had since the neoliberal stage in India have strongly affected the supply of adequate food for the population. Moreover, all this took place while the country lived a stage of strong GDP growth. The drivers the authors mention to explain this are: the orientation of production to exports, the focalization of food distribution policies, the decline in income of the rural and urban population, the expulsion of peasants from the land, the cutback of public expenditures in the agricultural sector.

Dialoguing with the issues mentioned earlier, Ana Carolina Oliveira and Maria Luiza Feitosa emphasize the importance of considering food to be a human right as well as the importance of public policies for achieving this right. The authors highlight the role that states should play in guaranteeing the right to food, which does not imply only secure access to food according to cultural guidelines but also individual emancipation and autonomy in the consumption and production of food. The authors thus contribute to the discussion of human security, as they consider food sovereignty to be a matter that goes beyond food security, rather than the reverse.

Note that the solution poses a challenge to the idea of "one Humanity": dividing in an attempt to achieve solidarity? That is, does sovereignty need to be valued as an element that makes communities independent, in order for those communities to better feed themselves in the face of transnational economic forces? Whatever the answer, it seems foolish to disregard national constitutions as a privileged instrument for guiding the adequate nourishment of the population. The trend in this regard is encouraging: several countries have incorporated the HRAF into their constitutions.

One example of the potential international interference in national agrifood systems is offered by Thiago Lima, Erbenia Lourenço and Henrique Menezes. They discuss the reasons behind international food aid from the US to African and Latin American countries containing genetically modified organisms. Although there are humanitarian motivations for the donations, there are also clear economic interests and a disrespect for the recipients' preferences. Certain international forums and dispute settlement environments may thus play a key role in shifting dysfunctional agrifood systems towards food sovereignty.

Indeed, it is not surprising to find that trade agreements and international organizations can reinforce the hierarchical relationship among countries in the North-South direction, keeping the latter vulnerable and dependent. However, international agreements and organizations can also be mobilized to spread solidarity among countries.

South-South cooperation to promote food and nutrition security is one example. In this context, the UN World Food Program's Centre of Excellence against Hunger, established in Brazil, excels at encouraging international cooperation in school food and nutrition. Clarissa Dri and Andressa Silva examine the Centre's actions through the principles of South-South cooperation, in terms of the autonomy of the countries involved and of strategic relations beyond the economic sphere. It is one example of how food security is more political than economic, as it does not depend as heavily on a country's ability to produce food but rather on deciding which food to produce and how to distribute it. South-South cooperation can therefore be a strategy for solidarity, which reinforces sovereignty.

In this vein, Felipe Albuquerque explains how policies to fight against hunger and poverty implemented in Brazil in the 2000s (at least until 2016) created a repertoire of success that enabled Brazilian diplomacy to make the country a relevant power for the region and for other developing countries. Throughout the text, Albuquerque shows how changes in the general direction of the economy (from President Lula to President Roussef and then to President Temer) impacted the country's external role as an international engine for policies to fight against hunger. This role is called into question by the movement that ousted President Dilma Roussef and brought her vice president, Michel Temer, to power.

A crucial food for Latin America is maize, and the history of its uses has much to do with the relations that Latin American countries have with developed countries. In their chapter, Andrea Santos Baca and Julia Cristina de Sousa e Berruezo show the role of maize in the world food market and the constructed image of it as a second class food, in a colonial attempt to sweep away the customs of the local people of Latin America and impose a mode of feeding similar to the European one, at the same time as spreading European uses of it worldwide. Furthermore, as the authors show, this crop has become one of the first to go through a process of hybridization and genetic modification, which responds to the "negative" image of food for animals (and not humans) that the Europeans gave to maize, as opposed to the images of wheat or rice as typically human foods. In other words, the apparent "advantage" of maize as a genetically modified food hides the value that the colonizing culture placed on it.

The relationship between economics, politics and food security is examined more deeply in the chapter by Agostina Costantino. This chapter brings us closer to the end of the book through a dialogue with the opening chapter on food security in India. The author reveals the irrelevance of Argentina's image as the "world's breadbasket," given the presence of thousands of undernourished or malnourished people in the country. Costantino shows how structural reforms implemented since the late 1970s—and more intensely since the 1990s—contributed to pushing aside the objective of food security, directing the entire economic structure towards the production of a (small) number of foods for export. In terms of international relations, this chapter offers a discussion of land grabbing by investors and foreign countries, which exacerbates food security and even calls the country's food sovereignty into question.

Closely related to the previous one, the chapter of Sol Mora deals with the general problem developed by Agostina Costantino, but in two specific case studies of Chinese investments in Argentina: an agri-food project and the building of an irrigation aqueduct. In both cases, it is about thousands of hectares that the Asian country intended to control in Argentina. Mora's hypothesis is challenging because most studies on land grabbing of national cases tend to focus separately either on the role of nation states, or on the social conflicts that have arisen, or on the interests of companies when setting up in other countries. This work not only addresses the problem comprehensively by including these three actors through the concept of governance, but also includes a protagonist not always considered in these studies: sub-national states, which are ultimately the ones that shape the relations that national governments end up having with other countries. The examples of Sol Mora show the effects that the current policy of relations with China can have on food security and the environment in the Southern Cone.

---//---

The biological constitution of the human being seems to be a perpetual prison or an eternal reminder that we are not only fragile but also intimately connected to nature. Developing bonds of solidarity not only among human beings but also with nature itself is a fundamental question. Along these lines, it is essential to understand the challenges and opportunities found in the context of international relations, in order to shape a political force capable of guaranteeing the HRAF for all people. We cannot accept, two decades into the twenty-first century, that "one in three women of reproductive age globally is still affected by anemia." Such data reveal the lack of care for our today and tomorrow, as anemia has "significant health and development consequences for both women and their children" (FAO, 2018, p.16). It is necessary to build agrifood systems that solve these types of problems. The further we move in this direction, the closer we come to glimpsing "one Humanity," not in the distressing sense of the Anthropocene but in the urgent sense of social justice.

The International Agri-Food Studies Network (*Rede de Estudos Agroalimentares Internacionais—Redagri*) and its collaborators wish everyone happy reading and lively debates!

References

ALKIRE, S. A Conceptual Framework for Human Security. **CRISE Working Paper**, Oxford, 2003.

BURKE, M. Climate Effects on Food Security: An Overview. In: BURKE, L. &. **Climate Change and Food Security:** Adapting Agriculture to a Warmer World. New York: Springer Dordrecht, 2010.

CHADE, J. **O mundo não é plano**. São Paulo: Saraiva, 2009.

CLAPP, J. Food Security. In: COOPER, H. &. T. **The Oxford Handbook of Modern Diplomacy**. [S.l.]: Oxford, 2013.

EVANS. Human Security and East Asia. **Journal of East Asian Studies**, 2004.

FAO. **The State of Food Security and Nutrition in the World 2018.** Building climate resilience for food security and nutrition. Rome, FAO, 2018.

_____. A statement by FAO Director-General José Graziano da Silva. **FAO** 2015. Available at: <https://bit.ly/2pQlFhv> Accessed 10 Oct. 2018.

_____. **Trade reforms and food security**. FAO. Roma. 2003.

G1. 1% mais ricos concentra 28% de toda a renda no Brasil, diz estudo. **Portal G1**. 14 set. 2017. Available at: https://glo.bo/2yDlOXn. Accessed 14 Oct. 2018.

HAMPSON et al. **Madness in the Multitude:** Human Security and World Disorder. Ottawa: Oxford University Press, 2002.

ICRC. Minas antipessoal: um panorama sobre o problema. **Comitê Internacional da Cruz Vermelha**, 2018. Available at: <https://bit.ly/2QL4V6G>. Accessed 17 Sept. 2018.

KALDOR, M. **Human Security**. Cambridge: Polity, 2007.26

KRAUSE, K. The key to a powerful agenda, if properly defined. **Security Dialogue**, p. 367–368, 2004.

KRAUSE, K. Critical perspectives on human security. In: MARTIN, M.; OWEN, T. **Routledge Handbook on Human Security**. New York: Routledge, 2014. p. 76–93.

LEÃO,M; MALUF, R. **A construção social de um sistema público de segurança alimentar e nutricional: a experiência brasileira**. Brasília: ABRANDH, 2012.

MACFARLANE, S. N.; KHONG, Y. F. **Human Security and the UN A Critical History**. Bloomington: Indiana University Press, 2006.

MCMICHAEL, P. **Global development and the corporate food regime. Prepared for Symposium on New Directions in the Sociology of Global Development**. XI World Congress of Rural Sociology. Trondheim: [s.n.]. 2004.

MCRAE, R; HUBERT, D. **Human Security and the New Diplomacy:** Protecting People, Promoting Peace. Montreal: McGill-Queen's University Press, 2001.

OWEN, T. The Critique That Doesn't Bite: A Response to David Chandler's 'Human Security: The dog that didn't bark'. **Security Dialogue**, p. 445, 2008.

RBA. Brasil pode voltar ao Mapa da Fome. ONU faz campanha pela segurança alimentar. **Rede Brasil Atual**. 14 mar. 2018. Available at: <https://bit.ly/2Aa4w8s>. Accessed 14 Oct. 2018.

ROCHA, R. M. A. O envolvimento internacional em questões de Justiça de Transição. **Revista de Economia e Relações Internacionais**, São Paulo, Jul. 2011. 107–127.

_____. O histórico da segurança humana e o (des)encontro das agendas de desenvolvimento e segurança. **Rev Carta Internacional**, 2017. p. 104–129.

SEN, A. **Desenvolvimento como Liberdade**. São Paulo: Cia das Letras, 2008.27

TADJBAKHSH, S; CHENOY, A. **Human Security Concepts and Implications**. Abingdon: Routledge, 2007.

TADJBAKHSH, S. Human Security: Concepts and Implications with an application to Post-Intervention Challenges in Afghanistan. **Les Études du CERI**, 2005. 117–118.

TAKASU, Y. Japan and Networked Human Security. In: MARTIN, M. &. O. T. **Routledge Handbook of Human Security**. Oxford: Routledge, 2015. p. 239–250.

UL HAQ, M. **Reflections on Human Development**. New York: Oxford University Press, 1995.

UNDP. **Human Development Report 1993: People's participation**. New York. 1993.

_____.. **Human Development Report. An Agenda for the Social Summit**. Oxford. 1994.

VIA CAMPESINA. Our World Is Not For Sale. Priority to Peoples' Food Sovereignty. **Bulletin**, November 1, 2001. Available at: <https://bit.ly/2yCpKdi> Accessed 10 Oct. 2018.

ZIEGLER, J. **Destruição em massa:** geopolítica da fome. São Paulo: Cortez, 2013.

CHAPTER 2
Contours of Food Security Challenges in Neo-liberal India

Praveen Jha[5], Santosh Verma[6], Manish Kumar[7]

Introduction:

The fact that since the early 1960s, global agricultural production has approximately tripled is well known. But in spite of such an increase in output, food security has remained a serious challenge in many countries across the world, partly due to unevenness in agricultural growth itself, but also on account of other important policy measures. Thus as per the current estimate, close to almost 800 million persons across the globe are reported to be suffering from chronic hunger, mostly in global South, along with many more being malnourished, and close to two billion suffering from micronutrient deficiencies. In short, trajectories of agricultural growth and policy regimes to address the food security have been inadequate and seriously deficient across many countries, particularly, in the so-called developing world.

As is often acknowledged, the four proximate pillars of food security are: availability, access, utilisation and stability, which depend fundamentally on overall macroeconomic policy regimes. Further, it is widely recognised that food availability at the macro-level cannot be equated with the food security at the household/individual level, and desirable outcomes can hardly be achieved by relying entirely on market processes. There is huge evidence from across the world, including from the so-called developed countries, that a variety of critical public interventions are important

---

5   Professor in Economics, Centre for Economic Studies and planning, Jawaharlal Nehru University, New Delhi.
6   Independent Researcher.
7   PhD. Research Scholar, Centre for Economic Studies and planning, Jawaharlal Nehru University, New Delhi.

in ensuring food and nutrition security (Dreze and Sen, 1989; Jha and Acharya, 2016). Given such a backdrop, the ascendancy of neo-liberalism since the 1970s, which in large parts of the world has resulted in significant compression of policy spaces for public intervention, several challenges have come to confront the objectives of adequate and assured food security.

Turning to India, as is well acknowledged, even the elementary markers related to food security paint a grim picture. For instance, as per the latest Global Hunger Index (GHI) Report (2019), out of 117 countries, which were surveyed, India has an alarmingly low rank of 102, much below some of its relatively poorer (in terms of per capita income) neighbours in South Asia, such as Nepal, Bangladesh, Pakistan. As it happens, this is in spite of reasonably robust GDP growth rates for almost four decades, in fact, second only to China which accounts for the fastest average GDP growth rates since the early 1980s, and has almost managed to banish hunger. This clearly tells us that relying simply on GDP cannot be a guarantee for ensuring even freedom from hunger, not to speak of food security. As we know from the huge and burgeoning literature on the subject, there are multiple correlates, economic-social-political, etc., of a robust and secure food system. Changes during the era of neoliberalism have created several adverse processes and mechanisms that have contributed to ongoing stress on the food front in a large number of countries, including India.

This paper seeks to investigate, in a political economy framework, some of the major causes underlying the deeply worrying food scenario in India. In particular, we examine important elements of the global and national economic policy architecture, which have been critical in shaping the overall context of the food system in the country. Growing internationalisation of food regime, *e.g.*, through WTO architecture, several multilateral/regional/bilateral treaties and conventions, and increase in power of multinational corporations to shape such a regime to their advantage, are among the most obvious 'external' factors that we need to take note of. Further, important constraints on national/domestic macro-economic policy space and autonomy, which again have important organic linkages with neo-liberalism and the above noted 'external' factors, need to be underscored for an adequate understanding of the current challenges on the food front. These include, *inter-alia*, compression of public expenditure in general and provisioning for food, (for instance through public distribution systems), in particular, move towards cash transfers, squeeze of support for agriculture and rural development through multiple channels such as adequate support prices, subsidies etc., and worsening of livelihood and employment prospects due to the nature and structure of the growth trajectory itself.

The paper engages with the dialectics underlying the above noted international and domestic correlates, which impinge on the issues relating to the food system in contemporary India. Given that the theme has a vast canvas and a range of complex connected themes that are relevant for any such discussion, we have had to be selective in focusing on only a few critical issues. The paper draws primarily on the available secondary information to provide a sketch of the current challenges and some policy reflections.

Food Security Situation in India:

The Food and Agricultural Organisation (FAO) estimates reveal that in 2014, the number of severely food insecure people in the world was 585 million, which increased to 704.3 million in 2018. If moderately food insecure people are also added to the number, it increased to 1696.3 million in 2014, and to 2013.8 million globally in 2018. Across most regions, the numbers for both severe and moderately food insecure have increased between 2014 and 2018. The South Asia also has witnessed a rise in numbers of severely and moderately food insecure people (Table 1) (FAO, 2019).

Table 1:   Number of Severely and Moderately Food Insecure People in Different Regions of the World

Regions	Number of Severely Food Insecure People (Millions)			Number of Moderately and Severely Insecure People (Millions)		
	2014	2016	2018	2014	2016	2018
World	585	600.4	704.3	1696.3	1801.9	2013.8
Africa	210.7	268.2	277	554.1	644.1	676.1
Asia	305.9	264.8	353.6	875.6	871.1	1038.5
Southern Asia	247.1	195.8	271.7	565.7	559.6	649.1
Latin America	45.1	46.5	54.7	141.2	170	187.8
Northern	16.1	13.4	10.6	105.2	95.8	88.7

Source: (FAO, 2019)

Across continents, the largest number of food-insecure people live in Asia, which is partly because of its high share in total global population. Further, as it happens, India, which accounts for 1.38 billion out of 7.46 billion of the global population, has the highest incidence of absolute hunger, and the situation has become more worrisome in the recent years. As a marker of food insecurity, Global Hunger Index, which is an initiative of International Food Policy Research Institute (IFPRI), Concern Worldwide and Welthungerlife, is a good indicator. This index uses three components, namely, undernourishment, child underweight and child mortality; it takes into account share of the undernourished population, the share of children under the age of five who have low weight against their height, share of children under the age of five who are stunted and mortality rate of children under the age of five. The Global Hunger Index (GHI) score[8] of India was 23.7 with the 67th position out of 81 countries in the list in 2011; this score went down to 29 and the country was ranked 80th out of 104 countries in 2015. As per the most recent estimate, in 2019, India's score further declined to 30.3 and it was ranked as 102 out of 117 countries. In other words, the GHI scores and ranking for India in recent years clearly show an extremely worrisome state of under-nutrition, child wasting and

8   Scores from 10.0–19.9 show moderate levels of hunger; Scores from 20.0–34.9 show serious levels of hunger.

stunting and unacceptably high mortality rates of children due to acute hunger.

As is obvious, food grains production is the major pre-requisite for the first pillar of food security, i.e. availability. As it happens, in the last thirty years of neoliberal policies, production of food grains output in India has increased at a slow pace, barely keeping ahead of the population growth; however, given the major policy reconfigurations during the period since the early 1990s, there has been a significant compression in food availability, going well beyond what may be explained by per capita production figures.

Figure 1 provides the annual food grain production in India and a comparison of per capita production and availability of food grains. In the period between 1990–91 and 2018–19, food grain production in India increased from 176 million tonnes to 285 million tonnes, with compound annual growth rate (CAGR) of 1.7 per cent. In the same period, per capita food grain production increased from 208 kg per year to 214 kg per year with a CAGR of 0.1 per cent. However, in the referred period, the per capita availability declined from 186 kg per year to 180 kg per year with CAGR of −0.1 per cent.

Figure 1:   Food Grain Production (Million Tonnes), Per Capita Production and Availability of Food Grains (Kg/person/year) in India, 1990–91 to 2018–19

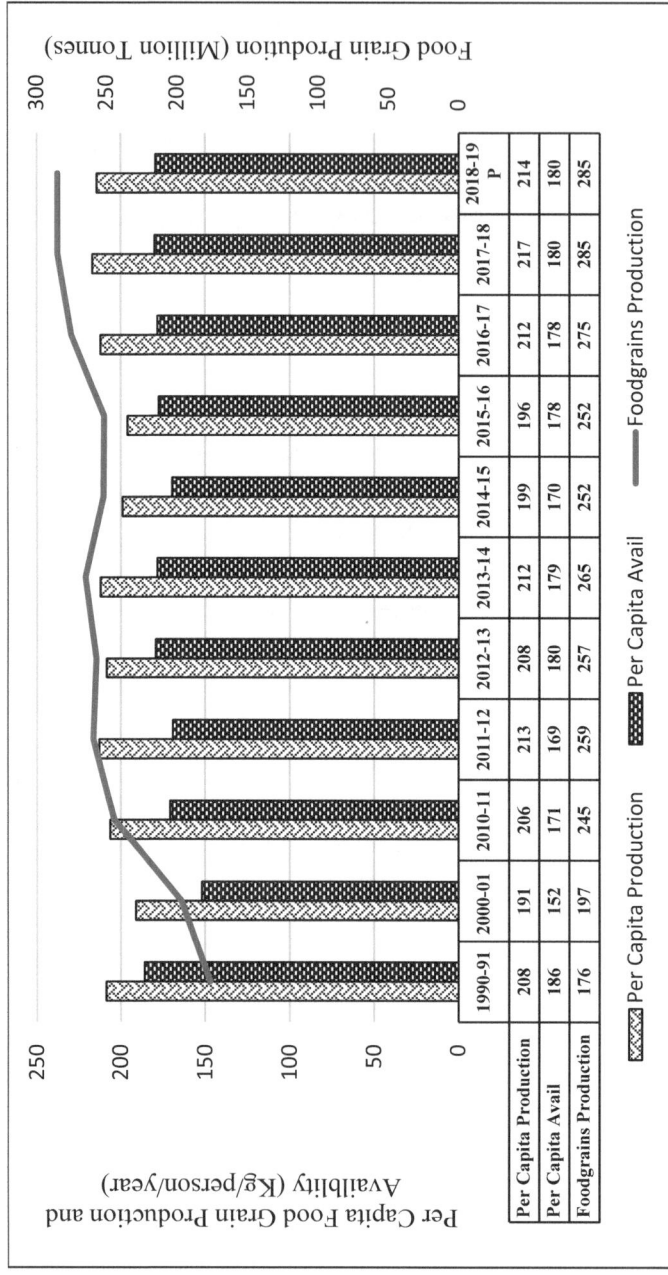

	1990-91	2000-01	2010-11	2011-12	2012-13	2013-14	2014-15	2015-16	2016-17	2017-18	2018-19 P
Per Capita Production	208	191	206	213	208	212	199	196	212	217	214
Per Capita Avail	186	152	171	169	180	179	170	178	178	180	180
Foodgrains Production	176	197	245	259	257	265	252	252	275	285	285

Per Capita Production   Per Capita Avail   Foodgrains Production

Source: Agricultural Statistics at a Glance—2019, Directorate of Economics and Statistics, Ministry of Agriculture, Government of India.

As regards, per capita availability of food grains, and in particular the growing gap between per capita production and availability, the factors responsible have very strong connects with the changes in the overall macroeconomic policy regime. One of the most important reasons is that of income deflation for a very large segment of the population, and consequently their ability to access food. Other important correlates that we need to take into account are: changes in agricultural subsidy and trade regimes, reconfiguration of the public distribution system, policies of stockholding, among others.

Table 2 presents the per capita availability and consumption of three major items and their related processed products, namely, rice, wheat and pulses. Between 1993–94 and 2011–12, the gap between availability and consumption of these items in India has widened considerably. This is based on different rounds of surveys done by the National Sample Survey Organisation (NSSO)[9].

Table 2:   Per Capita Availability and Consumption of Rice, Wheat and Pulses (Kg/year/person)

Year	Rice			Wheat			All pulses		
	Per Capita Availability	Per Capita Consumption		Per Capita Availability	Per Capita Consumption		Per Capita Availability	Per Capita Consumption	
		Rural	Urban		Rural	Urban		Rural	Urban
1993–94	75.7	82.6	62.4	58.2	52.6	54.0	13.6	9.3	10.5
1999–00	74.3	80.2	62.1	58.4	54.1	54.1	11.6	10.2	12.2
2004–05	64.7	77.6	57.3	56.3	51.0	53.1	11.5	8.6	10.0
2009–10	66.4	74.7	56.6	61.4	53.0	52.8	12.9	7.9	9.6
2011–12	69.4	74.6	56.7	57.8	53.9	52.6	15.2	9.5	11.0

Source: Agricultural Statistics at a Glance—2019, Directorate of Economics and Statistics, Ministry of Agriculture, Government of India.

---

9   The NSSO is a part of the Ministry of Statistics and Programme Implementation, under the Government of India. It carries surveys annually, quinquennially and decadal, on a large number of themes relating to Indian economy. Among these, the large quinquennial surveys on Employment, Unemployment and Consumption since mid-1970s have been an extremely valuable source to map trends relating to poverty, unemployment, consumption etc. It may be noted that these surveys are reasonably large and considered to be among the best in the world. As it happens, the current government decided to go in for a change in methodologies relating to these surveys based on the Pangaria Committee Report of 2016. Strictly speaking, the subsequent surveys of 2017–18 and 2018–19 are not comparable with the above noted quinquennial surveys.

Table 2 presents the average picture of the country; however, it is well acknowledged that neoliberalism tends to exacerbate inequality everywhere and the India story is no different. From the different rounds of the above noted quinquennial rounds of the NSSO, we are in a position to map per capita consumption and food intake across different deciles of the population between early 1990s and 2011–12. As per the estimates available for this period, it is clear that for the bottom 9 deciles in rural and the 6 deciles in urban India, per capita consumption is less than the official norms of adequate calorie benchmark, which are 2400 and 2100 calories per day respectively (refer Table 3) (Ram 2017). This shows extreme levels of food insecurity in both rural and urban India. In the next sections, the paper offers an analysis of some of the major reasons for persistent and growing food insecurity in India; essentially these correlate well with ascendency and consolidation of neoliberal policies in the country.

Table 3:   Estimated per Capita Calorie Intake per Day (in kcal)

Decile	Rural				Urban			
	1993–94	2004–05	2009–10	2011–12	1993–94	2004–05	2009–10	2011–
1	1465	1482	1545	1674	1453	1509	1558	1634
2	1731	1676	1712	1820	1703	1681	1700	1760
3	1850	1797	1819	1911	1800	1829	1760	1855
4	1975	1875	1882	1977	1900	1847	1846	1917
5	2057	1955	1980	2038	1997	1935	1912	1977
6	2165	2037	2022	2119	2080	2010	1977	2049
7	2278	2148	2110	2184	2189	2094	2074	2127
8	2411	2280	2181	2348	2287	2195	2164	2244
9	2588	2362	2323	2333	2462	2315	2290	2378
10	3035	2764	2610	2610	2844	2654	2527	2638
All	2156	2038	2018	2099	2072	2007	1981	2058

Source: (Ram 2017)

There are various studies that have analysed the trends and causes for decline in calorie-intake since the early 1990s (Deaton and Dreze, 2009; Patnaik, 2010a, 2010b; Nayyar and Nayyar, 2016: among others). Although there are some differences as regards the precise estimates of calorie deficient population across these studies, due to methodological differences, there is a broad similarity regarding the overall trends.

Neoliberalism and Its Impact on Food Security

It is well-acknowledged that the rise of neoliberalism has reconstituted the balance of power between the State and market forces, resulting in reduced commitments through a host of policy changes, towards citizens' welfare at large. It is well known that, as a theory of political and economic practice, neoliberalism promotes strong private property rights, free markets and free trade in order to achieve human well-being through entrepreneurial freedom and skills (Harvey, 2007). In these theories, the State is confined to the responsibility of creating and preserving an institutional framework conducive to the free markets (*ibid*). India shifted in a significant manner towards liberalisation with the adoption of so-called new economic policy (NEP) in July 1991 (Patnaik and Chandrasekhar, 1995; Patnaik, 2007). In line with the policy prescriptions of the Brettonwoods Institutions (e.g. the World Bank and the IMF), India went ahead with policies of fiscal stabilisation and Structural Adjustment Programmes resulting in significant curtailment of its development and social sector expenditure and promoting a whole range of market friendly measures; these have had substantial impacts of well-being of the masses in general such as poverty, food security, employment etc. along with increases in inequalities across different axes such as rural-urban, social and occupational groups, among others. In the following sections, we focus on policies that impacted, directly and indirectly, on overall food situation in the country.

A. Export Orientation

The trade liberalisation, which is an integral part of the neo-liberal policies, has facilitated the export of agricultural products from developing countries to developed countries, despite falling per capita availability and consumption in the latter (Patnaik, 2016). As mentioned earlier, the export of food grains from India is among one of the significant factors contributing to the gap between production and availability, as is clearly evident from the table below.

Figure 2:   Indian Export of Food Grains (Thousand Tonnes), 1990–91 to 2018–19

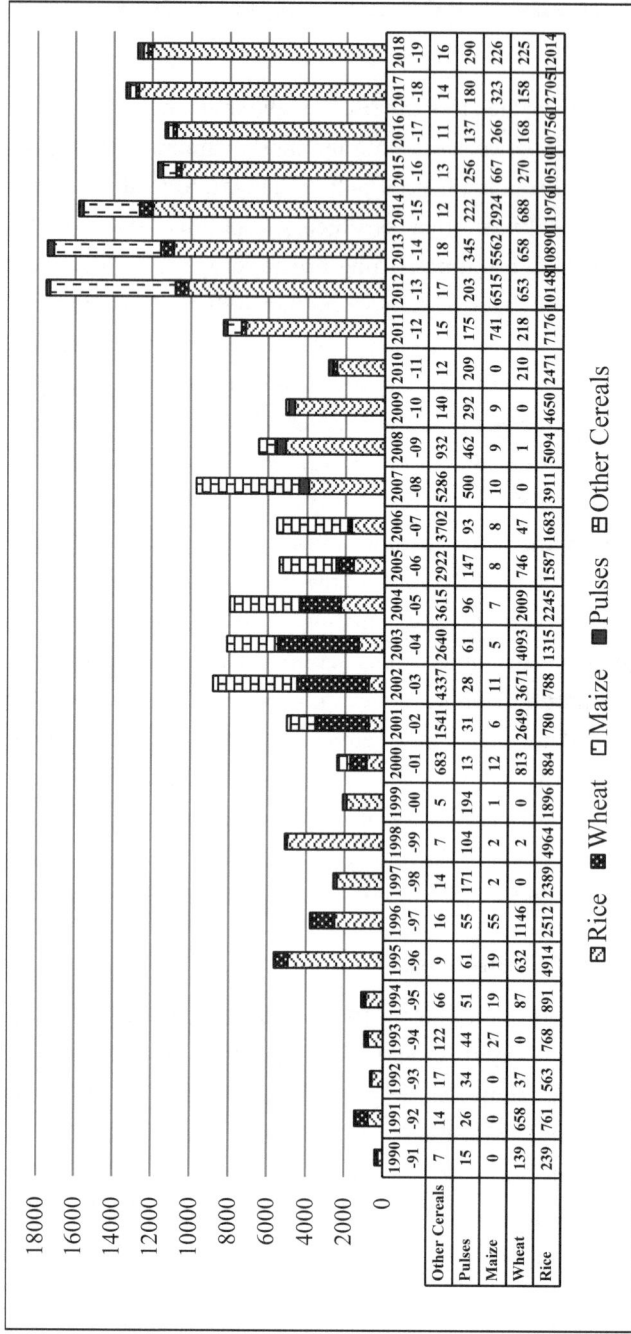

	1990-91	1991-92	1992-93	1993-94	1994-95	1995-96	1996-97	1997-98	1998-99	1999-00	2000-01	2001-02	2002-03	2003-04	2004-05	2005-06	2006-07	2007-08	2008-09	2009-10	2010-11	2011-12	2012-13	2013-14	2014-15	2015-16	2016-17	2017-18	2018-19
Other Cereals	7	14	17	122	66	9	16	14	7	5	683	1541	4337	2640	3615	2922	3702	5286	932	140	12	15	17	18	12	13	11	14	16
Pulses	15	26	34	44	51	61	55	171	104	194	13	31	28	61	96	147	93	500	462	292	209	175	203	345	222	256	137	180	290
Maize	0	0	0	27	19	19	55	2	2	1	12	6	11	5	7	8	8	10	9	9	0	741	6515	5562	2924	667	266	323	226
Wheat	139	658	37	0	87	632	1146	0	2	0	813	2649	3671	4093	2009	746	47	0	1	0	210	218	653	658	688	270	168	158	225
Rice	239	761	563	768	891	4914	2512	2389	4964	1896	884	780	788	1315	2245	1587	1683	3911	5094	4650	2471	7176	10148	10890	11976	10510	10756	12705	12014

⊠ Rice   ▧ Wheat   ☐ Maize   ■ Pulses   ⊞ Other Cereals

Source: Agricultural Products Export Development Authority, Government of India

In the last three decades, the export of food grains from India has increased with a CAGR of 12.7 per cent. Rice has the largest share in the total agricultural export from India; the share of wheat was relatively higher in the period between 2000 and 2006. The share of maize in total food grain export was significant only between 2011 and 2015. The increasing export orientation of food grains has happened in a context where the export price received for the major crops were less than the economic cost which is indeed a very strange phenomenon; further, apart from reducing availability, it obviously contributed to a compression of the income of the substantial segments of farmers. Thus, in a sense, it was akin to a "dual loss" to for the country as a whole (Kumar, 2019).

It is also well known that globalisation has tended to increase price volatility for agricultural products, contributing to major shocks in the recent decades; for instance, in 2006–08 and 2010–11. The FAO reported that food price index rose between 7 per cent and 27 per cent for 2006 and 2007 and for 2008, it was 24 percent above the level of 2007 (FAO, 2009). These upward spirals of global food commodity prices were due to the massive increase in financial speculation in the food commodity on the commodities future markets (Ghosh et al., 2012), which was largely due to crisis in the traditional financial sector around the same years.

In India, there was a continuous pressure on food prices from 2006–2013; as it happens, it was also a period of growing trade openness and integration with the global market for agricultural commodities. The share of agricultural trade to agricultural GDP increased from 5.2 per cent to 19 per cent in 2013–14 (Bhattacharya and Sen Gupta, 2017). The integration of India's agricultural market to global agricultural market led to a rising share of agricultural land being diverted to exportable crops having high-end prices. In 2007–08, when global prices were soaring to a very high level, the export of food items became lucrative than selling in the Indian domestic market. There was a significant increase in the share of exports in total Indian food production, i.e. from 6.2 per cent between 2003–04 and 2005–06 to more than 10 per cent in the period 2006–07 to 2008–09.

B. Open Market Sale of Public Food Stock

Driven by the logic of fiscal consolidation and expenditure compression, India's reasonably well-functioning Universal Public Distribution System (PDS) was converted to a Targeted Public Distribution System (TPDS) in 1997; incidently it also resulted in exclusion of a large number of eligible households from getting cheaper food grains and making them vulnerable for food security (Swaminathan and Mishra, 2001; Swaminathan, 2008). As shown in table 2, an important reason explaining the difference between availability and consumption of food grains is rising food stock with the government, which was obviously connected with universal PDS to TPDS.

Figure 3: **Stock of Food Grains in the Central Pool, January 1991–2020 (Million Tonnes)**

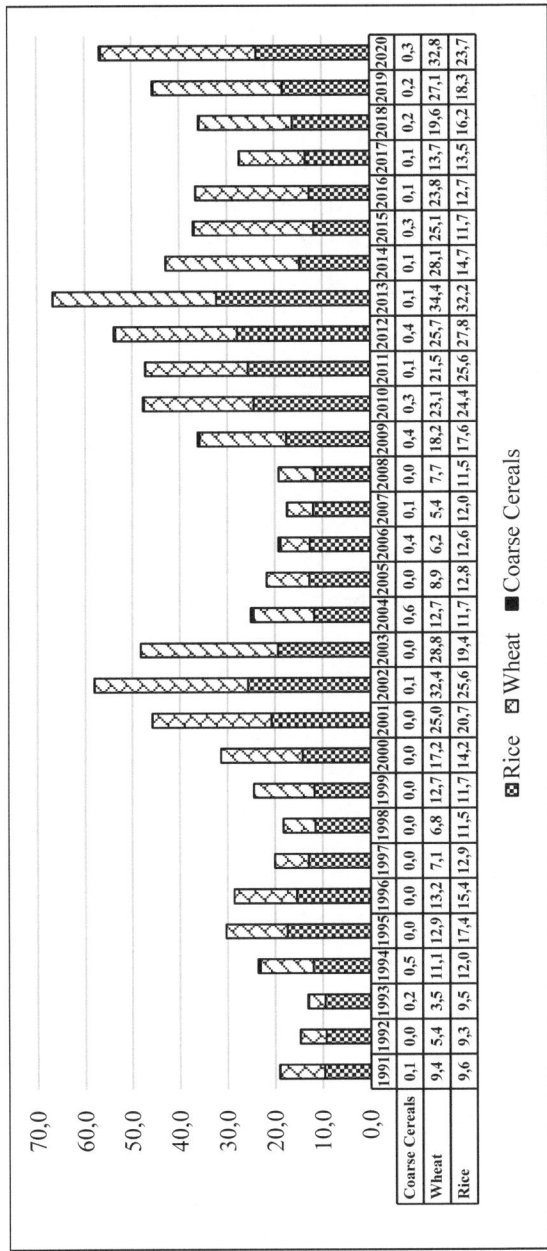

	1991	1992	1993	1994	1995	1996	1997	1998	1999	2000	2001	2002	2003	2004	2005	2006	2007	2008	2009	2010	2011	2012	2013	2014	2015	2016	2017	2018	2019	2020
Coarse Cereals	0,1	0,0	0,2	0,5	0,0	0,0	0,0	0,0	0,0	0,0	0,0	0,1	0,0	0,6	0,0	0,4	0,4	0,0	0,4	0,3	0,1	0,4	0,1	0,1	0,3	0,1	0,1	0,2	0,2	0,3
Wheat	9,4	5,4	3,5	11,1	12,9	13,2	7,1	6,8	12,7	17,2	25,0	32,4	28,8	12,7	8,9	6,2	5,4	7,7	18,2	23,1	21,5	25,7	34,4	28,1	25,1	23,8	13,7	19,6	27,1	32,8
Rice	9,6	9,3	9,5	12,0	17,4	15,4	12,9	11,5	11,7	14,2	20,7	25,6	19,4	11,7	12,8	12,6	12,0	11,5	17,6	24,4	25,6	27,8	32,2	14,7	11,7	12,7	13,5	16,2	18,3	23,7

⊠ Rice   ▨ Wheat   ■ Coarse Cereals

Source: Directorate of Economics and Statistics and Department of Food and Public Distribution, Government of India

Figure 3 provides the estimates of major food grains stocks in the central pool (i.e. with the government of India) between 1991 and 2020, As it is clear from the figure that the stock of food grains was rising in the central pool even before 1996, but after 1998 there was a sharp rise in the food grain stock. Between 2004 and 2008, under the United Progressive Alliance (UPA)-I government, in which Left Parties of India had a significant say, the food stock declined. After 2008, the stock of food in the central pool further increased until 2013. In 2013, the Government of India under UPA-II enacted National Food Security Act (NFSA), which guarantees subsidised food to the three-fourth of the rural population and half of the urban population (GoI, 2013a). The NFSA played an important role in increasing the base and reach of food grain distribution under TPDS. However, the incumbent regime led by the Bhartiya Janata Party (BJP) after 2014 made some changes in the architecture of NFSA as well as norms[10] of provisioning; these had an adverse impact on PDS system, leading to a decline in the distribution of food grains and build-up of stocks again. June stocks[11] for the last four years from 2017, were 55.5, 68.1, 74.3, and 83.5 million tonnes respectively. Such huge stocks are completely illogical and avoidable when experts agree that 20–30 million tonnes are adequate as buffer norms for any contingency. Except for adherence to the bizarre philosophy of neoliberalism, there is no reason why the government should persist with such levels of "excess supply" which end up depriving millions of poor, hungry from access to food.

---

10   Since, 2017 the Government of India made AADHAR card, a unique identification number-card, mandatory for availing TPDS (Mittal, 2017).

11   https://fci.gov.in/stocks.php?view=46

Figure 4: Sale of Wheat and Rice under the Open Market Sale Scheme (Domestic/Export from Central Pool) (Thousand Tonnes)

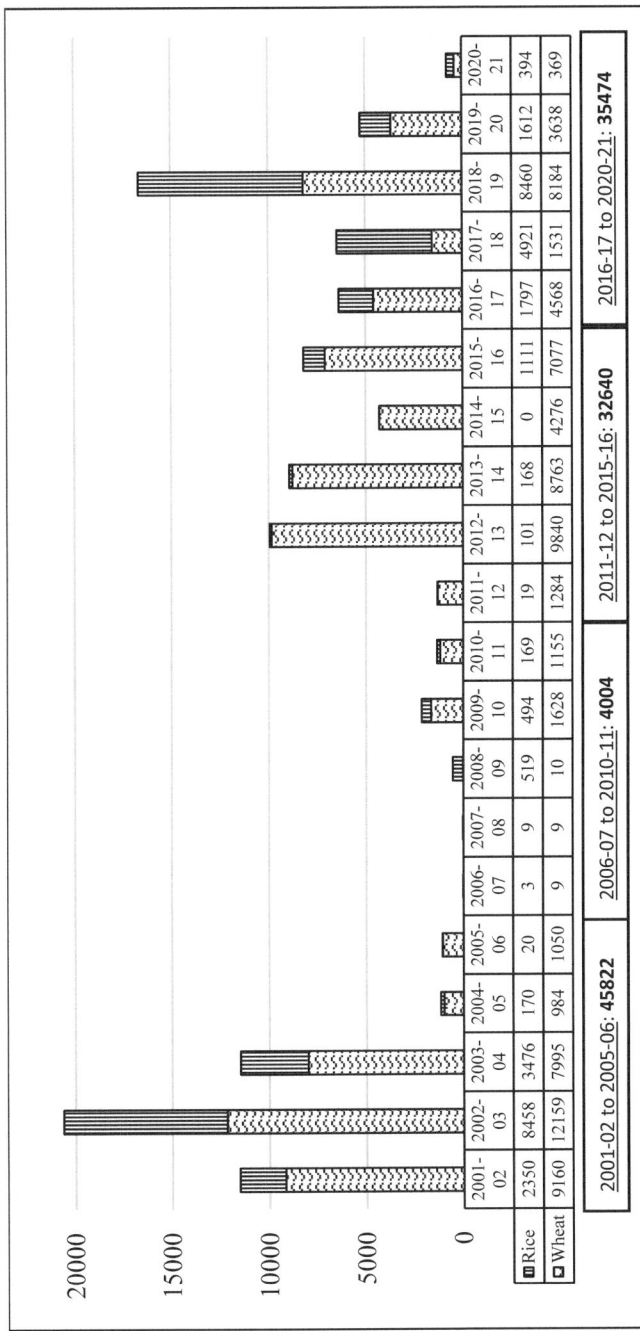

	2001-02	2002-03	2003-04	2004-05	2005-06	2006-07	2007-08	2008-09	2009-10	2010-11	2011-12	2012-13	2013-14	2014-15	2015-16	2016-17	2017-18	2018-19	2019-20	2020-21
Rice	2350	8458	3476	170	20	3	9	519	494	169	19	101	168	0	1111	1797	4921	8460	1612	394
Wheat	9160	12159	7995	984	1050	9	9	10	1628	1155	1284	9840	8763	4276	7077	4568	1531	8184	3638	369

2001-02 to 2005-06: **45822**

2006-07 to 2010-11: **4004**

2011-12 to 2015-16: **32640**

2016-17 to 2020-21: **35474**

Source: Department of Food and Public Distribution and various years' Economic Survey of India

Now we move to the policy of Open Market Sales Scheme (OMSS) which the Government of India had adopted for wheat in 1993 and for rice in 1994 (GoI, 2005); the relevant figures for sale under the scheme are presented in Figure 4. The scheme makes provision for sale of wheat and rice under the central pool, that is, out of food grains procured by the public agencies. The Food Corporation of India (FCI) sells food grains in bulk to private traders through tenders. The policy makers had rightly argued that keeping high stock in the central pool has a substantial economic cost, and hence it was prudent to offload part of it through open markets (domestic as well as export). Of course, the question arise: why not provision for higher levels of distribution through PDS to the needy population instead of opting for open market sales? Obvious answer lies in the logic of neoliberal framework.

As it happens, the OMSS resulted in the *Wheat Crisis in 2006*, when in April of that year (which is a month of wheat procurement), the stock of wheat in the central pool fell short of the buffer norm by 100 thousand tonnes (Aspects of Indian Economy, 2006); this forced the government to import wheat in that year. It was under United Progressive Alliance-I, which was a front led by the Congress and supported by the Left parties among others, that the OMSS was entirely stopped between 2004 and 2009; unfortunately, it again got a new lease of life subsequently. The trends for the OMSS during the last two decades are clearly evident from Figure 4.

C. Unemployment and Migration of Workers

The neoliberal model of economic development has created huge challenges for labour absorption in the country thus aggravating the pool of labour reserves. This again has many dimensions and multiple correlates. Many of these are connected with accelerated primitive accumulation, vis-à-vis the petty production, peasant agriculture and a whole host of activities broadly subsumed under informal production, who were earlier protected to a certain extent from the big capital (both foreign and domestic) under Nehruvian Socialism (*dirigiste regimes*) (Patnaik and Patnaik, 2019).

On the challenges of labour absorption in contemporary India, as we have argued earlier, there is "overwhelming dependence on agriculture which accounts for close to 50% of the total workforce. Significantly, as per the recent estimates, agriculture contributes only approximately one-sixth of the GDP of the country. This overcrowding of the workforce in agriculture and its 'underemployment' is structured by a high presence of wage labour and a declining number of people who report themselves as 'cultivators'. As regards the non-agricultural sector, its single most important feature (quite like agriculture) is the extremely high proportion of vulnerable informal employment. Though the non-agricultural sector accounts for about half the work force, it contributes approximately 80% to the total GDP, with a very small segment of less than 10% of workers, in the organized sector. Of the total employment in the organized sector, almost 65–70 per cent is in the public sector (including public administration and defense services). The unemployment among the youth, in particular among the 'educated', is substantially higher than the overall rate of unemployment" (Jha, 2019; *pp. 10–11*).

One of the significant promises with which neoliberal policies ascended in India was adequate and appropriate employment opportunities to the growing workforce. However, as is clear from Table 4, the overall outcome has gone in the opposite direction.

Table 4:   Unemployment rate (%) in India

	1993–94	1999–00	2004–05	2009–10	2011–12	2017–18
Rural (Male)	1.4	1.7	1.6	1.6	1.7	5.8
Rural (Female)	0.8	1	1.8	1.6	1.7	3.8
Rural (Total)	1.2	1.5	1.7	1.6	1.7	5.3
Urban (Male)	4	4.5	3.8	2.8	3	7.1
Urban (Female)	6.2	5.7	6.9	5.7	5.2	10.8
Urban (Total)	4.5	4.7	4.5	3.4	3.4	7.8

Source: Reserve Bank of India, Handbook of Statistics of the Indian States and NSS 2019. Periodic Labour Force Survey, 2019.

It is worth noting here that the massive and growing political outcry on the employment front, especially, in rural India during the first and half decades of economic reforms pushed the government to adopt the Mahatma Gandhi National Rural Employment Guarantee Act (MGNREGA) in 2005, which provided some succour to the most vulnerable segments of the rural population, and has been a life line for them. After the General Elections in 2014, the National Democratic Alliance (led) by the BJP formed government at the Centre and has pursued a range of policies which have been, on the whole, disastrous on the employment front as is evident for the figures from Periodic Labour Force Survey 2017–18.

Reasons for poor labour absorption have been analysed in great detail by a large number of scholars working on India; for reasons of space, it is not possible for us to get into a discussion of the relevant issues here and those interested in these may refer to Jha (2016); Patnaik (2016); Patnaik and Patnaik (2019) among others. It also worth noting that the huge swelling of labour reserves in the country has impacted on quality of employment. Table 5 presents the total number of workforce in India in the formal and informal sectors. Apart from a rising number of informal workers, the most worrying fact is—the rise in informal workers in the formal sector, i.e. informalisation of formal sector workers.

Table 5:   Distribution of Workers by Type of Employment and Sector

Sector/Worker	Total Employment (Million)		
	Informal/Unorganised Workers	Formal/Organised Workers	Total Workers
1999–2000 (NSS 55th Round)			
Informal/Unorganised	341.3 (99.6)	1.4 (0.4)	342.6 (100.0)
Formal/Organised sector	20.5 (37.8)	33.7 (62.2)	54.1 (100.0)
Total	361.7 (91.2)	35.0 (8.8)	396.8 (100.0)
2004–05 (NSS 61st Round)			
Informal/Unorganised	393.5 (99.6)	1.4 (0.4)	394.9 (100.0)
Formal/Organised sector	29.1 (46.6)	33.4 (53.4)	62.6 (100.0)
Total	422.6 (92.4)	34.9 (7.6)	457.5 (100.0)
2009–10 (NSS 66th Round)			
Informal/Unorganised	387.4 (99.4)	2.3 (0.6)	389.8 (100.0)
Formal/Organised sector	39.7 (56.5)	30.6 (43.5)	70.3 (100.0)
Total	427.5 (92.9)	32. 6 (7.1)	460.2 (100.0)
2011–12 (NSS 68th Round)			
Informal/Unorganised	398.8 (99.6)	1.4 (0.4)	400.2 (100.0)
Formal/Organised sector	48.2 (57.1)	36.3 (42.9)	84.5 (100.0)
Total	447.0 (92.2)	37.7 (7.8)	484.7 (100.0)

Source: 1. NSS 66th and 68th Rounds of Employment-Unemployment Survey. Computed.
2. The figure for 55th and 61st round are adopted from the *Report on Conditions of Work and Promotion of Livelihoods in the Unorganised Sector, 2007*. Note: Figures in brackets are percentages.

The informal sector workers (who are deprived of any kind of social security, paid leave etc.) are extremely vulnerable to any sudden economic shock. Further, even for the most protected category of workers (i.e. formal sector workers), there has been a substantial increase in vulnerability, as is evident from the Periodic Labour Force Survey (2017–18) conducted by the NSSO. The Survey indicated that among the regular wage/salaried employees, 69.2 percent in the rural areas and 72.4 percent in the urban areas and a total of 71.1 percent in whole India do not have written job contracts. The same survey also reveals that 56.2 percent in the rural areas and 52.8 percent in the urban areas and 54.2 percent at all India level, regular wage/salaried employees do not have any provision of paid leave; it also notes that, among the regular wage/salaried employees, 52.5 percent in rural areas, 47.7 percent in urban areas and 49.6 percent at all India level do not have any social security benefits.

Increasing challenges of labour absorption have contributed significantly to labour mobility. Unfortunately, there are serious data challenges relating to labour migration, which we are not in a position to pursue here. However, it is quite clear that during the period since the early 1990s, labour mobility in search of work has increased very substantially (Census, 2001, 2011; GoI, 2017; NSSO different rounds, Srivastava, 2020).

Compression of rural development expenditure, reduced access to land, growing landlessness among marginal and small farmers, increased vulnerabilities of peasant production, etc., which have strong organic connections with neoliberal policies, are obvious contributors to growing mobility in search of work; in short, much of labour migration in contemporary India is driven by distress. These *'footloose'*[12] workers are constantly moving not only from rural to urban but to rural to rural and urban to rural as well, many of them cot into multitasking and perennial circuits of circular migration.

---

12   The word "footloose labour" was coined by Jan Breman for a person who works on daily wages and is in search of a job on a daily basis unlike a permanent or semi-permanent job (Breman, 2010).

D. The Rise in Landlessness and Asset Inequality:

One of the major adverse outcomes of overall economic policies in rural India during the neoliberal era has been the rise in landlessness. Of course, there are other factors at work, such as, development and infrastructure projects, urbanisation, etc. which have put pressure on land for agricultural purposes. However, it is quite clear that a whole range of polices unleashed by neoliberalism have dramatically exacerbated the trend towards growing landlessness for at least the bottom half in the rural India and the trends for the recent years have been studied by several scholars (Rawal, 2008, 2013; Patnaik, 2012; Verma, 2015; Verma and Roy, 2019; GoI, 2013b). It is quite clear from the recent studies that more than 40 percent of households in rural India do not have access to cultivable land, (i.e. other than their homestead) (Rawal, 2008; GoI, 2009; Verma and Roy, 2019).

Table 6: **Number of operational holdings and rural households in India (in Million)**

Particulars	1990–91	2000–01	2010–11
Number of Operational Holdings	106.6	119.9	138.4
Number of Rural Households	108.2	132.4	179.7
Operation Holdings as Percent of Total Rural Households	98.56	90.58	77

Source: Agricultural Census, 1990–91 2000–01, 2010–11 and Census of India 1991, 2001, Socio-economic Caste Census, 2011.

Table 6 provides information on the number of operational holding and the total number of rural households in India. According to the official definition, "*operational holdings include all lands which are used wholly or partly for agricultural production and is operated as one technical unit by one person alone or with household members without regard to the title, legal form, size or location*" (GoI, 2019; pp 6). It is clear from the above table that access to land by rural households has drastically decreased in the period under consideration.

A study on asset inequality in India (Sarma et al., 2017), based on the All India Debt and Investment Survey (1991–92 (48th Round), 2002–03 (59th Round) and 2012–13 (70th Round)) shows the rise in asset inequality in rural and urban India. Decile-wise percentage asset holdings are given in Table 7. It shows that the assets held by the bottom 60 per cent in both the rural and urban areas have declined in the period from 1991–92 to 2012–13. Also, the assets held by the middle 35 per cent have declined. The top 5 per cent have witnessed an increase in their asset holdings both in rural and urban areas.

Table 7:   Percent Share of Assets Held by Asset Deciles

Deciles	Rural Households			Urban Households		
	1991–92	2002–03	2012–13	1991–92	2002–03	2012–13
0–10	0.21	0.23	0.25	0	0.01	0
10–20	0.84	0.95	0.89	0.02	0.05	0.04
20–30	1.56	1.68	1.50	0.25	0.45	0.30
30–40	2.52	2.53	2.26	0.99	1.38	0.98
40–50	3.75	3.61	3.23	2.09	2.55	1.96
50–60	5.25	5.09	4.51	3.72	4.20	3.40
60–70	7.39	7.13	6.31	6.08	6.67	5.45
70–80	10.62	10.33	9.16	9.67	10.74	8.76
80–90	17.17	16.88	15.39	16.94	18.42	15.38
90–100	50.70	51.57	56.50	60.24	55.54	63.72
Top 5 %	36.62	37.31	42.71	44.75	40	50.70
Middle 35%	49.25	48.60	44.65	48.18	51.36	42.62
Bottom 60 %	14.12	14.09	12.64	7.07	8.64	6.68

Source: Sarma et al., 2017

The inequality in land and other assets holdings is sharper if the data is further disaggregated by social categories (Sarma et al., 2017; Verma and Roy, 2019). It means that the Scheduled Tribes, Scheduled Castes and the other backward classes, who are historically vulnerable with respect to assets, especially, land and are thus more vulnerable to food insecurity.

48 JHA ET AL.

E. Withdrawal of Support to Agriculture

One of the worrying trends for Indian agriculture in the recent years has been overall subdued investments and the share of public investment has tended to slow down, as is evident from the table below.

Table 8: Share of Public and Private Investment in Agriculture (%)

Period	Public	Private
2002–2004	18	82
2004–2009	22	78
2009–2014	14	86
2014–2017	16	84

Source: Agricultural Statistics at a Glance, different years.

More importantly if we look at total investment and expenditure relevant for rural areas, overall situation subsequent to the 1980s has been seriously worrisome. Figure 5 maps the relevant situation graphically.

As per the Constitution of India, responsibility for different sectors are allocated to either the Union government (i.e. the Central government), or the State government (i.e. the governments heading the different provinces), or shared by both, (i.e. what is known as the "Concurrent List"). Agriculture in India has been largely in the domain of state government and hence most of the finances for agriculture and rural development come from state budgets. The figure above presents the share of the rural economy in the total expenditure of all Indian states. The broad category called rural economy here includes: spending on agriculture and allied activities, rural development, irrigation and flood control, special area programme, village and small industries. In 1990–91, the share of the rural economy in the total expenditure of all Indian states was 22 per cent, which decreased to 19 per cent during the 1990s and 15 per cent in the next decade (Jha and Acharya, 2011). Subsequently, during 2010–20, there was marginal improvement and the annual figures have fluctuated between 13 per cent and 17 per cent; however, important point to note is that compared to 1980s, the subsequent decades have witnessed substantial compression on rural economy as a whole, with obvious adverse implications for employment and livelihoods.

Combining the expenditures of Union and State governments on rural development, agricultural & allied activities and food subsidy for the period from 1990–91 to 2017–18, the relevant trends are shown in Figure 6. This entire period consists of sub-phases depending on a variety pulls and pressures due to economic and political challenges. The period from1990–91 to 2003–04, by and large shows a declining. During this period, apart from opening the economy to agricultural trade, several protective regulations were withdrawn, agricultural subsidies were cut, and the universal PDS was converted to TPDS (Patnaik, 2008). The growing crisis in rural India resulted in some policy redressal in the subsequent years, particularly, when UPA was in power. Apart from enactment of MGNREGA to provide 100 days of employment to every household in India in 2005–06, a couple of other major interventions included National Food Security Mission (2007–12) to increase production and productivity of wheat, rice and pulses, Rashtriya Krishi Vikas Yojana (2007) to provide much needed support for agriculture and allied sectors. All these flagship efforts led to some increase in Government's expenditure on rural development, agriculture and allied activities and food security in this period (see Figure 6, the period from 2004–05 to 2008–09). The period had also witnessed an increase in combined total revenue and capital expenditure of the central and State Governments on social sectors.

Figure 5: Share of expenditure on the "Rural Economy" in the aggregate expenditure of All Indian States in per cent.

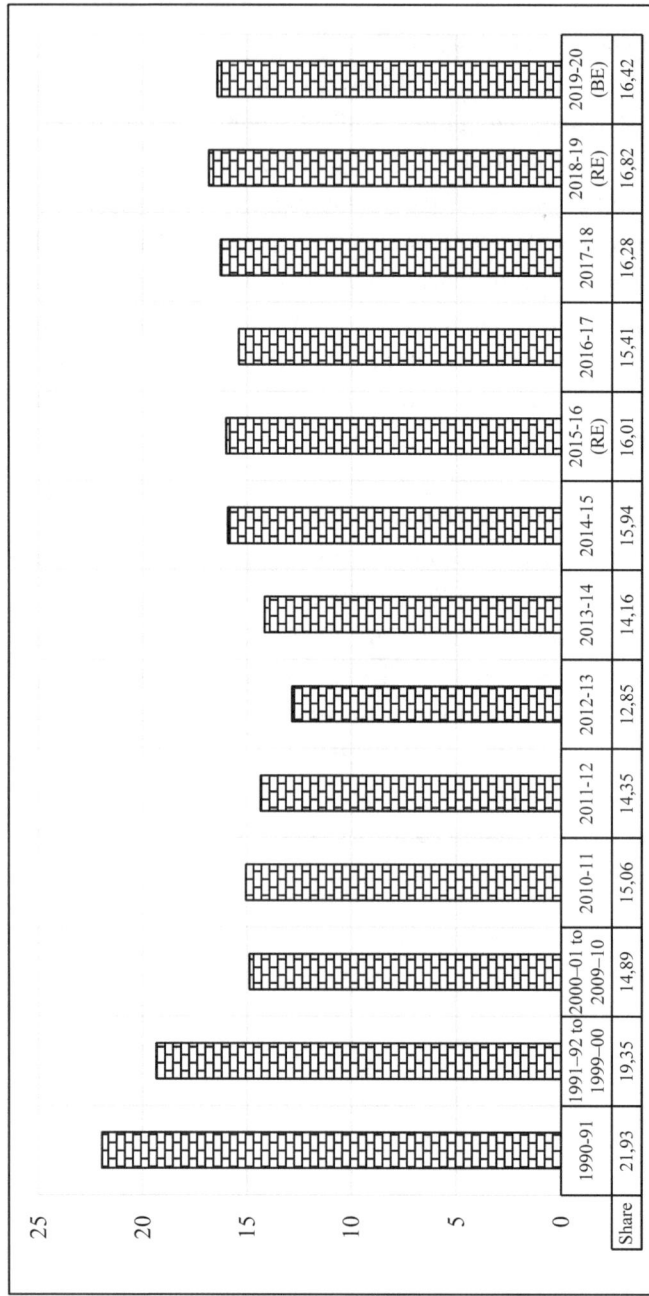

	1990-91	1991–92 to 1999–00	2000–01 to 2009–10	2010-11	2011-12	2012-13	2013-14	2014-15	2015-16 (RE)	2016-17	2017-18	2018-19 (RE)	2019-20 (BE)
Share	21,93	19,35	14,89	15,06	14,35	12,85	14,16	15,94	16,01	15,41	16,28	16,82	16,42

Source: Jha and Acharya, 2011 and Reserve Bank of India, Handbook of State Finance, different years. RE: Revised Estimates and BE: Budget Estimates

Figure 6: Combined Capital and Revenue Expenditure of Union and State Governments on Agriculture & Allied Activities (AG), Rural Development (RD) and Food Security (FS) (% of GDP and % of Total Expenditure).

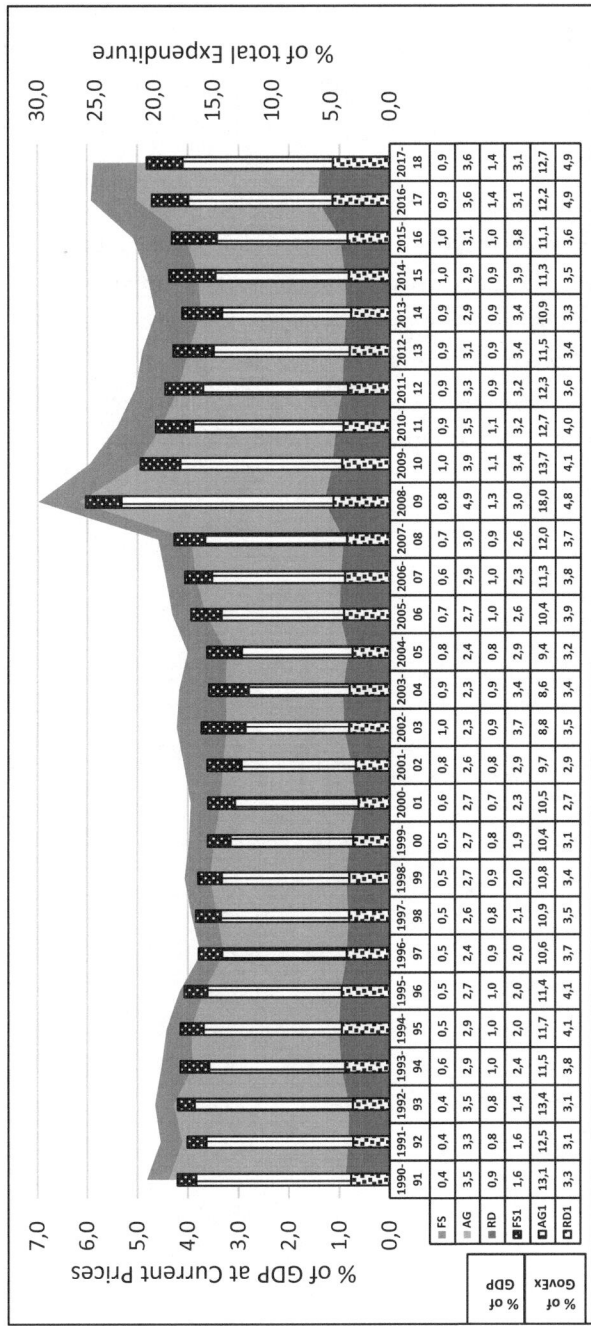

	1990-91	1991-92	1992-93	1993-94	1994-95	1995-96	1996-97	1997-98	1998-99	1999-00	2000-01	2001-02	2002-03	2003-04	2004-05	2005-06	2006-07	2007-08	2008-09	2009-10	2010-11	2011-12	2012-13	2013-14	2014-15	2015-16	2016-17	2017-18
FS	0,4	0,4	0,4	0,6	0,5	0,5	0,5	0,5	0,5	0,5	0,6	0,8	1,0	0,9	0,8	0,7	0,6	0,7	0,8	1,0	0,9	0,9	0,9	0,9	1,0	1,0	0,9	0,9
AG	3,5	3,3	3,5	2,9	2,9	2,7	2,4	2,6	2,7	2,7	2,7	2,6	2,3	2,3	2,4	2,7	2,9	3,0	4,9	3,9	3,5	3,3	3,1	2,9	2,9	3,1	3,6	3,6
RD	0,9	0,8	0,8	1,0	1,0	1,0	0,9	0,8	0,9	0,8	0,7	0,8	0,9	0,9	0,8	1,0	1,0	0,9	1,3	1,1	1,1	0,9	0,9	0,9	1,0	1,0	1,4	1,4
FS1	1,6	1,6	1,4	2,4	2,0	2,0	2,0	2,1	2,0	1,9	2,3	2,9	3,7	3,4	2,9	2,6	2,3	2,6	3,0	3,4	3,2	3,2	3,4	3,4	3,9	3,8	3,1	3,1
AG1	13,1	12,5	13,4	11,5	11,7	11,4	10,6	10,9	10,8	10,4	10,5	9,7	8,8	8,6	9,4	10,4	11,3	12,0	18,0	13,7	12,7	12,3	11,5	10,9	11,3	11,1	12,2	12,7
RD1	3,3	3,1	3,1	3,8	4,1	4,1	3,7	3,5	3,4	3,1	2,7	2,9	3,5	3,4	3,2	3,9	3,8	3,7	4,8	4,1	4,0	3,6	3,4	3,3	3,5	3,6	4,9	4,9

Source: Authors' Calculation, Compiled from Various Reports of Indian Public Finance Statistics

Subsequently, after 2009–10 to 2013–14, there is another round of compression in overall expenditure on rural development, agriculture and allied activities and the food subsidy. Such a decline aggravated the distress in the rural sector which also contributed to the defeat of the UPA government. For the period 2014–15 to 2017–18, there was an uptick in combined expenditure of central and State Governments as a percentage of GDP and total government expenditure on rural development and agriculture and allied activities, but a sharp decline in expenditure on food subsidy. The relevant information for the last couple of years, i.e. after 2017–18 which are not shown in the above figure, as these are not available from Indian Public Finance Statistics used as the source for this figure, indicate a reversal in the overall rural expenditure trends again.

Figure 7:   Share of 'Village and Small Industries' and 'Irrigation and Flood Control' in Total Expenditure of Indian States

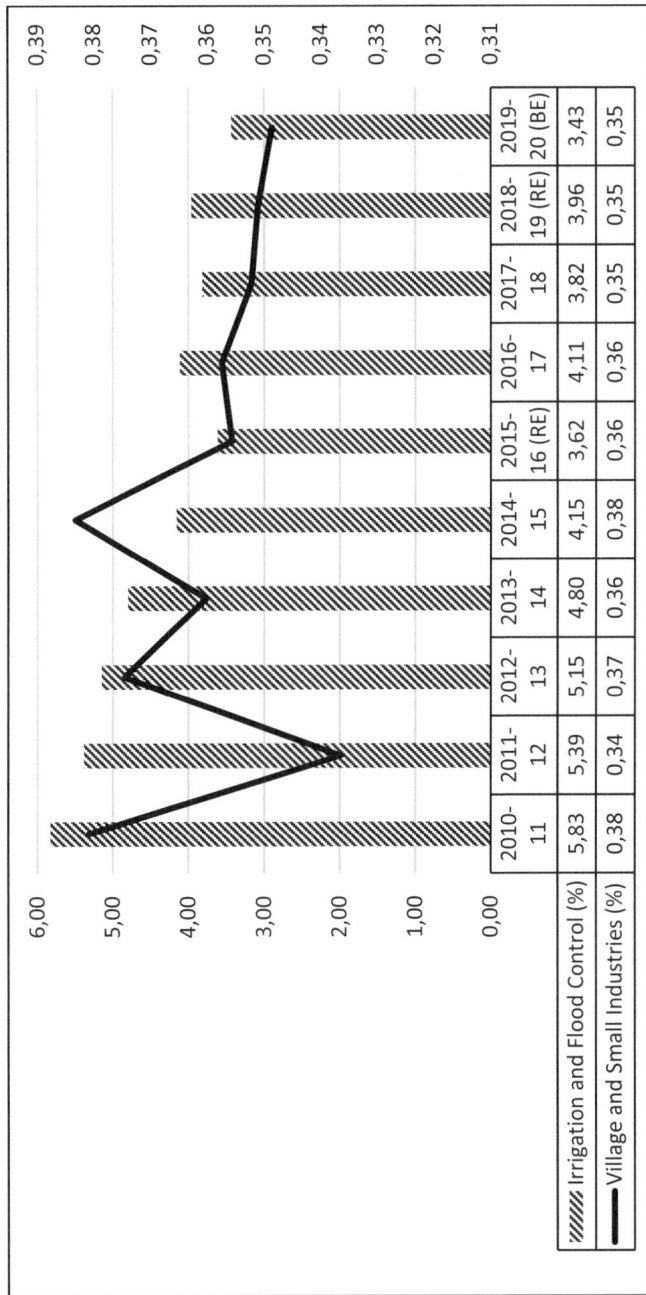

	2010-11	2011-12	2012-13	2013-14	2014-15	2015-16 (RE)	2016-17	2017-18	2018-19 (RE)	2019-20 (BE)
Irrigation and Flood Control (%)	5,83	5,39	5,15	4,80	4,15	3,62	4,11	3,82	3,96	3,43
Village and Small Industries (%)	0,38	0,34	0,37	0,36	0,38	0,36	0,36	0,35	0,35	0,35

Source: Reserve Bank of India, Handbook of State Finance, different years. RE: Revised Estimates and BE: Budget Estimates

As discussed above the share of public investment in agriculture had declined significantly in the last three decades, a similar trend is visible for irrigation. The figure 7 presents the share of irrigation and flood control in the total expenditure of Indian states. The 2010–20 decade has seen a sharp decline in the share. The share of irrigation was more than 10 per cent in the 1980s and 7.5 per cent in 1990s (Modak, 2018). The decline in the budgetary allocation is also visible in the physical outcome. The share of public sources in the net irrigated area in the country in the last three decades has registered a decline, and at the same time, private sources have increased. There is a shift from public canal irrigation to the private tubewell irrigation in India at large scale (*ibid*).

Various studies show that the cost of cultivation has increased significantly in the liberalisation period (Raghavan, 2008; Kumar, 2019). Hence, in the aggregate withdrawal of support to agriculture has led to continuous squeeze of farmers' income, and deepened the agrarian distress. As one would expect, all classes of farmers have been affected adversely, but the marginal and small farmers as well as the landless workers, accounting for almost 90 percent of the rural population, have been the worst hit (Patnaik, 2012; Sainath, 2018), and their food security has been dented further. Those replaced by agriculture could have been provided jobs in rural industries.

Concluding Remarks

The paper has tried to examine some of the most important markers and their causes relating to food insecurity in India. Given that Indian economy has been the second fasted growing economy in the world, for close to four decades now, and is unable to address the most basic indicator of human well-being, namely, adequate food, is indeed a cause of serious concern. As discussed in this paper, most of the important causal correlates for such a state of affair lie in the domain of overall macroeconomic policy regime. Ascendency of neoliberalism, through multiple policy channels, has impacted on different dimensions of food security in the country in very significant adverse ways, both from the demand side i.e. through the policies of income deflation for the large majority of working people and masses in general, and supply side i.e. through compression of expenditure (as a proportion of GDP and of public expenditure), trade policies, completely unreasonable holding of food stocks etc. *It is worth noting that for the first time in India since Independence, per capita consumption in the country for more than a quinquennium at a stretch (i.e. between 2011–12 and 2017–18) declined significantly[13]; in fact in rural India, the order of decline was close to 10 percent, which possibly is unprecedented anywhere in the world during so-called "normal" times.*

References:

Aspects of Indian Economy, (2006): How the Wheat Crisis of 2006 Was Created, Aspects of Indian Economy, No. 42, December, https://www.rupe-india.org/42/crisis.html.

Bhattacharya, R. and Abhijit Sen Gupta. (2017): Drivers and Impact of Food Inflation in India, Journal of Macroeconomics and Finance in Emerging Market Economies, Vol. 11, No. 2, 31 July.

Breman, J. (2010): Outcast Labour in Asia: Circulation and Informalisation of the Workforce at the Bottom of the Economy, Oxford: Oxford University Press.

Census of India. (2001): D-Series: Migration Tables, Government of India.

Census of India. (2011): D-Series: Migration Tables, Government of India.

Deaton, A and J Dreze (2009): Food and Nutrition in India: Facts and Interpretations, Economic & Political Weekly, Vol XLIV, No 7, 14 February.

Drèze, Jean and Amartya Sen (1989). Hunger and Public Action, Clarendon Press Oxford.

FAO, IFAD, UNICEF, WFP and WHO. 2019. The State of Food Security and Nutrition in the World 2019. Safeguarding against economic slowdowns and downturns. Rome, FAO.

FAO. (2009): The State of Agricultural Commodity Markets 2009, Rome. Available at http://www.fao.org/3/i0854e/i0854e01.pdf.

---

13 Along with the PLFS survey, a consumption survey was done in 2017–18 with the similar frame. But, the government presumably found it so embarrassing that in spite of the assurance that it would be released officially, but it was finally suppressed.

Ghosh, Jayati, James Heintz and Robert Pollin. (2012): Speculation on Commodities Futures Market and Destablisation of Global Food Prices: Exploring the Connections, International Journal of Health Services, Vol. 42, No. 3, pp. 465–483.

Global Hunger Index Report (2019): Global Hunger Index, The Challenge of Hunger and Climate Change. https://reliefweb.int/sites/reliefweb.int/files/resour ces/2019%20Global%20Hunger%20Index.pdf

GoI, (2005): Department of Food &Public Distribution, Highlights 2004–05, Department of Food and Public Distribution, Government of India, https:// dfpd.gov.in/1sGbO2W68mUlunCgKmpnLF5WHm/pdf/annual-2004-05.pdf.

GoI, (2009). Report of Committee on State Agrarian Relations and the Unfinished Task in Land Reforms, Department of Land Resources, Ministry of Rural Development, Government of India. https://dolr.gov.in/sites/default/files/ Committee%20Report.pdf.

GoI, (2013a): The National Food Security Act, 2013, Gazette of India, Government of India, https://dfpd.gov.in/fgAvAHcAcgBpAHQAZQByAGUAYQBkAG QAYQB0AGEALwBQAG8AcgB0AGEAbAAvAE0AYQBnAGEAegBpAG4 AZQAvAEQAbwBjAHUAbQBlAG4AdAdAAvAA==/1_405_1_NFSA_ACT.pdf

GoI, (2013b): Draft National Land Reforms Policy, Department of Land Resources, Ministry of Rural Development, Government of India, 18 July.

GoI, (2017): Economic Survey, 2016–17, Ministry of Finance, Government of India.

GoI, (2019): Agriculture Census 2015–16, Phase-I, All India Report on Number and Area of Operational Holdings, Department of Agriculture, Co-Operation & Farmers Welfare, Ministry of Agriculture & Farmers Welfare, Government of India.

Harvey, David. (2007): A Brief History of Neoliberalism, Oxford University Press.

Jha, Praveen and N. Acharya, (2011): Expenditure on the Rural Economy in India's Budgets since the 1950s: An Assessment, *Review of Agrarian Studies*, Vol 1, No. 2, July–December.

Jha Praveen and N Acharya (2016). Public Provisioning for Social Protection and Its Implications for Food Security, *Economic and Political Weekly*, Vol. 51, Issue No. 18, April 30.

Jha, Praveen (2019): Prospects for Labour and Contemporary Capitalism: An Assessment with Reference to India, The Indian Journal of Labour Economics, No. 62, September 24, pp. 319–340.

Kumar, Manish. (2019): India's Rice Export: What is in It for Farmers? Agrarian South: Journal of Political Economy, Vol. 8, No. 1–2, 30 July.

Mittal, P. (2017): Aadhaar made mandatory to ensure poor get food: Centre tells Delhi HC, Live Mint, 24 April, https://www.livemint.com/Politics/djFjNTe qvkzHVJ1G1mHQzI/Aadhaar-made-mandatory-to-ensure-poor-get-food-Centre-tells.html.

Modak, T. S.(2018): From Public to Private Irrigation: Implications for Equity in Access to Water, *Review of Agrarian Studies*, Vol. 8, No. 1, January–June.

Nayyar, G and Rohini Nayyar (2016): India's Poverty Numbers': Revisiting Measurement Issues, Economic and Political Weekly, Vol LI, No. 35, 27 August.

Patnaik, P. and C.P. Chandrasekhar (1995): Indian Economy under 'Structural Adjustment', Economic and Political Weekly, Vol. 30, No. 47, 25 November.

Patnaik, Prabhat. (2007): The State Under Neoliberalism, Social Scientist, Vol. 35, No. ½, Jan–Feb, pp. 4–15.

Patnaik, Prabhat. (2012). The peasant question and contemporary capitalism: Some reflections with reference to India. Agrarian South: Journal of Political Economy, 1(1), 27–42.

Patnaik, Prabhat. (2016). Imperialism and the agrarian question. Agrarian South: Journal of Political Economy, 3(1), 1–15.

Patnaik, U. (2008). Theorising Poverty and Food Security in the Era of Economic Reforms, In Globalization and the Washington Consensus: Its Influence on Democracy and Development in the South, pp. 161–200, available at http://biblioteca.clacso.edu.ar/clacso/sur-sur/20100707035029/12patna.pdf.

Patnaik, Utsa (2010a): Trends in Urban Poverty under Economic Reforms: 1993–94 to 2004–05. Economic & Political Weekly, Vol XLV, No 4, 23 January.

Patnaik, Utsa (2010b): A Critical Look at Some Propositions on Consumption and Poverty. Economic & Political Weekly, Vol XLV, No 6, 6 January.

Patnaik, Utsa. (2015): The Origins and Continuation of First World Import Dependence on Developing Countries for Agricultural Products, *Agrarian South: Journal of Political Economy*, 4(1) 1–21.

Patnaik, U. and P. Patnaik (2019): Neoliberal Capitalism at a Dead End, Monthly Review, Vol. 71, No. 3, July–August.

Raghavan, M. (2008): Changing Pattern of Input Use and Cost of Cultivation, Economic and Political Weekly, Vol. 43, No. 26–27, June.

Ram, Krishna (2017): Explaining Calorie Consumption Puzzle in India: An Empirical Study based on National and International Data-Sets since 1990s. Social Scientist, Vol. 45, No. 9/10 (September–October 2017), pp. 35–53.

Rawal, Vikas (2008): Ownership Holdings of Land in Rural India. Putting the Record Straight. Economic and Political Weekly, Vol. XLIII, No. 10, 8 March.

Rawal, Vikas (2013): Changes in the Distribution of Operational Landholdings in Rural India. A Study of National Sample Survey Data. Review of Agrarian Studies, Vol. 3, No.2, July 2013 to Jan. 2014.

Sainath, P. (2018): In India, Farmers Face a Terrifying Crisis, The New York Times, 13 April, available at https://www.nytimes.com/2018/04/13/opinion/india-farmers-crisis.html.

Sarma, Mandira, P. Saha and N. Jayakumar (2017): Asset Inequality in India: Going from Bad to Worse, Social Scientist, Vol. 45, Nos.3–4, March–April.

Srivastava, R (2020): "No Relief for the Nowhere People," Hindu, 4 May, https://www.thehindu.com/opinion/op-ed/no-relief-for-the-nowhere-people/article31495460.ece.

Swaminathan, M. (2008): Programmes to Protect the Hungry: Lessons from India, Economicand Social Affairs, DESA Working Paper No. 70, October, available at https://www.un.org/esa/desa/papers/2008/wp70_2008.pdf.

Swaminathan, M and Neeta Mishra (2001): Errors of Targeting: Public Distribution of Food in a Maharashtra Village, 1995–2000, Economic and Political Weekly, Vol. 36, No. 26, June30.

Verma, Santosh (2015): Subverting the Land Acquisition Act, 2013, Economic and Political Weekly, Vol. 50, No. 37, 12 September.

Verma, Santosh and Ranjana Roy (2019): Political Economy of Inequality in Ownership Holdings in India: An Analysis of 70th Round NSS Data, Man & Development, Vol. XLI, No. 3, September.

CHAPTER 3
Legal Dimension of the Human Right to Adequate Food and Public Policies

Ana Carolina Oliveira Lopes (UFPB);
Maria Luiza Pereira de Alencar Mayer Feitosa (UFPB)

1 Introduction

Seeing the act of nourishing oneself as a right is an exercise that goes beyond guaranteeing the consumption of a certain number of calories per day. It is essential to understand the right to adequate food as a vital extension of the right to life and a corollary of the principle of human dignity. Within the context of international human rights conventions, the concept of the human right to adequate food not only signifies the need to ensure access to food but includes aspects related to its production, conservation and distribution. It also encompasses the political dimensions of land reform, social and environmental sustainability and food and nutrition security—in the country and in the world—and a break with the mode of capitalist accumulation, all directed towards the greater objective of producing the equitable sharing of rights, including the human right to food, among other social rights.

In Brazil, according to studies by the Special Secretariat for Family Farming and Agrarian Development (*Secretaria Especial de Agricultura Familiar e do Desenvolvimento Agrário—SEAD*), 70% of food is produced by family farming. However, in order for small farmers to be able to produce increasingly more food and sustenance, it is necessary to maintain and improve credit and purchase programs, which guarantee the flow of production and the generation of income, as in the case of the Food Acquisition Program (*Programa de Aquisição de Alimentos—PAA*) and the National School Feeding Program (*Programa Nacional da Alimentação Escolar—PNAE*), both created in 2003.

The right to food was included—albeit belatedly—in the list of social rights protected by the legal system, in the context of what is called the third generation of public policies, which followed the macroeconomic stabilization policy reforms (first generation) and their administrative support (second generation). In 2006, Law No. 11,346, the Organic Law on Food and Nutrition Security (*Lei Orgânica de Segurança Alimentar e Nutricional—LOSAN*), was enacted, creating the National Food and Nutrition Security System (*Sistema Nacional de Segurança Alimentar e Nutricional—SISAN*), which brought together the three levels of government—federal, state and municipal—with the objective of implementing policies that would guarantee the right to adequate food.

In this scenario, legal and political aspects are intertwined in the guarantee and realization of rights. The objective of this essay is to extract approaches to the concept of the human right to adequate food from both international legal devices and domestic legislation, comparing the mechanisms in the LOSAN with the International Covenant on Economic, Social and Cultural Rights (ICESCR), in order to understand the equivalence between the constitutional and human dimensions of the right under analysis.

It is necessary to understand the public policies and coordinated actions of the three levels of government as a method for realizing the human right to food, based on the scope of the policy. The idea is to point out mechanisms adopted by Brazilian administrations in their attempts to realize the right to adequate food, as well as outline some of the challenges faced in implementing these policies, until arriving at the current crisis, following the impeachment of President Dilma Rousseff, who was replaced by an administration with rentier elements, subordinate to international financial capitalism.

The main methodological line will therefore involve the inductive approach, through a general analysis of the data collected and evaluated. The comparative procedure, using reading and discussion techniques for the selected legal, documentary and doctrinal material, will conclude the study, which is generally theoretical and descriptive, underpinned by a historical, critical and dialectical foundation. This chapter is the result of research carried out with funding from the Institutional Scientific Initiation

Scholarship Program (*Programa Institucional de Bolsas de Iniciação Científica—PIBIC*), linked to the Center of Legal Sciences at Federal University of Paraíba (*Universidade Federal da Paraíba—UFPB*), in the 2013–2014 cycle, under the work plan titled "Studies and Reflections on National Public Policies: Empirical Research," proposed and supervised by Professor Maria Luiza Pereira de Alencar Mayer Feitosa and carried out by the scholarship recipient Ana Carolina Oliveira Lopes.

2 The concept of the right to adequate food within the multiple dimensions of human rights

Internationally, the first major charter to protect human rights was the Universal Declaration of Human Rights (UDHR), which in Article 25.1 states "Everyone has the right to a standard of living adequate for the health and well-being of himself and of his family, including food [...]." Following the horrors of World War II, many countries were concerned with protecting the peace and well-being of humans, including the right to food in this context.

As it has no binding force on the signatory states, the UDHR was spun off into two covenants: the International Covenant on Civil and Political Rights and the ICESCR. The international protection of human rights, particularly the right to adequate food, is included in the latter document, with a broad and multidimensional perspective, not only linked to food itself or the initial notion of well-being but also integrated with several other aspects.

According to the ICESCR, the right to food has two basic components: the right to adequate food and the fundamental right to be protected against hunger are both enshrined in Article 11. The dimension of protection against hunger is linked to the right to life itself, understanding that the right to adequate food requires an appropriate environment, in economic, political and social terms, allowing individuals to purchase their food for themselves, in a context of food security.

According to Article 11 of the ICESCR:

1. The States Parties to the present Covenant recognize the right of everyone to an adequate standard of living for himself and his family, including adequate food, clothing and housing, and to the continuous improvement of living conditions. The States Parties will take appropriate steps to ensure the realization of this right, recognizing to this effect the essential importance of international co-operation based on free consent.

2. The States Parties to the present Covenant, recognizing the fundamental right of everyone to be free from hunger, shall take, individually and through international co-operation, the measures, including specific programs, which are needed:

    a) To improve methods of production, conservation and distribution of food by making full use of technical and scientific knowledge, by disseminating knowledge of the principles of nutrition and by developing or reforming agrarian systems in such a way as to achieve the most efficient development and utilization of natural resources;

    b) Taking into account the problems of both food-importing and food-exporting countries, to ensure an equitable distribution of world food supplies in relation to need.

The text contains important aspects regarding the concept of the human right to food. First, its essentiality, as the guarantee of adequate living conditions—such as food and clothing—is closely related to the principle of human dignity. Furthermore, within the context of the guarantee to adequate food, realizing the human right to food involves production, distribution, nutritional education, aspects of agricultural policy and land distribution, and the rational and sustainable use of natural resources.

Second, it emphasizes the fact that the guarantee to food is the responsibility and duty of states, which will need to adopt policies, programs and actions—guiding international cooperation—in order for this right to be fully realized. It is therefore not only necessary to "put food on the table" of the population but to guide and implement policies for everything from sustainable production—involving an equitable distribution of planting and harvest—to the rational consumption of food.

To this end, Comment 12 by the Committee on Economic, Social and Cultural Rights (CESCR) emphasizes that the right to food:

is realized when every man, woman and child, alone or in community with others, has physical and economic access at all times to adequate food or means for its procurement. The right to adequate food shall therefore not be interpreted in a narrow or restrictive sense which equates it with a minimum package of calories, proteins and other specific nutrients. The right to adequate food will have to be realized progressively. However, States have a core obligation to take the necessary action to mitigate and alleviate hunger as provided for in paragraph 2 of article 11, even in times of natural or other disasters (ONU, 1999).

The right to adequate food therefore encompasses the availability of food in sufficient quantity and quality to ensure the well-being of individuals, satisfying their daily needs. Based on the multidimensional view of the human right to adequate food, food should be free of harmful substances as well as be part of a context that respects the culture, customs and habits of a given population.

Along the same lines, out of respect for future generations, production must be sustainable, preserving the environment. Guaranteeing the right to food cannot jeopardize other human rights. With a perspective complementary to the comment by the CESCR, the first United Nations (UN) special rapporteur on the right to food, J. Ziegler, defined the concept of the right to adequate food as:

> the right to have regular, permanent and free access, either directly or by means of financial purchases, to quantitatively and qualitatively adequate and sufficient food corresponding to the cultural traditions of the people to which the consumer belongs, and which ensures a physical and mental, individual and collective, fulfilling and dignified life free of fear (FAO, 2001).

The complementarity of the comment demonstrates the distinct approach to human dignity offered by the normative postulate of the right to food. The legal concept of this right should thus include protection from hunger as a central element, as it is essential to exercising other human rights, such as the right to employment, housing, education and citizenship. This text therefore adopts the perspective of the interdependence and indivisibility of human rights, assuming that the inadequate protection of one right directly affects the realization of other rights (FERREIRA, 2011).

In reality, the right to food goes beyond purely "social" aspects. It signifies that even if it is considered a social right par excellence, the guarantee of any fundamental right includes other dimensions, such as civil, political and economic rights and even transindividual and intergenerational rights, requiring the state—as well as society—to respect individual freedoms and be concerned for future generations. In a broader perspective, any human right includes not only the binomial of civil rights and social rights—the dichotomy between abstentions and positive benefits from the state—but a set of rights—integrated with and interdependent on one another—understanding that one right is the basis for the realization of another.

Based on the preliminary understanding of a lack of hierarchy among human rights, this confirms that economic, social and cultural rights (ESCR) are located on the same level as other rights. For Flávia Piovesan,

> as important as freedom of expression is access to healthcare, education and employment. Dying from torture is as serious as dying from hunger. There is a parity with respect to the freedom axis and the equality axis and, not only that, but the integral view of human rights, i.e., the declaration comprises a catalog of civil and political rights and a catalog of economic, social and cultural rights, thus establishing a relationship of interdependence, interrelationship and indivisibility. Not only are they on an equal footing, but they depend on one another. There is no true freedom without equality, nor is there true equality without freedom (PIOVESAN, 2009, p. 108).

Human rights invoke the perception of movement, a series of transformations and achievements linked to the history of a people. As such, they cannot be conceived in a linear, limited or stagnant view but, rather, understood in the ongoing struggle for their affirmation, "the story of a struggle, of a fight and of social actions" (PIOVESAN, 2009, p.107). The recognition of human rights is particularly related to their possession, and thus, the right to food is a human right, as it is a corollary of the principle of human dignity.

Human rights are positivized in international constitutions, laws and treaties. From a positivist perspective, in the context of states, they comprise the text of constitutional charters, representing protections conferred upon the individual through the power of the state as well as recognition of the state's obligations to its people. This view corroborates the paradigm shift of the modern state, which is primarily responsible for the realization of those rights.

The paradigmatic turn begins with the Constitutions of Mexico (1917) and Germany, in the Weimar Republic (1919), which first granted a legal and political understanding of economic issues, creating the duties of the economic order and reinforcing the phenomenon of social constitutionalism (FEITOSA, 2012). States began to recognize the obligation to guarantee social rights within their political agendas, through government actions that would implement collective rights, such as education, health, employment and social security. This moment characterized the decline in the classical liberal model, leading the state to also redistribute income and structure investment policies (FEITOSA, 2012).

The so-called "new social constitutionalism" seeks to guarantee material equality through constitutional charters. What emerges is an active model of the state, which intervenes in economic activity and controls basic sectors, such as education, healthcare, housing, industry and banking, as well as general activities, such as transportation, water supply, electricity, fuel and the postal service. However, it is clear that the interventionist state that becomes consolidated—namely, after the New York stock market crash of 1929—begins to regulate economic activity rather than guaranteeing social rights.

Following World War II, there is further improvement of social constitutionalism and a consequent expansion of legal mechanisms for social protection. Constitutional charters then began to include social aspects, making states legally responsible for protecting those rights; the absence of the state may thus characterize a human rights violation. Within the scope of state responsibility, as stated above, is the right to food.

In the case of Brazil, despite state recognition of different international instruments protecting the human right to food, it was only on February 4, 2010, with the enactment of Constitutional Amendment No. 64, that food was included in Article 6 of the Federal Constitution, which addresses constitutionally protected social rights. This achievement was the result of pressure from society and social movements, including campaigns running on national television networks, which demanded the approval of Constitutional Amendment Project (*Projeto de Emenda Constitucional—PEC*) No. 47.

This does not mean that the right to food was not protected by the Brazilian legal system before the amendment's approval. It is common knowledge that International Human Rights Treaties have the status of a supralegal norm, as understood by the Federal Supreme Court[14], and are thus part of the Brazilian legal system, supporting the recognition of the right to adequate food. Moreover, in 2006, as mentioned above, the SISAN was created through the enactment of Law No. 11,346, to ensure the human right to food.

That law included the normative concept of "adequate food" in its text, granting it the status of a fundamental right, in line with the domestic legal system as well as with the human rights treaties ratified by Brazil. Thus, according to the caput and paragraphs of Law No. 11,346, Art. 2:

> Art. 2 Adequate food is a fundamental human right, inherent in the dignity of the human person and indispensable for the realization of the rights enshrined in the Brazilian Constitution, and the government should implement the policies and actions that may be necessary to promote and ensure the food and nutrition security of the population.
> § 1 The adoption of these policies and actions should take into account environmental, cultural, economic, regional and social dimensions.
> § 2 It is the duty of the government to respect, protect, promote, provide, inform, monitor, inspect and evaluate the realization of the human right to adequate food as well as guarantee the mechanisms for its enforceability.

Accordingly, the legal concept adopted in Brazil is in line with the description of the right to food used in the ICESCR, showing how the human right to food should be realized with a multidimensional perspective, with the state assuming the responsibility for promoting actions to achieve it. The normative concept thus reinforces the idea that all fundamental rights have a great structural affinity and that the realization of any right—civil, political or social—involves adopting a series of actions—with negative or positive benefits from the state and civil society—that complement and interact with one another. This thus breaks with the immediate conception of thinking about social rights solely as positive benefits from the state.

Brazil has assumed the obligation to respect, protect and promote the right to food. It also has the obligation to not discriminate, in order to guarantee the protection of the human right to food equally for all people.

---

14   In Portuguese, the *Supremo Tribunal Federal* (STF) (RE 466343-SP and HC 87585-TO)

The state must therefore act to use the maximum available resources in measures to fight against hunger and malnutrition, in addition to establishing a legislative and institutional framework, within the context of a judicial system capable of guaranteeing the right to food.

By law, the state must also promote access to natural resources and means of food production, such as land, water, seeds, rural credit, fisheries and livestock. It also has the obligation to specifically protect those subjects, such as children, the elderly and people with disabilities, who—for reasons beyond their control—are unable to access food on their own, as well as engage in international partnerships and cooperation to promote the human right to food, particularly in emergency and disaster situations, respecting the environment and ensuring the right to food for future generations by promoting a sustainable development model (FAO, 2001).

The list of state obligations involves an intercommunication between the duties of respecting, protecting and promoting the right to food, coordinating actions that imply both positive and negative benefits from the state, with the objective of guaranteeing full access to food, including all generations of human rights. This again reaffirms the maxim that a human right cannot be fully realized in solely a single generation or dimension, considering the indivisible and interdependent character of human rights.

Another important concept guiding Brazilian legislation is found in Article 3 of the LOSAN: the idea of food and nutrition security. The LOSAN represents the consecration of a comprehensive and intersectoral conception of Food and Nutrition Security as well as an affirmation of the principles that guide its application, namely, food security and the human right to food. The principles of the human right to adequate food thus incorporate the need for regular, permanent access to quality food as well as respect for the particularities and cultural characteristics of each region,

> without compromising access to other essential needs, based on healthy food habits, thus contributing to a dignified existence in a context of the integral development of the human being, preserving the conditions that guarantee the long-term availability of food (FAO, 2001).

Having first understood the importance of recognizing food as a fundamental human right, the state is now responsible for establishing mechanisms and carrying out actions to guarantee, protect and respect this right. Public policies and intersectoral, participatory government action complement the realization of the human right to adequate food, with mechanisms to demand the state's actions. This performance through public policies is in line with the concept of the right to food recognized by the signatory states of the ICESCR and—in the case of Brazil—enforces the infra-constitutional legislation that makes the state responsible for adopting measures to realize the human right to food.

3   Public policies and the human right to adequate food

The advancement of human rights discourse and the emergence of new rights also lead to discussions about the methods to guarantee them. Public policies are increasingly moving away from the field of management science and are now being discussed in the legal realm, as a way to realize ESCR, connected to administrative law, showing the extent to which the legal and political spheres must be in constant dialog. Maria Paula Bucci presents the following concept:

> public policies are programs for government action aimed at coordinating the means available to the state and private activities, in order to achieve socially relevant and politically determined objectives. Public policies are "conscious collective goals" and, as such, a public law problem in the broadest sense (BUCCI, 2002, p. 241).

With the advent of socioeconomic constitutionalism, the social question began to be confronted by the state. General and abstract norms gave way to a kind of governance through policies (BUCCI, 2002), which characterizes different types of state intervention in the private sphere, severing the dichotomy between public and private law, which began to dialog, under the guidelines of constitutional principles. This movement became known as the constitutionalization of private law—civil and commercial—and had significant repercussions in Brazil.

Constitutional principles guide the activity of interpreting and applying legal norms, in a phenomenon that incorporates branches traditionally linked to private law into the spirit of the Constitution, eliciting—in practice—a new constitutionalism. The 1998 Brazilian Citizen Constitution has a principle load that was common at the time; it is a programmatic document that outlines essential aspects of the state's structure, while establishing guidelines for the realization of fundamental rights, incorporated broadly in the text, with the subsequent inclusion of the human and social right to adequate food.

Discussions about guaranteeing the right to food in Brazil have always been linked to the discourse of the fight against hunger. In an attempt to resume the debate on the fight against hunger through the institutionalization of a food security policy, the National Council for Food and Nutrition Security (*Conselho Nacional de Segurança Alimentar e Nutricional—CONSEA*) was reestablished in 2003, in the first year of the Lula administration, following eight years with no activities (MACHADO, 2017). In this context, as a result of widespread debate and social pressure, the LOSAN was approved, creating the SISAN, opening up space for both the conception of a system of integrated public policies and the establishment of mechanisms to demand actions carried out by the state.

It is obvious that the law in itself does not solve the problem of hunger. However, the existence of the legislative instruments makes it possible to create conditions for the formulation of food security policies, with national action plans that involve goals, guidelines, resources, evaluation, monitoring and collaboration between sectors of government and civil society (MACHADO, 2017). The SISAN thus emerged as a demand from civil society with the greater objective of ensuring the right to adequate food in the country, bringing together all the social actors to implement the National Policy for Food and Nutrition Security (*Política Nacional de Segurança Alimentar e Nutricional—PNSAN*) (Art. 1 and 3 of the LOSAN), whose instrument is the National Food and Nutrition Security Plan (*Plano Nacional de Segurança Alimentar e Nutricional—PLANSAN*) (MACHADO, 2017).

According to Law No. 11346/2006, the SISAN is

a public system, with an intersectoral, participatory administration, that facilitates collaboration between different sectors and the three levels of government, as well as organized civil society, in order to implement and execute food and nutrition security policies. The law defines as members of this system: the National Conference on Food and Nutrition Security (*Conferência Nacional de Segurança Alimentar e Nutricional—CNSAN*), the National Council for Food and Nutrition Security (*Conselho Nacional de Segurança Alimentar e Nutricional—CONSEA*), the Inter-Ministerial Chamber on Food and Nutrition Security (*Câmara Interministerial de Segurança Alimentar e Nutricional—CAISAN*), the agencies and institutions for food and nutrition security in the nation, states, Federal District (*Distrito Federal—DF*) and municipalities, as well as for-profit or non-profit private institutions that express an interest in joining the SISAN. (CAISAN, 2011, p. 43)

This policy is guided by two principles that are part of the very structure of its institutions. The deliberative councils demonstrate the principle of social participation and intersectorality, through the collaboration of the three levels of government; the states and the Federal District joined the SISAN, followed gradually by the municipalities. Data from 2017[15] indicate that 276 municipalities are registered in the SISAN and that more than 400 are ready to join the system; 600 municipalities are expected to be incorporated by 2019, according to the 2016–2019 Multi-Year Plan (*Plano Plurianual—PPA*) (SANTOS, 2017). Similarly, for-profit or non-profit private institutions that express an interest in joining and respect the SISAN's criteria, principles and guidelines can also join the policy, although this has not been regulated by the Inter-Ministerial Chamber on Food and Nutrition Security (*Câmara Interministerial de Segurança Alimentar e Nutricional—CAISAN*) (MACHADO, 2017).

Other policies are part of the system for guaranteeing the human right to adequate food within the logic of the SISAN. They are the National School Feeding Program (*PNAE*) and the Food Acquisition Program (*PAA*), domestic policies developed within the framework of state-level Enterprises for Technical Assistance and Rural Extension (*Empresas de Assistência Técnica e Extensão Rural—EMATER*).

Created in 2003, during the first Lula administration, the PAA is a government policy that aims to combat and eradicate hunger and poverty

---

15   Data available at: <https://goo.gl/2CpTQZ> Accessed on: Sept. 25, 2018.

while strengthening family farming. A significant part of the food produced by family farmers, land reform settlers and indigenous, quilombo and traditional communities is thus purchased by the government, intended for soup kitchens, public hospitals, food banks and food baskets (grocery products that are considered essential to guarantee the sustenance of a family during a period of time). This food can also be purchased by family farming organizations to hold in stock, with periodically controlled sales. Furthermore, government agencies are advised to have at least 30% of their food come from family farms, purchased through the PAA[16].

The PNAE, in turn, has similarities with the PAA, inspired by the Vargas administration's School Lunch Campaign, created in 1954. The foundation of the PNAE is to guarantee at least one daily meal in the country's schools and it is now the largest food and nutrition program in South America, recognized internationally by governments and organizations.

Other key public policies include credit programs for purchasing equipment, for production or for the disposal of surplus at markets through associations and cooperatives. In Brazil, the implementation of these programs and investments in them, combined with other initiatives, formed a set of public policies that removed Brazil from the Hunger Map in 2014, making the country a global leader in the fight against hunger and poverty.

In the context of the PNAE, Law No. 11,947/2009 requires that at least 30% of the resources provided by the National Education Development Fund (*Fundo Nacional de Desenvolvimento da Educação—FNDE*) for school feeding must be used to purchase products from family farms and rural family entrepreneurs or their organizations, prioritizing land reform settlements, traditional indigenous communities and quilombo communities, according to Article 14. This is an institutional trade policy that seeks to guarantee that family farmers are able to sell their products at fair prices and includes the state and municipal education network (EMATER, 2013).

---

16   Data available at: https://goo.gl/S6ajFP Accessed on: Sept. 23, 2018.

The objective of the policy is for food to be purchased—whenever possible—in the same municipality as the schools. The demand from schools can also be supplemented by farmers from the rural territory, the state and the country, in that order of priority. The Law is regulated by Resolution No. 26, from the Deliberative Council of the FNDE, describing the operational procedures observed for the sale of family farm products to the Executing Entities.

With regard to the PAA, which, as mentioned above, promotes access to food by food insecure populations, the objective is to ensure social and economic inclusion in rural areas by strengthening family farming. The PAA also contributes to the formation of strategic stocks and to the supply of the institutional food market, which includes government food purchases for different purposes and allows family farmers to stock their products to be sold later at fairer prices[17].

The PAA offers the opportunity to purchase food from family farmers—with no bidding—at prices compatible with those on the regional markets. The products are intended for food actions carried out by institutions in the healthcare network and the Network for Public Food and Nutrition Supplies (*Rede de Equipamentos Públicos de Alimentação e Nutrição—Redesan*), such as low-income restaurants, soup kitchens and food banks for socially vulnerable families. Furthermore, these foods are used to create food baskets distributed to specific population groups, and thus, through Article 19 in Law 10,696/2003, the PAA was augmented with resources from the Ministry of Agrarian Development (*Ministério do Desenvolvimento Agrário—MDA*).

These are just a few examples of policies developed at the federal level to realize the human right to adequate food. There are also other actions, such as credit policies as well as welfare actions, that were developed to fight against hunger in the country (PACHECO, 2017). In some ways, the integrated and participatory action has broadened the dialog between society and the government, making Brazil a global leader in the context of public policies to fight against hunger (NIERDELE, 2017).

---

17   Data available at: https://goo.gl/fs2xDn. Accessed on: Sept. 20, 2018

However, despite the creation and implementation of a system of integrated public policies that seek to realize the human right to adequate food, this alone is not sufficient for achieving a high degree of effectiveness with regard to the human right to food, nor the fight against hunger in Brazil. Starting in 2003, with the restructuring of the CONSEA, there were significant advances in the area of policies to fight against hunger. However, as noted by Nierdele (2017), these policies are now being impacted and experiencing disruptions due to the abrupt change in the country's institutional policy, particularly beginning in 2014.

The realization of any social right depends on economic processes that broaden or restrict a policy's reach. As Santos (2016, p. 122) argues, "[...] depending on the political and economic environment, as well as social pressure through the labor movement, social policy measures may expand or be restricted". Brazil, with initiatives such as the cash transfer program Bolsa Familia (in English, Family Grant), has become an international leader in policies to fight against hunger, but all that can be undone.

The country's removal from the Hunger Map, according to the Food and Agriculture Organization (FAO) of the UN, which occurred in 2014, was a significant development but is now jeopardized by the political and economic anachronism that has befallen Brazil. The Hunger Map has been published by the FAO since the 1990s, and Brazil appeared on it every year until 2014. According to Nierdele (2017), the country's success in food security policies was the result of supporting family farming and creating policies to balance the rural exodus, creating jobs and controlling inflation in the domestic market. Following meetings by managers, academics and social movements, three groups of actions emerged from this set of measures: "agricultural policies (PRONAF, SEAF, PGPF); social welfare policies (rural housing, territories of citizenship, Brasil Sem Miséria [in English, Brazil Without Extreme Poverty], Bolsa Familia); and food security policies (PAA, PNAE)" (NIERDELE, 2017, p. 2).

The positive impacts of these policies revealed a clear reduction in poverty and undernourishment, as well as the encouragement of producer associations, due to the PAA, the PNAE and rural credit lines. However, there were some difficulties in this process, such as an inadequate implementation of the three groups of policies mentioned above; there were social sectors and certain regions where these policies simply "have not arrived," particularly those most in need of government action.

It is therefore essential to consolidate and improve the dialog and to intensify the actions in order to include sectors that are still underserved, adapting them to the contexts of each locality. It is what Paulo André Nierdele (2017) calls a "territorialization of policies," understanding that true productive inclusion comes from bringing the producer and consumer closer together, creating small retail networks and new strategies for selling products from family farms, along the lines of the PAA and the PNAE, which have shown positive results over the years.

Promoting productive inclusion means reducing the outsized role of welfare policies in the reduction in poverty and the guarantee to food, which is not solely the fight against hunger. Achieving the objective of food security within the perspective of the right to food involves cultural aspects, sustainable production, support for small producers, and a discussion of the country's land ownership structure.

However, although programs to fight hunger and protect the human right to adequate food in Brazil have been in effect for years and have had striking results and international recognition, they are now being threatened and are in danger of disappearing altogether. There is a strong movement by the Temer administration, which replaced the democratically elected government of Dilma Rousseff, to weaken policies for family farming, while attempting to serve and prioritize the demands of agribusiness. When the substitute administration took office in 2016, it shut down nine ministries, including the MDA, which was eventually incorporated into the Ministry of Social Development (*Ministério do Desenvolvimento Social—MDS*).

In 2017, the resources for the programs fell from 500 million reais to just 54 million reais, representing a cut of approximately 90%. According to the Brazilian Semi-Arid Region Network (*Articulação Semiárido Brasileiro—ASA*), the number of people assisted fell from 91,700 to 41,300, a

55% reduction in the number of families benefited[18]. Another significant factor was the approval of Constitutional Amendment No. 95, which froze social investments in the country for a period of twenty years—adjusting, when possible, for inflation—beginning in 2018.

The institutions belonging to the SISAN played an important role in creating a network of participatory policies with action from the three levels of government. However, in times of crisis, it is essential to remember that there is a well-founded fear of policies being dismantled, as

> The current government's decision to limit the rise in public spending to adjustments for inflation for twenty years was already present in the drastic cuts by the 2018 Proposed Budget Law, with the closure of the "Support Program for Sustainable Development for Indigenous Peoples, Quilombo Communities and Other Traditional Communities" and the 11% cut in the Bolsa Família program. Reducing the PAA's resources for the Purchase with Simultaneous Donation, Seed Purchase and Direct Purchase programs by 99.8% represents, in practice, the end of those modalities, which serve the poorest rural residents. It is also unacceptable that the resources for programs to support living in the semi-arid region are being drastically reduced during periods of prolonged drought (PACHECO, 2017).

In this scenario of uncertainties and social setbacks, it is essential to rethink and restructure certain social practices and policies, guiding greater popular participation towards the ongoing movement of demands. It is important to re-secure a government agenda of adjustments, rather than disruptions, to policies for food and the fight against poverty. If nothing is done, the financial hollowing-out of the programs will once again challenge the human right to adequate food, in the standards achieved by Brazil.

4 Final considerations

It is important to understand food as a right, rather than solely a basic need to be met by the state. This view implies that the state is responsible for protecting, respecting and promoting the human right to food through collaborative and interconnected actions. The right to food goes beyond the act of nourishing oneself or merely promoting the guarantee to food.

---

18   Data available at: https://goo.gl/oK5cB8. Accessed on: Sept. 23, 2018.

The idea is based on the principle of food and nutrition security, which solidifies the right to food through the ongoing, permanent availability of healthy food, respecting the cultural characteristics of each region, without compromising the guarantee to other rights.

In this scenario, public policies represent the primary instrument for the realization of human rights, such as the human right to food. These policies should be developed in an integrated way between the state and civil society, encouraging popular participation in a process of social transformation and productive integration, to promote not only the guarantee to food but also individual emancipation and autonomy in the consumption and production of food.

In times of crisis, more than ever, political action to guarantee rights is essential. Brazil cannot return to the Hunger Map after years of struggling to leave it. It is clear from this report that there is a need for action to ensure that the conditions for guaranteeing a multidimensional and complex right, such as the human right to adequate food, are maintained in a territory with continental dimensions and dependent and peripheral economic policies, as is the case of Brazil.

References

BRASIL. **Pacto Internacional de Direitos Econômicos, Sociais e Culturiais.** Decreto nº 591, de 6 DE julho de 1992. Presidência da República, Brasília, 06 de julho de 1992. Available at: https://goo.gl/53fkA8. Accessed on: Feb. 22, 2014

_____. **Declaração Universal dos Direitos Humanos.** Adotada e proclamada pela resolução 217 A (III) da Assembleia Geral das Nações Unidas em 10 de dezembro de 1948. Available at: https://goo.gl/q2DmH4. Accessed on: Feb. 23, 2014

_____. Lei nº 11.346, de 15 de setembro de 2006. **Cria o Sistema Nacional de Segurança Alimentar e Nutricional—SISAN com vistas em assegurar o direito humano à alimentação adequada e dá outras providências.** Brasília, 15 de setembro de 2006. Available at: https://goo.gl/2orvHt. Accessed on: Feb. 28, 2014

_____. Emenda Constitucional nº 64, de 4 de fevereiro de 2010. **Altera o art. 6º da Constituição Federal, para introduzir a alimentação como direito social.** Brasília, em 4 de fevereiro de 2010. Available at: https://goo.gl/T6obPx. Accessed: 5 Mar. 2014.

_____. **PAA.** Secretaria Especial de Agricultura Familiar e do Desenvolvimento Agrário. Available at: https://goo.gl/HnkmZ1. Accessed on: Sep. 26, 2018.

BUCCI, M.P.D. O conceito de políticas públicas em direito. In: BUCCI, M.P.D (org.). **Políticas Públicas: reflexões sobre o conceito jurídico.** São Paulo: Saraiva, 2006.

_____. Políticas públicas e direito administrativo. In: **Direito administrativo e políticas públicas.** São Paulo: Editora Saraiva, 2002. p. 241–227. Available at: https://goo.gl/3FasYe. Accessed on: Mar. 9, 2017.

CAISAN. Câmara Interministerial de Segurança Alimentar e Nutricional. **Plano Nacional de Segurança Alimentar e Nutricional: 2012/2015.** Brasília, 2011.52

EMATER. Empresa da Assistência Técnica e Extensão Rural do Estado da Paraíba. **Relatório de Atividades—2012.** Cabedelo, 2013.

CONTI, I. L. **Segurança alimentar e nutricional: noções básicas.** Passo Fundo, 2009. Available at: https://goo.gl/Y6imfH. Accessed on: Aug. 16, 2014.

FAO. Comission. **El derecho a la alimentación.** Informe presentado por el Sr. Jean Ziegler, Relator especial sobre el derecho a la alimentación (7 de febrere de 2001), Doc. E/CN.4/2001/53, párrafo 14.

FEITOSA, M. L. P. A. Direito econômico da energia e direito econômico do desenvolvimento. Superando a visão tradicional. In: **Direito Econômico da Energia e do Desenvolvimento—Ensaios interdisciplinares.** FEITOSA, M.L.P.A.M e PEREIRA, M.M.F (org.). São Paulo: Conceito Editorial, 2012.

FEITOSA, M. L. P. A. Direito econômico do desenvolvimento e direito humano ao desenvolvimento. limites e confrontações. In: FEITOSA, M. L. P. A.; FRANCO, F. C. O; PETERKE, Sven; VENTURA, V. A. M. F: **Direitos Humanos de solidariedade: avanços e impasses.** 1ª ed. Editora Appris—Curitiba, 2013.

FERREIRA, É. A determinação ontonegativa dos direitos humanos. In: **Cadernos de pesquisa marxista do direito.** KASHIUR JUNIOR, C.N, ET AL. (Ed.)—vol.1, n1. São Paulo, 2011.

GONZAGA. V. **Programas que fortalecem a agricultura familiar estão em risco na América Latina.** Jornal Brasil de Fato. 2018. Available at: https://goo.gl/jyhupT. Accessed on: Sep. 23, 2018.

LEÃO, Marília (org.). **O direito à alimentação adequada e o sistema nacional de segurança alimentar e nutricional.** Brasília: ABRANDH, 2013.

LIMA, G. M. Crítica à teoria das gerações (ou mesmo dimensões) dos direitos fundamentais.2003 p. 7. Available at: https://goo.gl/xutUij. Accessed on: Oct. 24, 2013.53

MACHADO, L.A. **O que é o Consea?** 2017. Available at: https://goo.gl/Wa2WAZ. Accessed on: Sep. 20, 2018.

NIERDELE, P. A. **Contextualização e análise de conjuntura.** 2017. In: https://goo.gl/54GxZ6. Accessed on: Sep. 20, 2018.

ONU. **CESCR General Comment No. 12: The Right to Adequate Food (Art. 11).** Adopted at the Twentieth Session of the Committee on Economic, Social and Cultural Rights, on May 12th 1999.

PACHECO, E. L. **11 anos da Losan—Hora de relembrar, celebrar e protestar.** 2017. Available at: https://goo.gl/6X6Lcu. Accessed on: Sep. 20, 2018.

PIOVESAN, F. **Direitos humanos: desafios e perspectivas contemporâneas.** In: Rev. TST, Brasília, vol. 75, no 1, jan/mar 2009. Available at: https://juslaboris.tst.jus.br/bitstream/handle/20.500.12178/6566/010_piovesan.pdf?sequence=5&isAllowed=y. Accessed on: Sep. 20, 2018.

SANTOS, M. **Estado, política social e controle do capital.** 1. ed.—Maceió: Coletivo Veredas, 2016.

SANTOS, P. **Mais 43 municípios aderem ao sistema de segurança alimentar e nutricional.** 2017. Available at: https://bit.ly/2C7hSUt. Accessed on: Sep. 25, 2018.

STF. **HABEAS CORPUS 87.585-8 TOCANTINS.** Relator: Ministro Marco Aurélio. DJ: 03/12/2008. Available at: https://bit.ly/2Nz41s4. Accessed on: Sep. 20, 2018.

CHAPTER 4
Brazil and the Diplomacy to Fight Against Hunger and Poverty

Felipe Leal Albuquerque
(Instituto de Ciências Sociais da Universidade de Lisboa—ICS-UL)

1   Introduction

Between 2004 and 2012, Brazil consistently reduced the percentage of the population living in poverty and extreme poverty, leading the Food and Agriculture Organization (FAO) of the United Organizations (UN) to declare that the country had left the Hunger Map. These successes, the result of macroeconomic stabilization and policies to fight against hunger and poverty, were translated into bilateral, regional, interregional and multilateral foreign policy initiatives. "The diplomacy to fight against hunger and poverty" became an instrument for Brazil's entrance into the international arena, particularly during the two terms of President Luiz Inácio Lula da Silva (2003–2010).

Beginning in 2013, the rates of extreme poverty in the country rose once again, revealing the persistence of a historical problem.[19] These inconsistencies were reflected in the topic being considered less important to the diplomatic agenda during the presidency of Dilma Rousseff (2011–2016). The reversal is completed under the presidency of Michel Temer (2016–2018), with an expansion of the fiscal austerity initiated by the previous administration and the closure of the General Coordination of Humanitarian Cooperation and Fight Against Hunger (*Coordenação-Geral de Cooperação Humanitária e Combate à Fome—CGFOME*) of the Ministry of External Relations (*Ministério das Relações Exteriores*, here referred to as Itamaraty, after the palace that houses the ministry), as well as the Ministry of Agrarian Development (*Ministério do Desenvolvimento Agrário—MDA*).

---

19   See: http://www.ipeadata.gov.br/Default.aspx, accessed on September 12, 2018.

The objective of this chapter is to present the foundations of the diplomacy to fight against hunger and poverty and identify how the evolution of domestic policies influenced foreign policy. The analytical model states that the internationalization of public policies had impacts not only on different aspects of the country's international engagement but also reverberated domestically. These effects were felt, for example, in the reorientation and rescaling of public policies and the reproduction of the rhetoric that identified Brazil as a nonindifferent actor.

The analysis focuses on the period 2003–2016, which coincides with the administrations of Lula da Silva and Rousseff, both part of the Workers Party (*Partido dos Trabalhadores—PT*). The two administrations are compared based on their foreign policy activity at three levels of analysis: multilateral, regional and bilateral. The chapter is divided into seven sections. It begins with a description of the analytical model. The second section traces the historical evolution of public policies to fight hunger and poverty, while the third discusses how this topic was incorporated into foreign policy. The next three sections provide examples of how the diplomacy to fight against hunger and poverty was present—albeit unevenly—in bilateral, regional and multilateral partnerships. I conclude by stating reasons for the collapse of this diplomatic front, such as the dismantling of domestic public policies as well as the interpretation that the topic was misused by a political group linked to the PT.

2 Analytical model

As shown in Figure 1, the analytical model is based on the assumption that public policies to fight hunger and poverty were transformed into instruments for international action. What I call "the diplomacy to fight against hunger and poverty" involves the set of policies actively and consciously used by decisionmakers in bilateral, regional and multilateral initiatives. It is thus a step towards achieving food and nutrition security and the human right to adequate food (HRAF). Foreign policy is seen as a process that begins domestically and reverberates internationally. Those external impacts can then lead to new domestic developments.

In the case of Brazil, the transformation of domestic public policies into foreign policy primarily involves the presidency and Itamaraty. Other ministries, subnational governments, nongovernmental organizations (NGOs) and civil society organizations also exert different degrees of influence. Although this transposition has become more plural and open to new actors, it is still largely controlled by the presidency and Itamaraty (ALBUQUERQUE, 2013).

The process of transformation is elucidated through different explanatory mechanisms, namely, South-South (SSC) and triangular cooperation initiatives; Brazilians being elected to leadership positions in international organizations, such as the FAO and Codex Alimentarius; combinations of votes with partners at those institutions; and the spread of technical and scientific knowledge developed by entities such as the Brazilian Agricultural Research Corporation (*Empresa Brasileira de Pesquisa Agropecuária—EMBRAPA*). It also involves immaterial components, such as the attempt to spread an "ideal model" of public policies and legitimize Brazil as a responsible actor working in solidarity with others. These courses of action are related to the more general foreign policy guidelines, which will be addressed in the following section.

Figure 1.   Analytical model

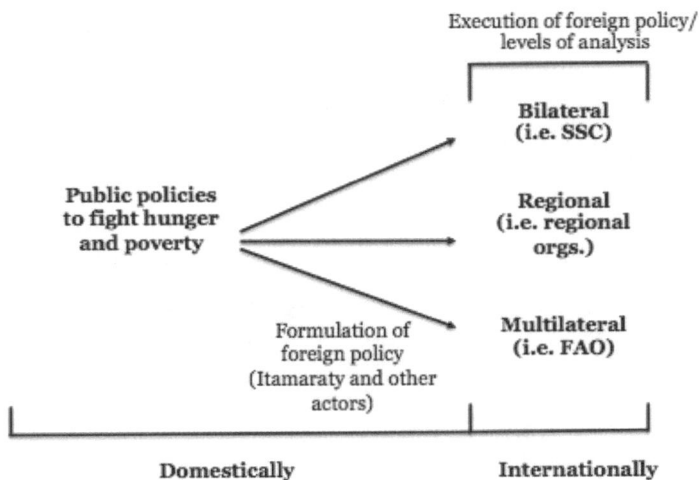

With regard to the possibility of there being a retroactive effect, the model is inspired by studies associated with the literature on public policy, such as Easton (1957), and foreign policy, such as Gourevitch (1978). Easton argues that domestic demands (inputs) involve decisions or "policies" (outputs) that then influence the development of new domestic demands. Considering the complementarity between national and international dynamics, Gourevitch uses the term "the second image reversed" to refer to the impacts that the external environment may have on domestic policy.

The context in which public policies are implemented domestically and used in foreign policy is crucial. In general, the sustainability of those policies and their importance depend on, among other things, the country's macroeconomic and political landscape as well as who is guiding foreign policy. Foreign policy does not occur in a vacuum, nor is it separate from domestic policy (PINHEIRO; MILANI, 2012). In theoretical terms, the argument is situated close to liberal perspectives and certain constructivist approaches to international relations, as it questions the idea that the state is a "black box."

The analytical model will be applied at three levels: bilateral, regional and multilateral. With regard to the bilateral level, I identify Brazilian South-South cooperation actions developed during the Lula da Silva and Rousseff administrations, as well as their continuities and discontinuities. As for the regional level, I describe moments when the diplomacy to fight against hunger and poverty was visible in initiatives of the Southern Common Market (*Mercado Común del Sur—MERCOSUR*), particularly the Specialized Meeting on Family Farming (*Reunião Especializada sobre Agricultura Familiar—REAF*), and of the Community of Latin American and Caribbean States (*Comunidade dos Estados Latino-Americanos e Caribenhos—CELAC*). Finally, the multilateral level focuses on the FAO.

The decision to carry out a qualitative comparison was made for two reasons: first, because it offers a broader view of foreign policy, making it possible to reveal continuities and inconsistencies and, second, because it prevents a merely descriptive exercise.

3 The fight against hunger and poverty: domestic dimension

In Brazil, the evolution of public policies related directly and indirectly to the fight against hunger and poverty occurs in an erratic, disjointed and fragmented way throughout history (ALBUQUERQUE, 2013).

During Lula da Silva's terms, new programs and ministerial departments received special budgets and purviews. In addition to reestablishing the National Council for Food and Nutrition Security (*Conselho Nacional de Segurança Alimentar e Nutricional—CONSEA*), the Extraordinary Ministry for Food Security and Fight Against Hunger (*Ministério Extraordinário de Segurança Alimentar e Combate à Fome—MESA),* the Ministry of Social Welfare (*Ministério da Assistência Social—MAS*) and the Executive Secretariat for the Bolsa Família (in English, Family Grant) program were created, later becoming part of the Ministry of Social Development and Fight Against Hunger (*Ministério do Desenvolvimento Social e Combate à Fome—MDS*); the duties of the MDA were expanded; and in 2007, the Parliamentary Front for Food and Nutrition Security (*Frente Parlamentar da Segurança Alimentar e Nutricional—FPSAN*) was reactivated (FRANÇA; MARQUES, 2017). The election of a center-left president was essential to the new centrality of these topics. The success of those choices reverberated into Lula's reelection in 2006 and into foreign policy initiatives.

One of the major landmarks is Fome Zero (in English, Zero Hunger), developed as the national strategy to guarantee the HRAF and eliminate hunger and extreme poverty. Launched in 2003, the program incorporates existing initiatives but breaks new ground by offering a systematic view. It was based on four axes: (i) access to food, which includes, for example, the Bolsa Família program, the National School Feeding Program (*Programa Nacional de Alimentação Escolar—PNAE*), the Workers' Food Program (*Programa de Alimentação do Trabalhador—PAT*), the Food and Nutrition Surveillance System (*Sistema de Vigilância Alimentar e Nutricional—SISVAN*) and the program to build water tanks in the semiarid region; (ii) strengthening family farming, which involves the National Program for

Strengthening Family Farming (*Programa Nacional de Fortalecimento da Agricultura Familiar—PRONAF*) and the Food Acquisition Program (*Programa de Aquisição de Alimentos—PAA*), linking the purchase of production from small farmers to the guarantee of food and nutrition security; (iii) income generation; and (iv) collaboration, mobilization and social control (Aranha, 2010).

The most widely known element of Fome Zero was the Bolsa Família program, which unified the Bolsa Alimentação, Vale Gás and Bolsa Escola programs—focused on food, gas and schools, respectively—formulated during the Fernando Henrique Cardoso government (1995–2002), with the newly created Cartão Alimentação food card. The initiative sought to expand access to food through conditional cash transfers to poor and extremely poor families and had a budget of R$ 13.4 billion in the last year of the Lula da Silva administration (BRASIL, 2010). As well as providing emergency support, it also served as a protective cushion at times of crisis. Some of the most common criticisms of the Bolsa Família program are its emphasis on emergency rather than structural actions; budgetary imbalances in some of its programmatic aspects; and the not-always-harmonious relationship among the bureaucratic entities responsible for the program.

In 2004, the Second National Conference on Food and Nutrition Security (*Conferência Nacional de Segurança Alimentar e Nutricional—CNSAN*) established that the topic is multidimensional and intersectoral. Subsequent conferences were held in 2007, 2011 and 2015, the latter two during Rousseff's presidency. The advances associated with Fome Zero contributed to the enactment of the Organic Law on Food and Nutrition Security (*Lei Orgânica de Segurança Alimentar e Nutricional—LOSAN*) in 2006, which established the National Food and Nutrition Security System (*Sistema Nacional de Segurança Alimentar e Nutricional—SISAN*), mandated in 2010. That same year, Constitutional Amendment No. 64 was published, amending Article 6 of the Constitution, including the right to food as a social right and transforming it into a state policy. Furthermore, the National Policy on Food and Nutrition Security (*Política Nacional de*

Segurança Alimentar e Nutricional—PNSAN) was established, with guidelines for the development of the first National Plan for Food and Nutrition Security (*Plano Nacional de Segurança Alimentar e Nutricional—PLAN-SAN*), in effect between 2012 and 2015.

The Rousseff administration began by continuing the series of policies that resulted in Brazil being removed from the FAO's Hunger Map in 2014 and, between 2002 and 2013, in a reduction in the percentage of the population living in hunger by 82.1%, exceeding the objective set in the Millennium Development Goals (MDGs).[20] In 2014, approximately 14 million families, or 46 million people, received benefits from the Bolsa Família program (BRASIL, 2014). Furthermore, there was an improvement in indicators of education and access to goods and services and a decline in income inequality, with the Gini index increasing from 0.570 in 2004 to 0.515 in 2014.[21] Launched in 2011, the Brasil sem Miséria (in English, Brazil without Extreme Poverty) plan aimed to go beyond Bolsa Família and sought to encourage productive inclusion, improve public services and lift approximately 16.2 million people out of extreme poverty. In 2012, the Brazil Carinhoso (in English, Affectionate Brazil) program was created, focused on supplementing the income of those served by the Bolsa Família program who had young children.

This positive scenario shows the first signs of reversal in mid-2014, due to factors such as the slowdown in economic growth; rising inflation and interest rates; recessionary fiscal and monetary policies; and falling international commodities prices. GDP stagnated in 2014 to decrease in 2015 (−3.5%) and 2016 (−3.3%). The unemployment rate increased in 2014, and indices such as average income, GDP per capita and entry into the formal

---

20   Between 2001 and 2012, the percentage of the population living in poverty fell from 24.3% to 8.4%, and the percentage living in extreme poverty fell from 14% to 3.5% (FAO, 2014). For data from the MDS, see: goo.gl/6nmj44, accessed on September 14, 2018. According to the World Bank, people living in extreme poverty are those with an average monthly income of up to R$ 133.72, and those in poverty, R$ 387.07. The guidelines of the Brasil sem Miséria plan indicate R$ 85 for extreme poverty and R$ 170 for poverty. In 2016, 52 million Brazilians were living in poverty, and 13 million were living in extreme poverty (IBGE, 2017).

21   See: https://bit.ly/2EyTKx3, accessed on September 15, 2018.

labor market worsened, which had impacts on policies to fight against hunger and poverty and led to a 11.2% increase in the number of people living in extreme poverty between 2016 and 2017[22]. This situation was not ameliorated by adjustments to the average benefit from the Bolsa Família program in 2011 and 2014, during the Rousseff administration, or in 2016 and 2018, in the Temer administration.

The reversal of those advances gained momentum during the presidency of Michel Temer (2016–2018). Bolsa Familia and programs such as the PAA were maintained, but in 2016, Constitutional Amendment No. 95 was approved, establishing a tax regime for the next 20 years in which primary expenditures—such as those on healthcare and education—would only be adjusted for inflation from the previous year. The measure was criticized by the UN Committee on Economic, Social and Cultural Rights, the UN special rapporteur on extreme poverty and human rights and the Inter-American Commission on Human Rights. The lower domestic dynamism negatively affected the diplomacy to fight against hunger and poverty.

4　Domestic dimension and foreign policy

The diplomacy to fight against hunger and poverty is part of the broader foreign policy developed during the presidential terms of Lula da Silva and—to a lesser degree—Rousseff. In this period, it is possible to identify traces of continuity in the general foreign policy objectives and in certain actions related to the area of food and nutrition security, although with a decrease in external activism.

More broadly, Lula da Silva's foreign policy was guided by an attempt to correct international asymmetries and democratize the decision-making bodies of multilateral forums. Brazil's actions would combine respect for the established parameters with the demand for more room to maneuver and preserve its own autonomy. In turn, that approach was underpinned by the defense of ideals of justice.

22　See: https://goo.gl/PCC1Px, accessed on September 16, 2018.

Lula da Silva's foreign policy established a series of strategies to achieve those objectives. Examples include the diversification of partnerships and the strengthening of relations with countries located in the "Global South." Associated with this effort was the creation of and participation in coalitions, such as the BRICS (Brazil, Russia, India, China and South Africa), the India-Brazil-South Africa (IBSA) Dialogue Forum, the G20 group of developing nations at the World Trade Organization (WTO), the Group of Twenty (G20) and the BASIC (Brazil, South Africa, India and China) (ALBUQUERQUE, 2016).

These foreign policy choices were combined with others, such as Lula da Silva's presidential diplomacy; the expansion of strategic partnerships with developed and developing countries, which began in the Cardoso administration; the expansion of the diplomatic corps and the opening and reopening of diplomatic offices, particularly in Africa and Latin America; the pursuit of regional integration through existing arrangements, such as MERCOSUR, and the creation of new ones, such as the Union of South American Nations (*União de Nações Sul-Americanas— UNASUL*) and the CELAC; and finally, the multiplication of South-South cooperation partnerships.

The diplomacy to fight against hunger and poverty made its way into the more general scope of foreign policy. It was the primary element of the discourse that Brazil's inclusion was based on the commitment to solidarity and on initiatives marked by nonindifference, an absence of conditionalities and horizontal relations. It also sought to achieve diffuse benefits, such as the expansion of soft power and diplomatic contacts with developing countries, as well as concrete results, such as drumming up votes in international organizations and securing trade advantages (INOUE; COELHO, 2018).

The intention was to ratify a "Brazilian model" to fight against hunger and poverty. The primary pillars of the Fome Zero strategy began to spread: emergency, visible in humanitarian cooperation actions; structural, present in technical cooperation and reverberating out into programs such as the PNAE and the PAA; and the central focus on the HRAF, advocated for by Brazil in multilateral forums, which was reflected in the activity of the CONSEA (RONDÓ; LOPES, 2016). The idea was to make foreign policy compatible with the transformations taking place domestically. This process should be broad enough that the discourse associated with the fight against hunger and poverty could be present on agendas not only within the field of food and nutrition security but also climate change, at the UN, and international trade, at the WTO.

This movement can be seen in Itamaraty's organizational chart with the creation of the CGFOME in 2004, as well as in the participation of other ministries—particularly the MDA, the MDS and the Ministry of Agriculture, Livestock and Supply (*Ministério da Agricultura, Pecuária e Abastecimento—MAPA*)—in the implementation of foreign policy through their international relations teams. The International Policy Centre for Inclusive Growth (IPC-IG), created in 2004, and the World Food Program (WFP) Centre of Excellence against Hunger, established in 2011, were important allies in the spread of domestic practices (FRAUN-DORFER, 2013).

As I will outline below, the "hyperactivism" of this foreign policy aspect has been associated with problems, such as (i) an excess of partnerships and cooperation projects, which led to discontinuities and frustration with promises made by Brazil; (ii) the widespread notion that the diplomacy to fight against hunger and poverty would be associated with a "partisan" foreign policy by the PT; and (iii) the fact that it was not clear to Brazilian society whether those choices would have benefits for Brazil.

Rousseff's presidency began with an intention to maintain the general shape of her predecessor's foreign policy. Due to changes in the domestic, regional and international conditions, however, it was necessary to make adjustments. The domestic instability resulted in a decrease in international travel and in the use of presidential diplomacy; late payments to international organizations; Itamaraty's lower share of the total budget;[23] a reduced number of new diplomats; and a change in foreign ministers.

---

23   https://goo.gl/eoxQkt, accessed September 29, 2018.

Compared to the previous period, the focus on domestic politics—particularly in Rousseff's second term—resulted in less international activism. Groups such as the IBSA lost dynamism. In contrast, the BRICS was privileged, as well as specific partnerships with developed countries, such as Germany and the United States, and developing countries, such as China. In short, this lower intensity existed alongside the maintenance of certain strategic courses, which in some cases led to a "continuity through inertia."

With regard to the diplomacy to fight against hunger and poverty, several South-South cooperation initiatives were continued, and others were completed, but there were no incentives to look for new partnerships. There was also a visible reduction in the importance of the Brazilian Cooperation Agency (*Agência Brasileira de Cooperação—ABC*). During Rousseff's presidency, there were discussions about transforming it into a Brazilian Cooperation Agency for Development (*Agência Brasileira de Cooperação para o Desenvolvimento—ABCD*), which would change its agenda, potentially incorporating trade and investments (LEITE; CAVALCANTE, 2016). The thematic focus became less important in the direction of Brazil's foreign policy, and it is no longer a cornerstone of its legitimation. This process was exacerbated during the presidency of Michel Temer.

5 Diplomacy to fight against hunger and poverty: multilateral dimension

In the multilateral dimension, the diplomacy to fight against hunger and poverty had a privileged locus of action, presenting traces of continuity throughout the presidencies of Lula da Silva and Rousseff. During this period, Brazilian government representatives used organizations such as the FAO to disseminate, legitimize and improve domestic policies and programs. This emphasis is part of a broader orientation towards spreading international awareness around the topic (CUNHA, 2010). The country's active participation in debates held at the FAO led to a Brazilian being elected as director-general of the organization, as well as the Fome Zero strategy and the Brazilian model of international cooperation receiving validation.

The fight against hunger and poverty was present in a number of multilateral initiatives and was understood as having a strategic role in defining the foreign policy of the new center-left administration. At the beginning of Lula da Silva's term, in a speech at the World Economic Forum in 2003, he called for a "crusade" against hunger by wealthy countries, a demand repeated at the G8 Evian summit. That same year, at the opening of the UN General Assembly, he repeated the word "hunger" 18 times, treating its elimination as a moral and political imperative and referring to Fome Zero. In 2004, presidential diplomacy would lead to his participation in the meeting on "Action Against Hunger and Poverty" at the UN.

At the WTO, the country advocated for fairer trade and more favorable treatment for developing and least developed countries. It was argued that rules on subsidies and anti-dumping and agreements such as those on agriculture (Agreement on Agriculture—AoA) were being applied in a discriminatory manner by developed countries. This widened trade discrepancies and, as a result, exacerbated poverty and hunger on a global scale.

Brazilian negotiators used this moral component in trade disputes, such as the cotton dispute with the United States, which began in 2002. In addition to serving the more immediate interests of domestic producers, it was argued that Brazilian activism would benefit countries whose economy depends on the product, such as the members of Cotton-4 (Benin, Burkina Faso, Chad and Mali), with which Brazil had carried out technical cooperation initiatives. In turn, the country's high agricultural competitiveness made it interested in opening up markets, which created contradictions between the discourse in favor of food and nutrition security and practice.

Brazil's actions at the FAO were inspired by the guideposts of Fome Zero, such as the protection of the HRAF and the development of integrated public policies. At the WFP, the country went from receiving food donations in the 1990s to being the seventh largest donor in 2012 (RONDÓ; LOPES, 2016). In the field of normative debates, Brazil had a prominent role in negotiations over the Voluntary Guidelines to Support the Progressive Realization of the Right to Adequate Food in the Context of National Food Security, finalized in 2004, which subsequently influenced the enactment of the LOSAN and the SISAN (CUSTÓDIO et al., 2011). Moreover, the country participated in the approval of the Voluntary Guidelines on the Responsible Governance of Tenure of Land, Fisheries and Forests, approved in 2012.[24] An important step in this process was the International Conference on Agrarian Reform and Rural Development, held in Porto Alegre in 2006.

Another example of the transposition of domestic experiences is the role of the CONSEA and the influence of its organizational structure during debates over the reform of the FAO's Committee on World Food Security (CFS). More specifically, the participation of civil society actors in the CONSEA enabled the Brazilian government to propose making the CFS more democratic and open (RONDÓ; LOPES, 2016). According to Cunha (2010), the initiatives and guidelines of Fome Zero, such as the focus on family farming and the HRAF, guided Brazil's position in debates at the CFS and the FAO.

Graziano da Silva's election to Director-General of the FAO in 2011, and his reelection by a large majority in 2015, illustrate how the trajectory of one individual confirms the hypothesis that domestic and multilateral dimensions are interrelated. One of the coordinators and formulators of Fome Zero, Graziano da Silva was appointed to the MESA, later serving as the FAO's regional representative for Latin America and the Caribbean. As Director-General of the FAO, he was elected with the expectation of strengthening South-South cooperation, reflecting one of the focuses of external action during the Lula da Silva administration and the votes received from African and Latin American partners. His election is part of an effort to elect Brazilians to key positions in international organizations. Although they are not carrying out a specifically Brazilian agenda, those representatives corroborate Brazil's adherence to the set of norms and rules that delineate the current order (ALBUQUERQUE, 2013; MILHORANCE, 2013).

---

24   Similar activism took place in 2014, during discussions on the Principles for Responsible Investment in Agriculture and Food Systems at the CFS and, that same year, in support of the UN General Assembly's declaration of the International Year of Family Farming.

With regard to cooperation initiatives between Brazil and the FAO, the Brazilian model of South-South partnerships and public policies like the PAA, the Bolsa Família program and the PNAE were highlighted on a number of occasions and shared through joint initiatives with partners from Latin America and the Caribbean.[25] The Brazil-FAO International Cooperation Program, which began in 2008 and is still ongoing, for example, demonstrates how Brazilian experiences are seen as a guideline for the development and execution of regional projects.

While there is continuity at the multilateral level between the diplomacy to fight against hunger and poverty developed during the Lula da Silva and Rousseff administrations, the same cannot be said of Temer's presidency. Although Brazil has contributed to the adoption of the Decade of Action on Nutrition (2016-2025) by the UN General Assembly and maintained a dialog with the FAO, the country has been criticized by civil society organizations and international representatives. The UN special rapporteur on extreme poverty and human rights, Philip Alston, referred to the "socially retrogressive" potential of Constitutional Amendment no. 95.[26]

6 Diplomacy to fight against hunger and poverty: regional dimension

At the regional level, the diplomacy to fight against hunger and poverty was carried out particularly with Latin America and the Caribbean and with Africa. With regard to the former region, Brazil's role as a provider of good practices and an articulator of common positions was aligned with regional integration initiatives, such as MERCOSUR, the REAF, created in

---

25 References to Brazil as a national and regional success story appear in subsequent documents from the FAO and the CFS. See, for example, a reference from the International Alliance Against Hunger on the occasion of the 30th meeting of the CFS (2004): https://goo.gl/PhMqJZ. Another positive mention is in the report "The State of Food Insecurity in the World" (2014). See https://goo.gl/9bx8nD, accessed on September 28, 2018. Also mentioned is the "Zero Hunger" challenge, inspired by Fome Zero and launched by the UN in 2012.
26 See: https://goo.gl/BdU5nA, accessed on October 4, 2018.

2004, and the CELAC. For the African continent, engagement took place with the region as a whole.

The sharing of knowledge took place in three gradual and complementary stages: it began with the REAF, grew through bilateral cooperation agreements with Latin American and Caribbean partners and then expanded to the CELAC, becoming continental. Throughout those developments, regional experiences were shared in multilateral forums, such as the FAO, through the Group of Latin American and Caribbean Countries (GRULAC), and in partnerships with extraregional actors. There was thus a growing public ownership and legitimation of Brazil's discourse and practices.

Among its objectives, the REAF seeks to systematize and align the different regional public policies for family farming as well as strengthen the institutions responsible for the topic, becoming a space for dialog between civil society and governments. In 2008, the MERCOSUR Family Farming Fund (*Fundo da Agricultura Familiar—FAF*) was created, funded by member countries and focused on ensuring the sustainability of the REAF and the funding of programs. In the case of Brazil, the MDA—and the Special Secretariat for Family Farming and Agrarian Development (*Secretaria Especial de Agricultura Familiar e do Desenvolvimento Agrário—SEAD*) during the Temer administration—acted as a leader for the domestic branch of the REAF and shared public policies such as the PNAE and the National Policy of Family Farming (*Política Nacional da Agricultura Familiar—PNAF*). Throughout its history, the REAF received "constant requests" for cooperation to organize national registries for family farming, from both MERCOSUR countries and nonregional actors (MALUF; LOPES, 2015: 44). The entity also contributed to the 2016 Model Law on Family Farming of the Latin American and Caribbean Parliament (*Parlamento Latinoamericano e Caribenho—PARLATINO*).[27]

---

27 It is also worth mentioning the Framework Law on the Right to Food, Food Security and Food Sovereignty of 2012 and the Framework Law on School Feeding, approved in 2013.

In addition to MERCOSUR, during Lula da Silva and Rousseff's administrations, the country shared experiences and helped strengthen the normative framework for the fight against hunger and poverty, influencing the approval of national laws by regional partners (RONDÓ; LOPES, 2016). This engagement was in line with the activism in forums such as the REAF and the FAO, such that initiatives in one aspect of foreign policy echoed in others.

The Hunger-Free Latin America and the Caribbean Initiative (*Iniciativa América Latina e Caribe sem Fome—IALCSH*), launched during the Latin American Summit on Chronic Hunger (2005) and supported by the FAO, for example, was presented by Lula da Silva on the occasion of the institution's 60th anniversary. The following year, it became a priority work topic for the FAO Regional Office, then headed by Graziano da Silva. In 2007, it received support from MERCOSUR. The initiative became one of the three guiding lights of the FAO's work, and following the creation of the CELAC, it became a regional priority, taking on a broader scope with the approval of the Plan for Food Security, Nutrition and Hunger Eradication 2025, whose objective surpasses what was stipulated in the UN Sustainable Development Goals (SDGs). Beyond the IALCSH, references to the HRAF, food sovereignty, and family, peasant and indigenous farming are frequent in the final documents from the CELAC summits and the meetings of CELAC agricultural ministers, although there are noticeably different views on the concept of food and nutritional security within the bloc. Compared to the CELAC and MERCOSUR, the topic received less attention at the UNASUL.

With regard to Africa, a number of initiatives also originated in domestic public policies and programs, such as Mais Alimentos (in English, More Food), the PAA and the Brazil-Africa Cooperation Program on Social Development (*Programa Brasil-África de Cooperação em Desenvolvimento Social*). The international aspect of the Mais Alimentos program is inspired by a PRONAF credit line created in 2008 and is focused on equipment financing and the rendering of agricultural services. According to the program, the requesting country has access to credit to purchase tractors and equipment produced in Brazil, later leasing (with subsidies) or renting them to local producers. Cabral (2016) discusses whether the initiative could lead to agricultural specialization and affect family farming in the receiving countries.

Purchase from Africans for Africa (PAA-Africa) promotes the local purchase of food from small rural producers for school feeding and operates in five African countries: Ethiopia, Niger, Malawi, Senegal and Mozambique. The program's second phase was implemented between 2014 and 2016, and the third ran until 2019. The Mais Alimentos program and PAA-Africa originated in the Brazil-Africa Dialogue on Food Security, Fight Against Hunger and Rural Development (*Diálogo Brasil-África sobre Segurança Alimentar, Combate à Fome e Desenvolvimento Rural*), which took place in 2010. Also focused on the African continent, the Brazil-Africa Cooperation Program on Social Development was coordinated by the MDS and was based on promoting technical assistance for the development of social policies. Finally, the internationalization of Brazil's strategy for fighting against hunger and poverty found a home in the African Union, which adopted the Brazilian model for school feeding in 2016, and in the Community of Portuguese Language Countries (*Comunidade dos Países de Língua Portuguesa—CPLP*), which approved the Food and Nutrition Security Strategy (*Estratégia de Segurança Alimentar e Nutricional—ESAN*) in 2011.

7   Diplomacy to fight against hunger and poverty: bilateral dimension

The third aspect of the internationalization of domestic experience took place through bilateral cooperation initiatives. Latin American, Caribbean and African countries were the most frequent recipients of Brazilian cooperation for international development (*cooperação brasileira para o desenvolvimento internacional—Cobradi*), indicating that it complements the regional dimension. Between 2005 and 2013, the Brazilian government spent R$ 7.9 billion through the different modalities of Cobradi (IPEA; ABC, 2016). Technical cooperation and humanitarian cooperation were associated with the diplomacy to fight against hunger and poverty, involving a multiplicity of actors from the federal bureaucracy, coordinated by Itamaraty through the ABC. In the period 2011–2013, it involved 128 countries and 88 federal government agencies.

Technical cooperation is motivated by external requests and is undertaken on a noncommercial basis, through the dissemination of Brazilian knowledge and experience. It involves official visits, technical missions, participation in international and Brazilian events and workshops and research grants for foreigners. A broad range of initiatives have attracted the interest of other countries, such as human milk banks, the unified registry for social programs, Bolsa Família, Brasil sem Miséria, the PNAE and rural development programs. Throughout the Lula da Silva and Rousseff administrations, there were partnerships with Portuguese-speaking countries on the African continent, particularly Mozambique and Guinea-Bissau, as well as the Cotton-4 group of countries.[28] In Latin America and the Caribbean, technical cooperation initiatives were prioritized with El Salvador, Haiti and Guatemala. The recipients were considered important to the Brazilian foreign policy developed between 2003 and 2014 as a whole (ALBUQUERQUE, 2015).

As shown in Figure 2, federal government spending on technical cooperation totaled approximately R$ 565 million between 2005 and 2013, predominantly for countries in Latin American and the Caribbean as well as Africa (IPEA, ABC, 2016). Expenditures were increased during Lula da Silva's administration, particularly during his second term, when spending on this modality peaked. Beginning in the Rousseff administration, there was a decline in the budget allocation as well as in the number of projects and partnerships.

---

28   Technical cooperation programs such as ProSavana, carried out in Mozambique, replicate the duality of the Brazilian agricultural model.

Figure 2.   Expenditures, in R$ million, on technical cooperation (2005–2013) (IPEA and ABC, 2016)

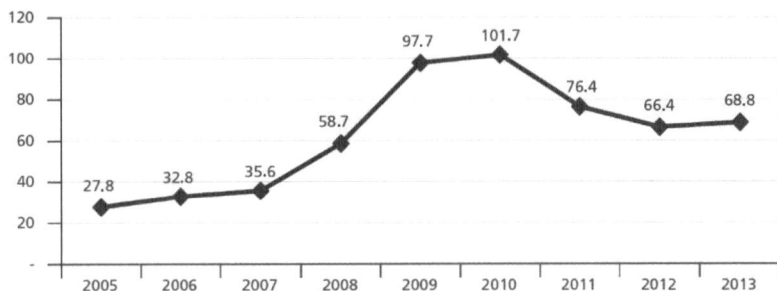

Trilateral cooperation involves the presence of two other actors, usually a developing country and a developed country. It may also involve a developing country and an international organization or informal cooperation arrangements bringing together three developing countries, as is the case with the IBSA and its fund for poverty and hunger alleviation, created in 2004.

Humanitarian cooperation refers to Brazil's engagement in emergency situations, through the transfer of funds to specialized organizations in the UN system, sending experts and donating food, medicine and basic necessities. This list of activities includes actions originating in domestic programs, such as strengthening family farming, local food purchases and school feeding. The work by the CGFOME and the Interministerial Working Group on International Humanitarian Assistance (*Grupo de Trabalho Interministerial sobre Assistência Humanitária Internacional—GTI-AHI*), created in 2006, aim to coordinate these activities.

Figure 3 illustrates that in the period 2005–2013, approximately R$ 822 million was invested in this type of cooperation, particularly in 2010, when Brazil assisted Haiti following a major earthquake (IPEA, ABC, 2016). It also shows a sharp drop in 2013. Throughout this period, the CGFOME acted primarily through contributions to actions and programs from entities such as the FAO and the WFP and through donations of basic necessities. The recipients of humanitarian cooperation included Cuba, Haiti, Cape Verde, Guinea-Bissau and Mozambique.

Figure 3.   Expenditures, in R$ million, on humanitarian cooperation (2005–2013) (IPEA, ABC, 2016).

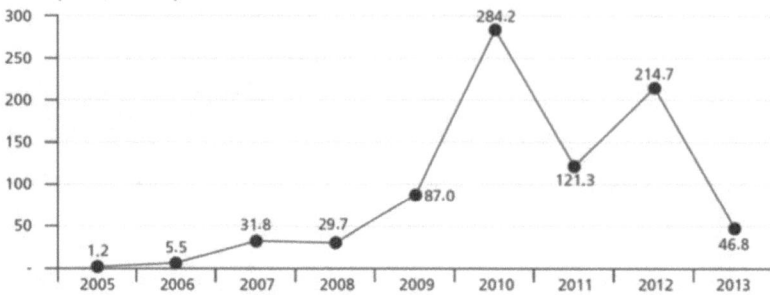

Although official data are only available through 2013, Cobradi was down-sized during the Rousseff years, reflecting a smaller emphasis on relations with other developing countries and the first signs of a domestic economic crisis (LIMA; SANTANA, 2020).[29] The expansion of external engagement during the Lula da Silva administration, which would lead to "exaggerated interpretations" about the nature of Brazilian cooperation, also required that no agreements would be made to begin new projects without completing those that were currently in progress (IPEA, ABC, 2016: 16).

8   Final considerations

This chapter demonstrates that Brazil articulated different dimensions of the Fome Zero strategy throughout Lula da Silva's presidency, as part of the diplomacy to fight against hunger and poverty. The successes of domestic public policies and programs—particularly Bolsa Família, the PNAE and the PAA—led to the internationalization of those practices. This occurred in three different dimensions: multilateral, through engagement in forums such as the FAO; regional, by developing partnerships with and making use of regional blocs; and bilateral, which involved South-South technical and humanitarian cooperation initiatives.

---

29   http://www.abc.gov.br/projetos/pesquisa, accessed on September 27, 2018.

The spillover of the domestic experience was a result of the expertise accumulated by federal bureaucratic entities and collegiate bodies, such as the CONSEA and the GTI-AHI. Other nonstate actors participated in the process, although they had secondary importance. Given this plurality of interests and actions, Itamaraty sought to act as a unifying agent, with the CGFOME and the ABC as its primary lines of action.

It is not clear exactly when the process of internationalization began. There is speculation, however, that it was driven by a number of factors: external requests from countries and institutions; interest from bureaucracies in expanding practices related to their ministerial departments; and the understanding by those in the foreign policy-making core—notably Itamaraty, the ministries and the presidency—that the diplomacy to fight against hunger and poverty could become a powerful instrument to enter into the international arena and receive validation for decisions made domestically. The structure of the REAF and the subsequent presence of Graziano da Silva at the FAO's regional office in Santiago were important initial steps.

I have demonstrated that the three levels of analysis are interrelated. South-South technical cooperation initiatives are endorsed by the FAO and/or the WFP. Collaborations at the South American level, carried out through the REAF, reverberate into the dialog with African partners and at the multilateral level. More importantly, sharing the same experiences with a multitude of actors helps give legitimacy to those experiences, the federal agencies responsible for their formulation and the Brazilian government. This dynamism assured a state of permanence for the public policies and endorsement of the discourse of Brazil as an actor committed to a development agenda focused on social inclusion. Foreign policy is therefore part of a system that begins domestically and echoes beyond the country's borders.

It is essential to note that the diplomacy to fight against hunger and poverty went beyond mere rhetoric. Brazil was able to meet the targets of the MDGs, as well as those of the World Food Summit (WFS), and lift a significant portion of the population above the poverty line. When copied by other countries, these practices also proved to be effective in many cases. This "material" component ensured that the Brazilian discourse was not empty. International organizations have endorsed those public policies, a positive image that gained momentum through the election of one of those responsible for Fome Zero to the position of Director-General of the FAO.

The Lula da Silva-Rousseff transition ensured the continuity of the diplomacy to fight against hunger and poverty, albeit with a smaller emphasis, which suggests what I call "continuity through inertia." The bilateral aspect specifically has become weaker, with many projects being concluded and few being created, thwarting the expectations of partners who had invested in strengthening bonds and contributed to electing Graziano da Silva to the leadership of the FAO. The deepening of the economic crisis has affected this dimension more directly due to budget cuts. Subsequently, it also had impacts on Brazil's contributions to the WFP and the FAO. Moreover, the withdrawal of presidential diplomacy and foreign policy dynamism undermined the maintenance of this strategy. Nonetheless, the interest of foreign delegations in social policies—including those created under the Rousseff administration, such as Brasil sem Miséria—continued despite the new scenario.

At that moment, some shortcomings of this diplomatic strategy became more evident. First, both PT administrations found it difficult to explain to the population why that particular aspect of foreign policy would be beneficial to the country. Although there was clearly a dimension of self-interest in the initiatives carried out, the decisionmakers avoided bringing it to the forefront, so as not to affect the discourse of solidarity. Second, contradictions in the dual model of agriculture developed in Brazil were exported to other countries, which sparked criticism and required a discursive exercise in order to bring them in line with the term "food and nutrition security." Third, there was a delayed understanding that internationalizing the same programs for partners with different realities might not yield the expected results. The transformative potential of those public policy "packages" could be diminished. Last, part of public opinion and certain political parties—particularly the center-right and right—accused that diplomacy of being a partisan and ideological project of the PT, reiterating the argument that social policies such as Bolsa Família had electoral and other nonexplicit objectives. This led to direct measures to reverse the diplomacy to fight against hunger and poverty during the Temer administration, such as the closure of the CGFOME, and indirect measures, through broader foreign policy decisions, such as lowering the political profile of the CELAC.[30] Furthermore, since the end of the second Rousseff administration, it has become more difficult to sustain the effectiveness of domestic programs, and a portion of the population has begun once again to live in a state of poverty and misery in Brazil.[31]

References

ALBUQUERQUE, F. L. R. de. **Atores e agendas da política externa brasileira para a África e a instrumentalização da cooperação em segurança alimentar (2003–2010).** Dissertação de mestrado em Relações Internacionais. Rio de Janeiro: Instituto de Filosofia e Ciências Humanas, Universidade do Estado do Rio de Janeiro. 2013.

_____. Cooperation on Food Security with Africa as an Instrument of Brazil's Foreign Policy (2003–2010). **Brazilian Journal of International Relations**, vol. 4, n. 3, 2015. pp. 558–581.

_____. A cooperative Global South? Brazil, India, and China in multilateral regimes. **Carta Internacional**, vol. 11, n. 1, 2016. pp. 163–187.

ARANHA, A. Fome Zero: A Construção de uma Estratégia de Combate à Fome no Brasil. In: Brasil. **Fome Zero: Uma História Brasileira**. Brasília: Ministério do Desenvolvimento Social e Combate à Fome. 2010.

BRASIL. **Fome Zero: Uma História Brasileira**. Brasília: Ministério do Desenvolvimento Social e Combate à Fome. 2010.

BRASIL. **O Brasil sem Miséria**. Ministério do Desenvolvimento Social e Combate à Fome. Brasília. 2014.

---

30   Nonetheless, the country remains active in the REAF, several South-South cooperation initiatives are still ongoing, and foreign delegations continue having meetings.

31   The World Bank has estimated that Brazil saw an increase of up to 3.6 million people living in poverty by the end of 2017. See: https://bit.ly/2NDeClV, accessed on September 26, 2018.

CABRAL, L. V. **Actors, interests and discursive politics in Brazil's agricultural development cooperation programmes with Mozambique.** Ph.D. thesis. Institute of Development Studies. Sussex: University of Sussex. 2016

CUNHA, B. L. A projeção internacional da Estratégia Fome Zero. In: Brasil. 2010. **Fome Zero: Uma História Brasileira,** vol. 3. Brasília: Ministério do Desenvolvimento Social e Combate à Fome. 2010.

CUSTÓDIO, M. B.; FURQUIM, N. R.; SANTOS, G. M. M. dos; CYRILLO, D. C.. Segurança alimentar e nutricional e a construção de sua política: uma visão histórica. **Segurança Alimentar e Nutricional,** vol. 18, n. 1, 2011. pp. 1–10. 81.

EASTON, David. An Approach to the Analysis of Political Systems. **World Politics,** vol. 9, n. 3, 1957. pp. 383–400.

FAO. **The State of Food Insecurity in the World:** Strengthening the enabling environment for food security and nutrition. Food and Agriculture Organization of the United Nations. Rome. 2014.

FRANÇA, C. G. de; MARQUES, V. P. M. de A. **O Brasil e a implementação das Diretrizes Voluntárias da Governança da Terra, da Pesca, dos Recursos Florestais:** aspectos da experiência recente. Paper apresentado ao III Seminário Internacional de Desenvolvimento Econômico e Governança da Terra. Unicamp, 7 a 9 de junho de 2017.

FRAUNDORFER, M. Fome Zero para o mundo—a difusão global brasileira do programa Fome Zero. **Austral: Revista Brasileira de Estratégia e Relações Internacionais,** vol. 2, n. 4,2013. pp. 97–122.

GOUREVITCH, P. Second image reversed: the international sources of domestic politics. **International Organization,** vol. 32, n. 4, 1978. pp. 881–912.

IBGE. **Síntese de Indicadores Sociais: uma Análise das Condições de Vida da População Brasileira.** Instituto Brasileiro de Geografia e Estatística. Rio de Janeiro. 2017.

INOUE, C. Y. A.; COELHO, N. B. R. Quando a fome encontra a diplomacia: a segurança alimentar na Política Externa Brasileira. **Meridiano 47,** vol. 19, 2018. pp. 1–20.

IPEA e ABC. **Cooperação Brasileira para o Desenvolvimento Internacional:** 2011–2013. Instituto de Pesquisa Econômica Aplicada; Agência Brasileira de Cooperação. Brasília: IPEA: ABC. 2016.

LEITE, A. C. C.; CAVALCANTE, T. F. A cooperação brasileira para a África: da diplomacia presidencial de Lula da Silva à diplomacia comercial de Dilma Rousseff. **Brazilian Journal of International Relations,** vol. 5, n.2, 2016. pp. 343–370.

LIMA, T; SANTANA, J. Q. Enlarging the donor base: an analysis of the World Food Programme's reform process and the Brazilian bridge diplomacy. **Rev. bras. polít. int.**, vol. 63, n.2, 2020. pp. 1–21.

MALUF, R.; PRADO, B. Atuação brasileira na América Latina e Caribe relacionada com a soberania e segurança alimentar e nutricional. **Textos para Discussão**, n. 8. CERESAN. Rio de Janeiro: Universidade Federal Rural do Rio de Janeiro (UFRRJ), 2015. pp. 1–62.82.

MILHORANCE, C. A política de cooperação do Brasil com a África Subsaariana no setor rural: transferência e inovação na difusão de políticas públicas. **Rev. Bras. Polít. Int.**, vol. 56, n. 2, 2013. pp. 5–22.

PINHEIRO, L.; MILANI, C. R. S. (org.). **Política Externa Brasileira: as práticas da política e a política das práticas.** Rio de Janeiro: FGV Editora. 2012.

PINTO, H. S. **A segurança alimentar e nutricional no Brasil (parte 1):** a modernização do Estado e os avanços na superação da fome. Brasília: Núcleo de Estudos e Pesquisas/CONLEG/Senado. 2014.

RONDÓ, M.; LOPES, M. Política externa e democracia: a construção de novos paradigmas em segurança alimentar e nutricional. **Friedrich Ebert Stiftung Brasil**, análise 18. 2016.

SILVA, A. C. da. De Vargas a Itamar: políticas e programas de alimentação e nutrição. **Estudos Avançados**, vol. 9, n. 23, pp. 87–107. 1995.

SILVA, S. P. **A trajetória histórica da segurança alimentar e nutricional na agenda política nacional: projetos, descontinuidades e consolidação.** Rio de Janeiro: IPEA. 2014.

VASCONCELOS, F. de A. G. de. Combate à fome no Brasil: uma análise histórica de Vargas a Lula. **Revista Nutrição**, vol. 18, n. 4, pp. 439–457. 2005.

CHAPTER 5
Practicing the Principles of South-South Cooperation: The Methodology of the Centre of Excellence Against Hunger

Clarissa Franzoi Dri (UFSC); Andressa Molinari da Silva (UFSC)

"This is Brazil: Centre's work has Brazilian origins and spreads Brazilian experiences, but sometimes I feel like Brazil doesn't see the importance of this policy."

Employee at the Centre of Excellence against Hunger in an interview with the authors, 2017

1 Introduction[32]

The Centre of Excellence against Hunger was created in 2011 as an initiative of the Brazilian government in partnership with the World Food Program (WFP) of the United Nations (UN). The Centre exists within the context of South-South cooperation and works to spread Brazilian experiences in the fight against hunger to other developing countries. It aims to encourage the creation of sustainable national policies for school feeding, social protection and improved nutrition. This work is carried out by providing technical assistance to other countries in order for them to develop the necessary skills to find solutions to hunger and poverty, particularly in the context of school feeding. The institution is based in Brasilia, is

32 The authors thank the professionals interviewed for their generosity and availability. We are also grateful for the support of the National Council for Scientific and Technological Development (*Conselho Nacional de Desenvolvimento Científico e Tecnológico—CNPq*) through the Call for Proposals *(Edital Universal)* and the Coordination for the Improvement of Higher Education Personnel (*Coordenação de Aperfeiçoamento de Pessoal de Nível Superior—CAPES*) through graduate funding. A very warm thank you goes to Mariana Rocha for her essential support to this research.

primarily funded by the Brazilian government, seeks to share Brazilian experiences and is part of the institutional framework of the UN. The Centre currently works with 28 countries, particularly in Africa and Asia, offering ongoing support, with frequent technical follow-up and policy advice, in an attempt to engage local governments in the programs.

This chapter will describe the Centre's methodology and the extent to which it is consistent with the theoretical principles of South-South cooperation. It argues that the Centre clearly follows the guidelines laid out in the literature on South-South cooperation but makes its own contributions, resulting from Brazilian domestic practices for fighting against hunger and poverty. Methodologically, the study is based on twelve semistructured interviews conducted by the authors between April and May 2017. Nine of those interviews were selected for this study: one with a diplomat who has experience in food security and eight with professionals working at the Centre of Excellence against Hunger. Those interviews were selected because of the interviewees' experience with monitoring the developed projects. The interviews were conducted face-to-face in Brasilia or via conference call. The analysis is also based on official documents describing the Centre's projects.

While there may be no consensus on the concept of South-South cooperation, with the exception of the fact that it involves developing countries (LEITE, 2012, p. 1), the principles that guide these practices are also presented or interpreted by analysts in different ways. This chapter seeks to take stock of the guidelines listed in the literature and compare them with the instruments used by the Centre of Excellence against Hunger. This may be a typical case of practice modifying theory, shaping and enhancing it. The actions that are gradually being applied and reformulated by the team at the Centre are based on work carried out by part of that same team at the National Education Development Fund (*Fundo Nacional de Desenvolvimento da Educação—FNDE*), affiliated with Brazil's Ministry of Education (*Ministério da Educação—MEC*). Those old practices demonstrate a certain connection with Paulo Freire's principles of popular education and communicative action and are supplemented—at the international level—by the guidelines for South-South cooperation provided by the Brazilian Cooperation Agency (*Agência Brasileira de Cooperação—ABC*). The characteristics of the Centre's projects seem to increase the list of guidelines, to the extent that the WFP is incorporating this new model into its institutional framework and expanding upon it.

This chapter does not intend to assess the effectiveness of the Centre's work. Other studies have already done that (see MAGALHÃES and BUANI, 2017), and there is room in the literature for further analyses along these lines, given the number of countries where the Centre operates. Nor does it intend to examine the process of the Centre's creation and organization (see DRI and DA SILVA, in press). The focus here is on how the institution intends to carry out the cooperation projects. This work seeks to contribute to a recent literature that has been studying the institution (FRAUNDORFER, 2015; MARCONDES and DE BRUYN, 2015), other than broader analyses of food and nutrition security and Brazil's role in this system.

The text is organized as follows. The first part provides a literature review of the principles that characterize South-South cooperation and differentiate it from other forms of international cooperation. The second part describes the development and implementation of the programs operated by the Centre in partner countries. This part is divided into five sections, based on the steps that are followed after contact is made with the countries and the core features of each of them, which shapes the Centre's contribution to South-South cooperation. This unique model is summarized in the conclusions.

2   Guidelines for South-South cooperation

The context for the emergence of South-South cooperation is linked to the recognition of the Global South as a symbolic concept, rather than a region. It appeared for the first time in international relations at the Afro-Asian Conference in Bandung in 1955. This event marks the starting point for political dialog among developing countries. At that moment, solidarity among them becomes a goal to be achieved and a tool to reduce asymmetries in the international system (PINO, 2009, p. 2). The Non-Aligned

Movement, emerging in 1961, is considered to be a direct consequence of the dialog that began at that conference and represents the refusal of a number of countries to align with one of the two Cold War superpowers (DE BRUYN, 2013, p. 11).

The G77 was formed alongside that movement, as a result of the political coordination provided by the "Conference on the Problems of Economic Development," which took place in Cairo in 1962, and the creation of the United Nations Conference on Trade and Development (UNCTAD) in 1964 (DE BRUYN, 2013, p. 11). The UN General Assembly institutionalized its support for technical cooperation among developing countries in 1974, creating a special unit to address the topic, now called the Unit for South-South Cooperation. The UNCTAD Buenos Aires Plan of Action was adopted in 1978 to promote technical and economic cooperation among developing countries, as a way to supplement the transfer of technology between the Global North and South. South-South cooperation in that plan is understood broadly, including trade, investment, humanitarian aid, loans and debt negotiation, capacity-building and the transfer of technology and knowledge (NEST, 2015, p. 10–11). From that moment on, the international community began to recognize that the experiences of the less developed countries could contribute to the development of other nations. This type of cooperation was considered a way to expand the collective self-sufficiency of developing countries, increase the effectiveness and sustainability of projects and reduce the costs of cooperation originating in more developed countries (FAO, 2017).

The logic of South-South cooperation assumes that the responses to certain problems become more efficient and sustainable when they are shared among countries with common characteristics and which have similar perceptions about the challenges they need to overcome (SILVA, 2010, p. 2). It would thus be possible to strengthen public policies through the transfer of experiences, knowledge and techniques. Governments with convergent understandings of their development goals could leverage South-South cooperation. South-South cooperation therefore also aims to reform the international order by creating solidarity among partner countries, seeking to guarantee the domestic self-sufficiency of each country for integration into the world economy (LECHINI and MORASSO, 2015, p. 116). "Furthermore, it has one particularly important motivation: to develop autonomy in order to increase the bargaining power of Southern countries in international forums and in their interactions with the core countries" (LECHINI and MORASSO, 2015, p. 117).

Among the principles that differentiate South-South cooperation from traditional North-South cooperation, Pino (2009, p. 1–2) lists

- noninterference in domestic affairs;
- greater sensitivity to specific contexts;
- equality among partner countries, including respect for their independence and national sovereignty;
- promotion of self-sufficiency;
- diversification of ideals, approaches and methods for cooperation;
- no explicit conditionalities;
- preference for using local resources that generate broader elements of ownership;
- greater flexibility, simplicity and speed of execution;
- "unrelated" character, not involving the purchase of goods and services from the offering country;
- adaptation to domestic priorities;
- preservation of diversity and cultural identity; and
- lower cost and greater impact.

De Bruyn (2016, p. 19–33) adds to that list, among other aspects, the following:

- nonhierarchical horizontality in relations between partners, demonstrated by the fact that cooperation is guided by request; follows concepts of sovereignty and noninterference; seeks positive results for all the actors involved; and is based on solidarity among nations;
- the pursuit of an alternative source of "profit," in the sense that cooperation for development is a foreign policy instrument which

brings benefits that are not financial but, rather, political: countries that promote cooperation may have a better position in the international arena;

- a mix of funding instruments, including government funds, private individual or corporate funds, as well as budget from global or regional international agencies and organizations;
- the importance of private sector participation, with financial and technical involvement in cooperation projects;
- discourse defending the modality of cooperation by its protagonists, based on the sharing of certain ethical principles[33], the use of the term "partnership" and the refusal to use the terminology of "donor and recipient" countries as well as "international aid" in their cooperation actions;
- no conditionalities for the implementation of a cooperation project;
- the seeming absence of civil society, which is generally related to low social participation in foreign policymaking;
- the inclusion of specific knowledge, expertise and technologies through the development experiences of the countries that offer this form of cooperation, based on a shared identity, historical ties and similar socioeconomic characteristics between partner nations;
- the concentration of cooperation in sectors related to social issues and the fight against poverty, seeking to increase economic productivity based on the idea of economic growth as an engine for development; and finally,
- increased coordination and integration among the developing countries that promote cooperation projects, through platforms for dialog and joint studies and programs encouraged by multilateral organizations.

---

33   "The core principles [...] can be summarized as follows: equal partnerships, mutual benefits, solidarity, no conditions, no interference, demand driven and sharing of own experiences. The Brazilian development cooperation define their policies as 'horizontal cooperation'" (DE BRUYN, 2013, p. 21).

Leite (2012, p. 28–33) understands South-South cooperation for development as the point of intersection between South-South cooperation, which includes development and trade, in accordance with the Buenos Aires concept, and international cooperation for development, which also encompasses North-South relations. Combining a theoretical and historical review of the latter two, the author plucks several characteristics that have a more pragmatic bias from the former, bringing them closer to North-South cooperation:

- direct, solidarity-based exchanges between partner countries or indirect exchanges in which participating countries seek recognition from third parties;
- reciprocity without an expectation of economic exchange—the nature of the reward is not defined or bargained in advance;
- pursuit of symmetry in the benefits achieved, which encourages the performance of the parties engaged in cooperation initiatives; and
- multiplicity of intrastate actors and a consequent plurality of objectives, with the executive branch of the requested country playing a special role in the expansion of cooperation initiatives.

More specifically in the case of Brazil, the country's involvement in international cooperation evolved from its symbolic presence in the field of technical cooperation in the 1960s and 1970s to the aim of promoting development based on efforts institutionalized during the Lula government. For Quadir (2013, p. 322), the country was attempting recognition as a prominent actor in international development at that moment, interested in transferring technical knowledge and capacities to other countries, particularly in Africa and Latin America. There was thus a "reemergence" of Brazil, alongside China and India as countries offering cooperation in the midst of an increasing number of regional and global meetings among developing countries, growth in trade and investment and an expansion of relations and diplomatic visits among those countries (DE BRUYN, 2013, p. 12).

Hirst (2010, p. 26–28) argues that South-South relations set a qualitative turn in international cooperation, with the intention of rearranging

actors' roles, power and influence. This would structurally change the traditional dynamics of international aid, giving agency to countries that were
once the recipients of cooperation and thus democratizing the international system. For the author, Brazil's cooperation with other countries in
the Global South follows several principles, including solidarity and co-
responsibility, which lead to horizontal cooperation as well as absence of
conditionality and direct financial gains (HIRST, 2010, p. 29). Another
principle refers to the non-aid character of the cooperation projects and
incorporates the idea of autonomy through an institutional strengthening
of all the nations involved (HIRST, 2010, p. 29–30). These characteristics
are possible for the partner countries share common histories, identities,
challenges and socioeconomic realities, which bring them closer together
and increase the chances of a successful transfer of experiences and initiatives for development.

Pino and Leite (2010, p. 20) indicate that Brazil is one of the most
active agents in South-South cooperation, contributing primarily through
the transfer of innovative solutions for development in different areas simultaneously, through international cooperation initiatives involving countries in the Global North and international organizations, as well as other
developing countries, favoring a third group of countries receiving foreign
aid. Leite, Pomeroy and Suyama (2015, p. 1451) argue that Brazil's involvement in South-South cooperation for development gained momentum in
the early 2000s with the rise to power of a left-wing government and the
state taking on a greater role in domestic development. The social policies
practiced domestically gained strength and legitimacy when they were exported to other countries, at the same time that South-South cooperation
offered the country an arena to internationally promote its image.

The impetus for domestic social development was therefore reflected
in the South-South cooperation initiatives led by Brazil. The topics addressed most frequently include food security, the right to food, family
farming, land reform, small-scale fisheries and dialog with civil society
(HIRST, 2010, p. 35). The initiative to establish the Centre of Excellence
against Hunger is part of this context, as an expression of South-South co-

operation instituted by the Brazilian government in partnership with international agencies. Its functioning will be described and analyzed in the following section and then compared with the principles of South-South cooperation presented in this section.

3 Guiding instruments and stages of the Centre's activities[34]

According to the WFP Strategic Plan 2008–2013, the Centre was established with the overall objective of "supporting developing countries in the design, management and expansion of sustainable and healthy national school feeding programs" (WFP, 2010, p. 4; WFP, 2013, p. 4). Its specific objectives are the following:

- to promote good school feeding practices through training and capacity-building activities aimed at national governments;
- to provide direct technical assistance to develop the domestic capacity to design and implement sustainable school feeding programs;
- to promote research and innovation and support the expansion of the global knowledge on school feeding; and
- defend and promote school feeding as an effective solution to the problem of hunger (WFP, 2010, p. 5).

To achieve these goals, the Centre follows a number of working methods derived in the beginning from FNDE's cooperation experiences. "At the FNDE, we spent a lot of time working on the best ways to welcome delegations. [...] And the Centre was initially created based on that methodology, which was to say: 'Well, there are WFP programs that the WFP isn't going to continue, so the governments need to take charge. We have the know-how on designing sustainable school feeding programs based on what Brazil has done; we can offer that support [...] So, it wasn't the kind of work that the WFP did; it was the kind of work that the Brazilian government did" (Employee 1). "The Centre's methodology was created by

---

34 This section will not follow standard conventions for block quotations, for ease of reading.

the FNDE, over time [...] and we taught them: the technicians are ours, the knowledge is ours" (Employee 2). The ABC's participation in the projects afterwards contributed to a structured incorporation of the established principles of South-South cooperation into those practices. Although it has been periodically adjusted since its creation, the methodology has maintained some core characteristics. They will be presented and discussed next and are organized based on the stages that typically take place in projects developed by the Centre.

3.1 Request for partnership and the Centre's visit to the requesting country

First, to initiate a partnership with a country, the Centre must receive a request. In other words, the Centre does not do anything until it receives a governmental demand, which contacts it through the Brazilian embassy or the WFP office in that country. At the beginning, a list of priority countries was agreed upon by the Brazilian government and the WFP. If the requesting country is on the list, there is a budget, which allows the Centre to make a visit to the country using funds invested by the Brazilian government. If the country is not on the list, its own government bears the costs of the visit, which occurs frequently: there are 23 priority countries, but over 40 countries have participated in study visits (Employee 7). "Over time, the name of the Centre of Excellence, and the opportunities it supported, of countries coming to Brazil to learn about our experiences and then continuing to receive remote or local support to develop their policies, all this spread very fast, which is also a sign of pent-up demand in the field of international cooperation" (Employee 4).

Next and based on an initial diagnosis of the problems and challenges made by the requesting country, the Centre generally organizes a technical visit in order to understand the local situation and its specific problems and demands as well as to provide detailed information about the policies that compose the Brazilian system of food and nutrition security, with an emphasis on school feeding. "This is very different from what the UN did in the 1970s, for example. You were in Washington; you wrote up a project to be carried out in a country like Senegal, where you had never been. [...] Here, there is a component where people come to Brazil, but then all the work is done in that country. We have to truly understand the reality of the country, truly understand the politics, the nuances, to be able to work. [...] Today, everything is changing. You pay very close attention to the country, what the country wants, what the country needs. National governments want autonomy; that whole colonization thing is over. [...] When you really want commitment from people, you work horizontally, without dictating. That's the way it has to be" (Employee 3). As part of that first contact, a terms of reference is created in collaboration, comprising the initial objectives of the partnership and the expected developments, "depending on the political actors you're dialoging with, on what they want: if they want to develop a school feeding program, which is the most typical case, if they want support for social protection or to create government agencies for food and nutrition security, for example" (Employee 4). When it is not possible to make that visit, support is requested from the local WFP office, which has a deep understanding of the domestic reality and the demands of the government and intermediates the work on the terms of reference. Support from the WFP offices for the Centre's activities has gradually become more important.

When the priorities are being defined, one of the goals is to include government actors: ministers and leaders of the institutions in charge of education, agriculture, health, social development and finance, among others, as well as officials working on the technical teams at those ministries. Another central feature of the Centre's activity is therefore direct contact with those responsible for public policies. "Our focus is on governments. [...] If I am moving from emergency aid to development, I need to have a mass of people who can take on those responsibilities. So at some point, I need to work not only on the capacity of the WFP staff who are working there, but I need to transfer that capacity to the government. That was the type of change that took place at the WFP: that there would have to be a sustainable transition, that the government has to produce domestic programs, and in order to produce all that, it has to have a trained staff" (Employee 1). One of the cornerstones of South-South cooperation is respect for national sovereignty and priorities. In the case of the Centre, dialog with government officials is also based on public management experiences in Brazil. "The Brazilian government often works that way: there are meetings with state and municipal governments, managers come together and work as a group, discuss a number of things together, try to develop things together. […] As we participate in activities with other partners, we have found that this way of working, which we consider normal, is seen by others as an innovation. This is an example, putting governments in a role, using workshops and activities, in a role that they were not used to having, in a more active leadership role" (Employee 4).

Government leadership is expected to generate the necessary political and regulatory support for both implementing and sustaining the new policy, which will be described in more detail ahead. "School feeding does not exist in many African countries. It is provided by agencies, be it the WFP, the World Bank or other agencies. So, the Centre actually tries to work along these lines: to create an awareness within the government about developing this project. In other words, it isn't just developing a strategy, a school feeding policy; it's coming up with public funds to start this movement. This is advocacy" (Employee 5). Then, the great challenge is "how to move from awareness, from documents, from laws, to practice. How to make this transition? How to develop the state's capacity to cultivate programs, not just implement a program at a school and consider it done? It involves balancing legitimacy and functionality. […] It is pointless to approve public policies, strategies, laws, have it all on paper, but then when you go to a school, the children aren't being fed. […] It is also pointless to make a program that works 100% if people don't recognize it; so, you have to balance those two variables: legitimacy and functionality" (Employee 5). This feature is so crucial to the work that it can be considered more than a method—it is in fact seen as one of the core objectives of the Centre's team. "I think that a measure for success for our work is to have a good relationship with the local partners, i.e., we can talk to ministers directly, have a direct line to government technicians. This has already happened in Senegal, Benin, Togo, Kenya, Zimbabwe, for example" (Employee 5).

3.2   Visit to Brazil by the requesting country and multisectoralism

In a second stage, a delegation from the requesting country visits Brazil and comes into contact with a school feeding program operating in schools located in a region chosen by the Centre based on social, economic, cultural and environmental similarities with the visiting country (Employee 6). The delegation spends approximately two weeks learning about strategies for developing and implementing this Brazilian public policy directly in schools, as well as visiting other government agencies and social institutions involved in this process. The aim of the visit is to offer a concrete and multidimensional perspective of the Brazilian experience, making it possible for the partner country to imagine ways of adapting the instruments of interest to their local reality. "It is as if, little by little, school feeding has become part of a somewhat systemic approach. In addition to education, it has links with health, agriculture, social protection. [...] In Brazil, there are programs that have worked, programs that haven't worked, and programs that are somewhere in the middle. So, they can see the entire range. I always say that this relationship with Brazil involves observing and making sure that they don't have to start from nothing, that they can think: 'Brazil did that, and it didn't work; should we try it?'" (Employee 1).

The Centre's encouragement of a multisectoral approach to the topics is intended to make future food policy more effective. "How does this translate into practice? This is very much the Brazilian approach to food and nutrition security: the creation of mechanisms for collaboration among initiatives and programs, in order to allow them to reinforce one another, help one another and maximize the other's impact. And we promote this approach in the countries where we work, beginning with the people who are part of the delegations that come here. We don't say, 'only the Ministry of Education can come because they are responsible for school feeding;' we say 'agriculture should come, gender should come' because they can all be involved, in one way or another. This intersectoral approach is what sets our work apart" (Employee 7). In fact, the Brazilian program is cross-sectional, insofar as

[…] [i]t brings together three major areas: education, food and nutrition security and productive inclusion. Besides enhancing school enrollment rates, it reduces short-term hunger, helps in cognitive and psychosocial development, helps to break the cycles of poverty and disease. It also contributes to decrease public health expenditure on the long term, since the beneficiaries tend to acquire healthy eating habits, and make them less susceptible to illness. School feeding, when linked to local agriculture production, can provide a stable market access to small-holder farmers and stimulate rural agriculture development, which in turn improves food security […]. Bringing education, health, agriculture, and social development to work together can reap economic benefits in developing countries around the world (WFP, 2013, p. 3).

In this respect, the training of domestic human resources is another essential step in the methodology. "Something that I find challenging and innovative at the same time is helping them make their own decisions. They are the ones who have to engage. If they are going to hold a workshop, it takes six months, a year, because it is the government that is organizing it, taking the lead. We facilitate and support, but they are the ones who organize. What I've seen in all the seminars we've done is the government taking the lead and asking: 'is this right?' In most of the workshops, the government has created committees, subcommittees; they are trying to organize everything. I think Africa in particular has a need for this work. It's as if they spent many years having voices that went unheard; they were silent and accepting, and suddenly you give these people a voice: 'I am listening to whatever you have to say, what you have to say is interesting, and I want to listen.' So, this person looks around and thinks: 'this is amazing. I have something to contribute; I also have the ability to act' […]. If you look from the beginning up to today, you can see how much they have grown in terms of their capacity … they now have the capacity to facilitate a workshop; they have learned, they are on another level. If you could measure their learning, it would be truly impressive" (Employee 1). This prioritization of capacity development is centered on encouraging the institutional and political elements that were crucial to the success of these policies in Brazil, with adaptations to the different contexts (MARCONDES and DE BRUYN, 2015).

Then, based on the perceptions of the actors making the visit and the challenges faced domestically, each country—with technical support from

the Centre's staff—produces a draft plan of action, which is used to institutionalize the desired policy. This document is prepared after the delegation returns to their home country but can also begin to be outlined during
their visit to Brazil or in seminars organized by the Centre. "There are
times when we ask the government participants to sit down together and
discuss elements that will become part of that document, and they write,
they begin to develop it here. This simple idea of bringing these government people together to develop, to put the idea down on paper, the proposals that will later become part of the document, this shocks some people
working at international agencies, as something they have never seen before" (Employee 4). The draft plan of action differs from the terms of reference in the first phase, as it identifies the objectives and future prospects
related to school feeding and/or food and nutrition security that are desired by the national government as well as focuses on the actions that
should be taken. "The Centre helps the delegation develop this document,
and the objective is to include medium-term and maybe long-term activities related to establishing and improving public policies" (Employee 4).

3.3   Upon return to the implementation site, the challenge of sustainability

The plan of action becomes more than a draft when it passes through a
process of domestic validation, with internal approval from the country's
government. There is generally a consultation with the political actors responsible for implementing projects, which is important for creating an
environment that will affirm a political commitment to the implementation and progress of the strategies being planned (WFP, 2013, p. 10).
Alongside this process, in order to follow up on the cooperation project
and seeking to implement the plan of action, the Centre offers continued
support to the country in the form of hiring consultants to collaborate on
the development of specific programs, holding seminars and workshops
and providing technical support for evaluation and monitoring (WFP,
2014, p. 19). "We don't like to use the term 'consultant' because it refers to
a way of working that occurs often enough that I can say it is the traditional
way that countries [in the Global North] provide support to governments,

while we want governments to lead, to participate" (Employee 4). The team attributes this difference in methods to Brazil's previous experiences as a recipient of international aid, leading it to prioritize horizontal interactions and respect the autonomy of each nation as they develop their projects. "Brazil is very young in terms of international relations. [...] When the Lula administration decides to engage in South-South cooperation, what would that be like? Let's see what would be nice; let's take the lessons we have learned about what we don't want, what other countries have done that we wouldn't want to do" (Employee 3).

This adaptability to the needs and rhythms of the partner country creates a flexibility in the cooperation model that has received criticism, primarily due to the difficulty of measuring results. However, rather than delivering a unilaterally defined product or meeting quantitative goals, the Centre makes its preference clear by creating conditions for the sustainability of domestic projects without international aid, even in the long term. "These countries often have entire areas of social protection or school feeding that are managed or implemented by international development agencies or NGOs, without the government's participation. The Centre's objective is to encourage countries to take on the challenge of seeing what is on the horizon, for example, a domestic, governmental school feeding program, with established policy documents, with a well-defined medium-to-long term plan for expanding school feeding, that sort of thing. So, our support is concentrated in this area, analyzing context, the challenges of family farming, what would be the best way to think about institutional arrangements, which sectors of government, who would be responsible for what, how to look for budget to sustainably fund this program, how to plan the implementation of this program over time. You don't start a program all at once, trying to cover the entire country; so, deciding which region to prioritize and why" (Employee 4).

One way to ensure that initiatives have continuity over time and become state policies is to institutionalize them through legal means. Legislative changes that have standardized school feeding and included food security in the Brazilian Federal Constitution usually impress partner countries during their visits (Employee 3), namely, the National Policy for Food and Nutrition Security (*Política Nacional de Segurança Alimentar e Nutricional—PNSAN*), approved in 2003, which resulted, in 2006, in the Organic Law on Food and Nutrition Security (*Lei Orgânica de Segurança Alimentar e Nutricional—LOSAN*), establishing the National Food and Nutrition Security Plan (*Plano Nacional de Segurança Alimentar e Nutricional—PLANSAN*). Added to this framework is the enactment of Constitutional Amendment 64/2010, which amended Article 6 of the Federal Constitution to include the social right to food as a human right to be defended by the country. This level of legal protection can prevent a policy from lapsing due to changes in the government, which is a persistent problem reported by the Centre's staff. In fact, "political instability and institutional fragility are two of the most complex issues. The constant change in governments is an enormous challenge. However, we have also seen that precisely because of those constant changes, there is a somewhat central body that remains. It is almost an incipient birth of a state bureaucracy. Sometimes it's one person, or two, and those people sort of just stay on, perhaps because no one else has their knowledge" (Employee 1). While working to design permanent policies, the Centre seeks to identify those employees and maintain contact, even in times when they are adapting to a change in government.

The difficulties in measuring the impact of the Centre's work over its first decades of operation are due to three main factors derived from this methodology, particularly with regard to the autonomy of states and the encouragement of permanent public policies. First, the data that may emerge on school feeding or food and nutrition security is derived from policies implemented by governments, not directly by the Centre. "The impact [...] depends much more on continuity and on what governments will do with the information we share with them" (Employee 6). Second, development does not happen quickly. Its evolution is long, unlike emergency aid, where it is possible to measure, for example, the amount of food delivered. "History is slow. If you think about developed countries, 60 years ago there was no social protection, and it takes time to formulate, debate, create friction for discussions in the country and evolve. And our projects are long term" (Employee 5). "Things take time to truly be effective. [...] Donors usually want you to solve a country's problem in six months or a year and deliver a report that everything has improved. That isn't always possible. [...] Europe didn't begin 50 years ago; it began 500 years ago. [...] This is one of the Centre's challenges: showing that it will have a result, but not today, not tomorrow. We're building something that lasts. It isn't just a pilot project, where when the money runs out, the partner leaves and the project ends the next day" (Employee 3). Third, the Centre does not determine the effective implementation of the project. "I don't know if it will actually be implemented. This is not in our mandate. The ideal would be to build tools and support so that [the policies] were always implemented, but what happens is that implementation depends on resources and the government itself. Because in capacity-building, I don't go there and implement anything; the idea is that the government takes ownership and implements it, and we have very little control over it" (Employee 1).

3.4 Multilateral action to encourage networks of cooperation

The Centre's scope of activity has gradually expanded from being solely trilateral (involving the Brazilian government, the WFP and the country requesting technical support) to becoming multilateral. This strategy was designed to optimize resources, allowing the Centre to work with different countries on a single visit, both in Brazil and abroad. Moreover, multilateralism encourages contact between the requesting countries, generating new synergies beyond interaction with Brazil or the WFP. The Centre has thus been promoting meetings, seminars and courses with the participation of different partner countries, who develop similar programs and share problems and challenges. The objective is to support the creation of regional and global networks to exchange knowledge and promote joint initiatives in order to coordinate efforts. "Hence, the idea of a hub and networks. Because the idea is that you should have this global knowledge and be capable to exchange. [...] This kind of interregional, interstate dialog was greatly encouraged by the Centre of Excellence. [...] First because we had a very busy schedule and we had to accommodate a lot of delegations. Then, after developing our theoretical foundations, we saw that this is the best way. We had, for example, Niger and Guinea Conakry, Benin, Togo and Burundi; those countries are still moving along the same path, they are still interacting. It was incredible; they began to see that they had the same problems with rice, the same problems with donors, with planting. The potential of these exchanges is impressive, and there is also the issue of visibility, of reporting to the international community, a concrete and visible program for which the country is able to stand as a country that has a certain amount of leadership or certain best practices and lessons learned" (Employee 1).

This practice of connecting countries in the Global South can also be considered one of the Centre's innovative methods. In addition to encouraging the exchange of experiences and the collective design of projects aimed at strengthening South-South cooperation, it also promotes less interference from material interests in the initiatives. These are basically "trade interests. The way it is now is: I give you [aid] because I'm interested in your ore and would like you to buy my product X. So, it's always like that. Because the United Kingdom, the United States, there are trade interests in everything; cooperation is not a disinterested cooperation, it is cooperation because of interests. They say 'look, I'll give you money to do project X if you start opening up your markets to my companies, to my industry, to my contractor,' like it is with China; they are everywhere there [in Africa], building. I think that networks reduce this [problem] because, when you have a diversity of actors, no one talks openly. [...] It's time for us to understand that we no longer should focus on bilateral cooperation because that generates a lot of interests from one country to the other" (Employee 8).

To encourage and strengthen these networks, the Centre holds events in partnership with local and international organizations, notably the Global Child Nutrition Forum (GCNF), organized annually by the Global Child Nutrition Foundation and supported by the Centre since 2013 (WFP, 2015, p. 31). The Forum brings together senior officials as well as technicians from more than 40 countries, international and regional organizations, nongovernmental organizations and different institutions who exchange knowledge through workshops, technical consultancy and discussion panels, facilitating the improvement and expansion of school feeding programs in the participating countries (WFP, 2015, p. 8). "But it was a small event held in the US, with a small number of people. After the Centre got involved, there was this idea about moving it away from the US, starting to hold it in developing countries, and this created a much larger mobilization. Today, there are 250 people attending the event every year, including a number of ministers; there are representatives from international organizations, different levels of government. And all of them, for one week, discussing the progress of their programs, making commitments, agreeing on partnerships for technical assistance" (Employee 7).

In 2014, the government of Niger, which has been working with the Centre since 2011, invited the Francophone African countries participating in the Forum—which was being held in South Africa—to attend a parallel meeting where a Francophone African School Feeding Network was proposed (Employee 6). "This had a huge impact. The countries were excited about the idea, and it was eventually expanded to an African School Feeding Network, linked to the African Union. [...] Representatives from the African Union requested that Brazil make a study visit; so, we visited representatives from different African countries and commissioners from the African Union [...], and they understood what we do and why so many countries make that request. So, they decided to take over this advocacy process for school feeding in Africa" (Employee 6). Subsequently, the countries in the bloc signed an agreement to increase funding for school feeding and the Africa Day of School Feeding was created (Employee 6). The Ministers of Education approved a continental recommendation saying that all countries should adopt a joint and coordinated approach to school feeding, through the bloc (WFP, 2016, p. 5). "Instead of working with each individual country, we are working with the entire African Union, which has an enormous persuasive power with countries in Africa" (Employee 6). Another consequence of working in networks is therefore the increased potential for the awareness and mobilization of political leaders on the topic of school feeding.

3.5   Beyond aid, the creation of rights

Another important characteristic of the work carried out by the Centre of Excellence is the consideration of nutritional food as a human right. This approach differs from food as aid to vulnerable populations, not only because it is part of a long-term, governmental perspective, but also because it goes beyond poverty and includes guarantees for all social classes. "Based on the Centre's activity with the government technicians we work with, social protection is seen as a right, rather than charity, which is a big debate in developing countries. You are providing a public service, and the population has the right to access those services. They used to be seen for a long time as services benefiting only a part of the population that didn't have proper access to food, so as a form of charity" (Employee 5). The discourse created by Brazilian foreign policy in the Lula administration made it possible to affirm this view at the international level, beginning with the president's history of life, which he shared in his international speeches (FRAUNDORFER, 2015, p. 96–97). Brazil's contribution to international initiatives to fight against hunger and poverty is thus strongly grounded in a rights-based strategy, emphasizing issues such as accountability and transparency (VELASCO, 2017, p. 337).

"We work with law, the promotion of rights. […] Foreign policy responds directly to domestic policy. […] You can only affect foreign policy if you have a consistent domestic policy; otherwise, it is impossible. […] This concept of school feeding was constructed by Brazil, because what the World Bank advocated was focusing only on the poorest people. And we said: 'no, food is a right. And food is not just the act of eating; it is communion, it is much more.' And then, interestingly, there were several excellent articles in The Guardian showing that children in England prefer to lie, to go hungry rather than admit they are they are below the poverty line because it's embarrassing. In a capitalist country, being poor is embarrassing; so, they would rather go hungry. And that's exactly what we said: 'who is going to eat if they are being discriminated against?' You can eat food, but what effect will this food have? Psychologically, it is a kind of violence. So, we managed to reverse that at the world forums, the WFP, the FAO" (Diplomat 1).

However, this construction of rights must be encouraged through partnerships with governments, rather than through mechanisms such as denunciation or censorship. One employee at the Centre develops this idea through the different dimensions of human rights. First, there is the dimension of respect, which means that the state cannot interfere with rights—it cannot take food away from people, for example. Second, there is the dimension of protection, which corresponds to protecting rights from the interference of third parties. In addition, there is a third dimension: fulfillment. This dimension means that the state has an obligation to guarantee rights. Therefore, for the state, ensuring food security for its citizens is not a favor; it is the accomplishment of a right that is recognized in many fundamental laws. In this respect, the Centre's work is guided by the right to adequate food. International human rights organizations usually have the demand-approach, i.e., asking the state to fulfill its obligations. In the case of the Centre, the perspective is different: it understands that states should have the ability to ensure that their population has a sufficient amount of adequate food and thus assists them with developing policies. The Centre does not adopt the coercion perspective, but rather the idea of partnership. The goal is that the state develops policies in order to be self-sufficient in the long term (Employee 7).

The employees at the Centre mention studies by Paulo Freire and Luigi Ferrajoli as important theoretical frameworks in this methodology, particularly in terms of two-way learning and the shared construction of solutions: "no one educates anyone else, nor do we educate ourselves, we educate one another in communion, in the context of living in this world" (FREIRE, 1981, p. 79). "It is an approach that clearly states that the solution is not given from the outset but, rather, that the response to the problem will only be created during the process. And that means you will cooperate with countries, you will discover the questions and answers with them" (Employee 4). "This right does not need to be codified. If it is a human right, it is universal, which is very important for common law countries, as this right is unlikely to be codified. For us, in terms of foreign policy, it was great" (Diplomat 1).

4   Conclusion: new paradigms for South-South cooperation?

After comparing the principles of South-South cooperation listed at the beginning of the chapter with the methodology for implementing projects at the Centre of Excellence against Hunger, it is clear that the institution follows all the guidelines mentioned by the authors. It is important, however, to describe the meaning of those guidelines in this case. With regard to the principles of acting upon request, horizontality, respect for the autonomy of nations and the use of local resources, the local visits made by the Centre's staff and the subsequent hiring of technicians to support governments during the implementation of the actions are particularly noteworthy. This understanding of the domestic reality creates a stronger potential for horizontal dialog. Moreover, direct contact with government leaders at different levels, intended to encourage the creation of domestic methods to recognize and guarantee rights, rather than short-term aid projects, emerges as a central condition for horizontal cooperation.

With regard to the pursuit of self-sufficiency in cooperation projects, encouraging the design of public policies based on legal and institutional changes seems to be essential. This is in line with one of the Centre's primary objectives: training domestic human resources to manage the processes with legitimacy and proficiency. The involvement of different governmental sectors also contributes to the effectiveness of policies to fight against hunger, considering the complexity and multidimensionality of the phenomenon. With regard to reciprocity, the absence of trade interests does not imply—as the theory mentions—a complete absence of interests. Brazil may, for example, be seeking international recognition, among other elements, but those rewards have not been previously agreed upon and thus do not condition the actions. Furthermore, the establishment of multilateral platforms, besides promoting the integration of developing countries, decreases the space for potential bargains for benefits resulting from cooperation.

One feature of the Centre's work that evades theoretical prediction refers to the multiplicity of intrastate actors involved in the requesting country and the plurality of objectives for cooperation. Defying this assumption, this new institution emerged precisely to centralize the diffusion of school feeding and nutrition practices. There is a coordination of efforts with the Ministry of Foreign Affairs (*Ministério das Relações Exteriores*, here referred to as Itamaraty), which manages the financial resources and assists with designing projects through the ABC, but there is no fragmented action or overlapping of goals, as may occur in other areas of cooperation offered by Brazil. This institutional method has facilitated the stability of international collaboration in this field, through an autonomous and collective building—by the team—of the trajectories to be tested. While the activities of the Centre of Excellence against Hunger confirm and solidify the theoretical principles of South-South cooperation, they also qualify and modify their emphases. In working with methods that are at the same time objectives, the institution challenges the immobility and ambiguity of certain guidelines for cooperation. Contact with governments, the creation of public policies, the encouragement of local capacity, working in networks and the construction of rights seem to be distinctive features of that cooperation and are more significant than the simples reference to horizontality or nonconditionality, for example.

One offshoot of the innovations proposed by the Centre in terms of instruments and materials is its proliferation within the framework of the WFP. The agency has gradually been replacing the idea of aid with prevention, increasing the organization's focus on cooperation for development, compared to humanitarian aid activities. Considering the Centre's close contact with local WFP offices, which in some cases gives continuity to projects that are in progress, the interviewees indicate that the Centre's methods have influenced changes at the WFP (Employees 1, 3 and 6). Rather than acting only in emergency situations, the WFP has been adopting ways of working on emergency aid and development simultaneously. Centers of excellence with models similar to the Brazilian model have been organized in China, India and Russia, demonstrating the potential for a successful transfer of public policies among the Global South and a foreign policy that values domestic experiences in the pursuit of social development.

Interviews

Interview with Employee 1 from the Centre of Excellence against Hunger, Brasilia, April 6, 2017, 48 min.

Interview with Employee 2 from the FNDE, conference call, May 18, 2017, 1h 14 min.

Interview with Employee 3 from the Centre of Excellence against Hunger, conference call, May 11, 2017, 1 h 11 min.

Interview with Employee 4 from the Centre of Excellence against Hunger, conference call, April 25, 2017, 1 h 6 min.

Interview with Employee 5 from the Centre of Excellence against Hunger, Brasilia, May 2, 2017, 42 min.

Interview with Employee 6 from the Centre of Excellence against Hunger, Brasilia, May 2, 2017, 1 h 12 min.

Interview with Employee 7 from the Centre of Excellence against Hunger, Brasilia, May 2, 2017, 44 min.

Interview with Employee 8 from the *Centre* of Excellence against Hunger, Brasilia, April 5, 2017, 44 min.

Interview with Diplomat 1, Brasilia, May 2, 2017, 1 h 37 min.

References

DE BRUYN, T. **Challenging Development Cooperation?** A Literature Review of The Approaches of The Emerging Powers. Leuven: KU Leuven, Hiva Research Institute for Work and Society, 2013.

_____. **Deconstructing the South-South Cooperation Partnership**: Insights from 14 projects of India, China and Brazil with Mozambique and Malawi. Leuven: KU Leuven, Hiva Research Institute for Work and Society, 2016.

DRI, C.; DA SILVA, A. Política externa brasileira para o sul global: a criação do Centro de Excelência contra a Fome. No prelo.

FAO. **¿Qué es CTPD?** 2017. Available at: <https://bit.ly/2ElA9A4>. Accessed 6 Apr. 2017.

FRAUNDORFER, M. Brazil's emerging role in global governance: health, food, security and bioenergy. London: Palgrave Macmillan, 2015.

FREIRE, P. **Pedagogia do Oprimido**. 9. Ed. Rio de Janeiro: Paz e Terra, 1981.

HIRST, M. America Latina y la cooperación Sur-Sur: Reflexiones conceptuales y políticas. In: PINO, B; SURASKY, J. (Coords.). **La cooperación Sur-Sur en Latinoamérica**: Utopía y Realidad. Madrid: Catarata, 2010. p. 17–40.

LECHINI, G; MORASSO, C. La cooperación Sur-Sur en el siglo XXI: Reflexiones desde América Latina. **Anuario de Integración Regional de América Latina y Caribe,** v. 11, 2015. p. 114–133.

LEITE, I. C.; POMEROY, M.; SUYAMA, B.. Brazilian South-South Development Cooperation: The Case of the Ministry of Social Development in Africa. **Journal of International Development,** v. 27, issue 8, 2015, p. 1446–1461.116.

LEITE, I. Cooperação Sul-Sul: Conceito, História e Marcos Interpretativos. **Observatório Político Sul-Americano (IESP/UERJ),** v. 7, n. 3, 2012. p. 1–40.

MAGALHÃES, B.; BUANI, C.. Cooperação sul-sul para segurança alimentar: influências do Centro de Excelência do Programa Mundial de Alimentos nas relações Brasil-África. **Monções,** v. 6, n. 11, 2017. p. 437–475.

MARCONDES, G.; DE BRUYN, T.. Brazil's South-South Cooperation in food security: capacity building approaches of the Centre of Excellence against hunger. **Food Security,** v. 7, issue 6, 2015. p. 1153–1164.

NEST Africa. Developing A Conceptual Framework for South-South Co-Operation. **Working Document,** September 2015.

PINO, B. **Cooperación Sur-Sur:** Innovación y Transformación en la Cooperación Internacional. Madrid: Fundación Carolina, 2009.

_____. LEITE, Iara. La cooperación Sur-Sur de Brasil: Proyección Solidaria y Política Exterior. In: PINO, Bruno; SURASKY, Javier (Coords.). **La cooperación Sur-Sur en Latinoamérica:** Utopía y Realidad. Madrid: Catarata, 2010. p. 69–101.

QUADIR, F. Rising Donors and the New Narrative of 'South-South' Cooperation: What prospects for changing the landscape of development assistance programmes? Third World Quarterly, v. 34, n. 2, 2013. p. 321–338.

SILVA, M. How Did We Get Here? The Pathways of South-South Cooperation. **Poverty in Focus.** IPC-IG, Brasília, 2010.

VELASCO JR, P. A diplomacia do combate à fome e a contribuição brasileira para a segurança alimentar e nutricional no seio da ONU e da FAO. In: SCHMITZ, Guilherme; ROCHA Rafael (Orgs). **Brasil e o Sistema das Nações Unidas: desafios e oportunidades na governança global.** Brasília: IPEA, 2017. p. 307–344.117.

WFP, Centro de Excelência contra a Fome. **Relatório Anual 2012.** 2013. Available at: <https://bit.ly/2OXaIss>. Accessed 17 Feb. 2017.

WFP, Centro de Excelência contra a Fome. **Relatório Anual 2013.** 2014. Available at: <https://bit.ly/1lOXMzh>. Accessed 17 Feb. 2017.

WFP. Programa de Execução PAM/BRASIL para a Promoção da Cooperação Sul-Sul de Apoio ao Desenvolvimento de Programas Sustentáveis de Alimentação Escolar. Nova York, 2010.

WFP. **Relatório Anual 2014**. 2015. Available at: <https://bit.ly/2QGVOUs>. Accessed 17 Feb. 2017.

WFP. **Relatório Anual 2015**. 2016. Available at: <https://bit.ly/1YWqDCq>. Accessed 17 Feb. 2017.

CHAPTER 6
Maize and the World Market: a History of Racism, Commodification, and Resistance

Andrea Santos Baca[35]
Julia Cristina de Sousa e Berruezo[36]

Introduction

Maize, rice, and wheat are considered the three plants of civilization. In the words of the French historian Fernand Braudel: "Wherever it began, agriculture had from the start been obliged to opt for one of the major food-plants; and had been built up around this initial choice of priority on which everything or almost everything would thereafter depend" (Braudel, 1982, p.107). With this, Braudel makes an interesting contribution, despite the serious Eurocentric limits of his study (not even mentioning Africa and Middle East wheat civilizations or any word about sub-Saharan civilizations) and the possible controversial origin of this classification (as will be mentioned below). From a strong materialism point of view, he suggests us to think that the fate of human civilizations is linked to the most mundane materiality such as food or, as he called, the long-term structures of everyday life. Thus, a plant of civilization can fall into disuse and even be forgotten when the civilization who cultivated it succumbs to internal, ecological or conquest crises: "In short, what we may think of as the success of a plant may also, perhaps, largely be the success of a culture (…). Plants, like men, can only survive when circumstances favor them. In this case, the mainstream of history passed them by" (Braudel, 1982, p.107).

---

35 Andrea Santos Baca, Ph.D. in Economics and professor at the Universidade Federal do ABC (UFABC, Brazil) E-mail: santos.baca@ufabc.edu.br
36 Master's Degree student in Development Studies at the University of Passau, Germany. E-mail: desous04@ads.uni-passau.de

In contrast to these Braudelian ideas, some authors have pointed out (Gray and Patel 2015; Grey and Newman, 2018) that the capitalist-modern confluence of different food cultures had always involved a contradictory double movement: domination (and often extermination) of cultures and recognition/appropriation of its culinary heritage (Grey & Newman, 2018: 717). So it seems that the success of food plants and the fate of their culture/civilization could be separate and even in opposition. Culinary colonialism, a process of conquest and destruction of communities and their indigenous food systems, followed by forced western diet assimilation and, finally, a commercial revaluation/appropriation of what was left and survived:

> Culinary colonialism: a historical transit from destruction and denigration of ingredients and cuisines, to forced assimilation to a settler gastronomic norm, to cultural appropriation of indigenous food and dishes ... Indigenous food enters the mainstream as alienated commodities. (Grey & Newman, 2018: 726)

In this chapter, we will explore how the Braudelanian ideas and those of culinary colonialism operate in the case of maize, specifically in the study of the fate of this plant within the capitalist agri-food system. This case is particularly fascinating, not only because maize is a traditional indigenous plant of civilization, but it is also a plant that went through, what we identify as, the dialectics of colonial universalism like few others.[37] But our proposal is to understand this dialectic as composed not just by the domination/appropriation pair but also by the mestizaje/resistance one.

An inevitable reference in this task is the work of Arturo Warman, a Mexican anthropologist, who in 1988 published the results of a ten-year investigation: *Corn and Capitalism: How a Botanical Bastard Grew to Global Dominance*. In addition to the constant reference to his work, his explanation of why he chose the word "bastard" as the adjective for maize coincides with the spirit of this work:

> I also use *"bastard"* in the sense of a person who has moved outside his former social orbit, one who remains outside the system of accepted norms. Corn entered the

---

37   This plant is called both corn and maize. Here the term "maize" (Zea Mays) will be the only one to be used and "corn" will be applied only if it corresponds to the original text quotation.

world system exactly this way. Enlightened elites used corn in this sense: as a contemptible object, subject to discrimination. Corn carried the stigma of being alien, strange, and poor. The wealthy judged corn and declared it to be guilty. The poor, on the contrary, opened their doors to it, embraced it, and adopted it. (Warman, 1989, p. xiii)

1 Maize as a world commodity

At first glance, maize might seem like an "exceptionally successful" food plant. It survived the modern capitalist whirlwind, violently opened by the conquest of Maize's Civilizations, and acquired a universal appeal: "maize is known, renowned, and used all over the world" (Warman, 2003, p. 12). Authors had called it *King Corn* (Pollan, 2002), *America's most Quintessential Crop* (NCGA), and the *Bastard King* (Warman, 2003). Data are presented below to illustrate the worldwide rising trajectory of this plant.

In 2018, almost 200 million maize hectares were harvested worldwide, less than the area dedicated to wheat and surpassing rice from 2010 onwards (figure 1). For the first time, the acreage for maize cultivation in Asia equaled those in America, each one with 35% of the total world maize acreage (in the 1960s, it was 41% in America vs 26% in Asia). In terms of quantity produced, the three main types of cereal showed similar growth throughout the 20th century, but as we entered the 21st century, maize stood out and surpassed the amount of rice and wheat (figure 2). In terms of yield, all three major types of cereal have presented a growing trend since the 1960s but historically maize ranked first. Although 174 countries sow maize, its production is very concentrated. Only four countries, the USA, China, Brazil, and Argentina concentrate 67% of the total world production in 2018 (FAOSTAT).

Unlike other commodities, only a small part of maize production crosses national borders. In 2013, maize international trade accounted for around 13% of production (in the 1960s it was 10%), a smaller share when compared to wheat (26%), and soybean (35%) (FAOSTAT). However, this does not reduce its importance on international markets, being one of the most important traded commodities. Maize international trade is highly concentrated, within only four countries: the United States, Brazil, Argentina, and Ukraine (currently accounting for 88 percent of total maize exports). Also, 45% of maize imports come from only five countries: Mexico, Japan, Vietnam, South Korea, and Spain. Since the 1960s, the USA has been the maize export leader, with export participation higher than 70% between 1976 and 1994. As of 1994, this participation has been declining with the emergence of new exporters, such as Ukraine, Brazil, and Argentina. After three decades of relative stability in the maize world market, both value and quantity increased sharply from the first decade of the 21st century (Figures 3 and 4).

Maize is also central in the operations of the ABCD[38] world grain traders, companies that dominate around 70% of international trade and operate all along the agri-food supply chain (Murphy, Burch, & Clapp, 2012 p. 8). And is also crucial for a wave of contemporary agricultural development initiatives driven-by multinational agricultural seed/biotechnology companies, such as Monsanto-Bayer and DuPont Pioneer (Tenaillon & Charcosset, 2011; Eddens, 2017).

According to the FAO, direct maize consumption is present in 136 countries, but only in 17 the average caloric contribution (kcal/capita/day) is bigger than 25% (FAOSTAT)[39]. Also, only 14% of total maize produced around the world is used as direct food with a caloric contribution around 7% worldwide, which is inferior to those of wheat (20%), rice (11%), and even sugar (9%) (FAOSTAT). However, this depends mainly on the country, while in countries like the United States, only 10% of maize production is used directly for food purposes, in Sub-Saharan Africa, 80% of the maize produced is for human consumption (FAOSTAT). Currently, maize's main destination is animal feed, 60% of maize produced aims to supply cattle, pigs, poultry, and pet food industries (Figure 5).

---

38   ADM (USA), Bunge (USA), Cargill (USA), Louis Dreyfus (Netherlands) and recently Cofco main Chinese buyer of Brazilian soy and corn.

39   These countries are Lesotho, Zambia, Malawi, Zimbabwe, Mexico, Guatemala, Kenya, Honduras, Timor-Leste, South Africa, Republic of Moldova, El Salvador, Eswatini, Togo, Burkina Faso, Nicaragua, and the United Republic of Tanzania (FAOSTAT).

Also, this crop is being increasingly used as a starch, flour, oil, or fructose, on different food, and non-food industries. Maize is a common ingredient in processed foods, not as the main ingredient but as a kind of "hidden" input in salad dressing, prepared soups, meat extenders, desserts, candies, etc. As a starch, it is increasingly used in the beer industry and as a high fructose corn syrup in soft drinks production[40]. Besides, maize derived products are used to produce explosives, soaps, paper products, adhesives, drugs (aspirin and antibiotics), inks, fireworks, insecticides and disinfectants, and, perhaps the most important: ethanol fuel (figure 6). Its incorporation into non-food sectors, particularly, shows a significant growing trend, from 3% in 1960 to 20% in 2018.

Figure 1.

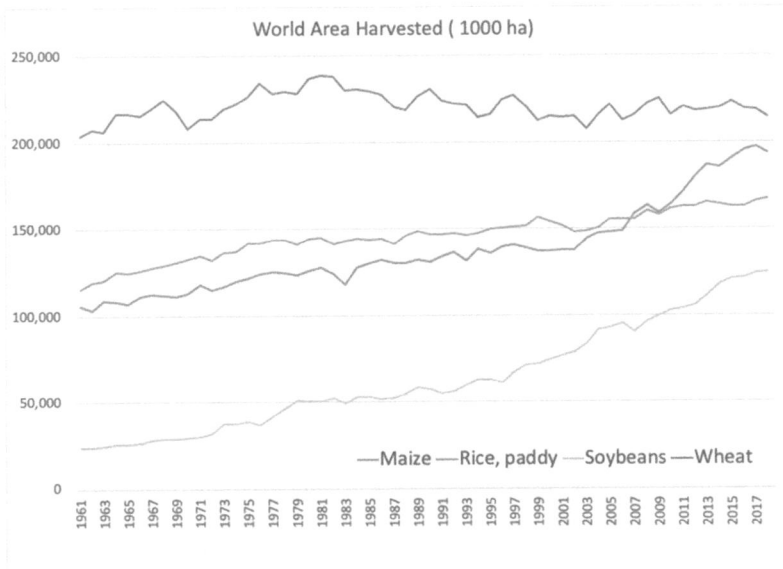

World Area Harvested (1000 ha)

—Maize —Rice, paddy —Soybeans —Wheat

Source: FAOSTAT—Crop.

---

40   Another important hidden ingredient is palm oil.

Figure 2.

Source: FAOSTAT—Crop.

Figure 3.

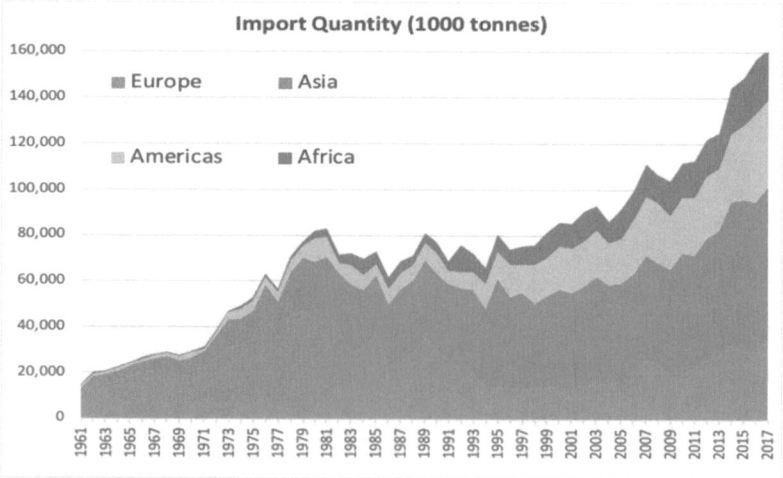

Source: FAOSTAT—Crop.

Figure 4.

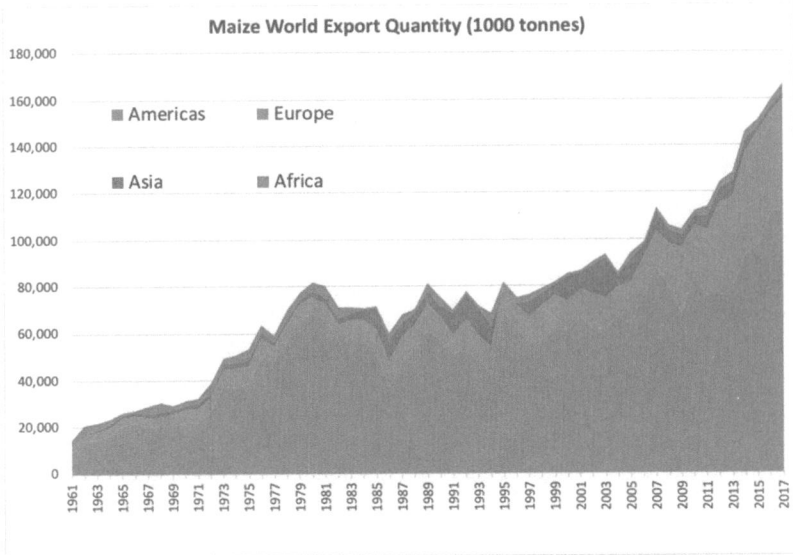

Maize World Export Quantity (1000 tonnes)

Source: FAOSTAT—Crop.

Figure 5.

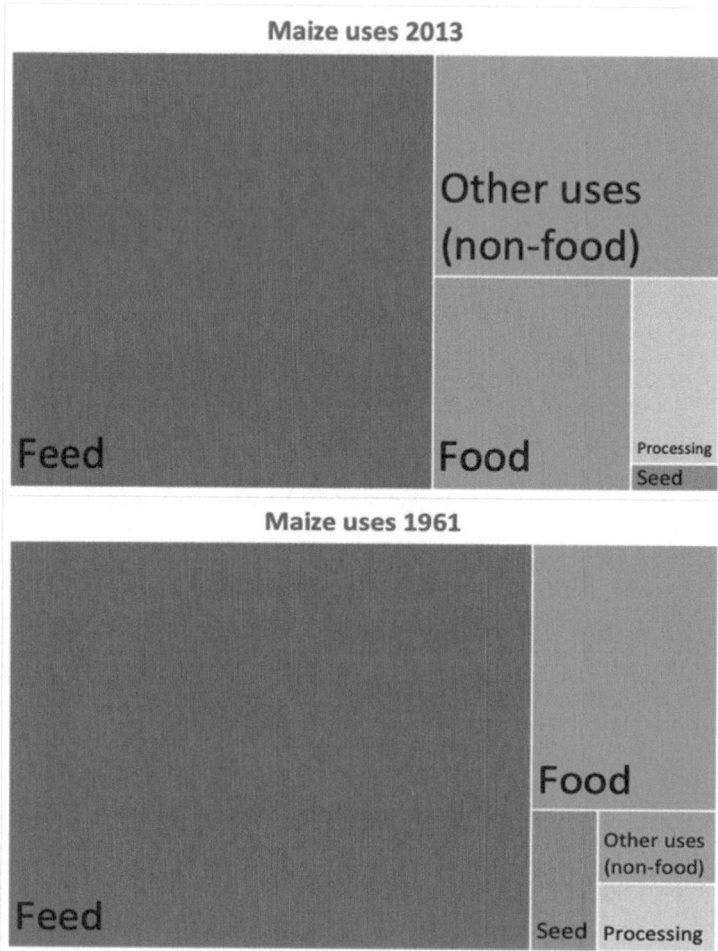

Source: FAOSTAT—Food Balances (old methodology and population).

Figure 6.

Maize

FOOD

Cob & Kernel: baby corn, pickled baby corn, boiled sweet corn, canned corn, frozen packaged. **Whole Kernel Products:** popcorn, soup mixes, canned hominy. **Alkali cooked:** tortilla, corn chips. **Dry Milled Corn:** breakfast cereals, fortified foods, snack foods, breads & bakery products, fermented beverage, unfermented beverage pet foods, baking. **Flour:** meat extenders, thickening agents, desserts, gravis & sauces, salad dressings; pie fillings. **Starch:** baking powder, brewed beverages, chewing gum, chocolate drinks, meat products, prepared condiments, precooked & frozen meals, prepared soups, powdered sugar, canned vegetables, candies, alcoholic beverage, acidulant, flavor enhancers, soft drinks. **Oil:** vitamin carriers, lecithin, cooking oil, margarine, mayonnaise, potato chips, salad dressing, sauces, shortenings, soups. **Sweeteners:** Fructose .

FEED

Whole Kernel Products:. Livestock feed.   **Dry Milled Corn:** livestock feed. **Wet-milled Corn:** cattle feed, poultry feed, zein production. **Starch:** amino acids.

INDUSTRIAL

Cob or Stover: polishing media, liquid spill recovery media, dust adsorbent, construction board, cosmetic powders. **Dry Grind Ethanol:** Distillers dried grains with soluble. **Dry-milled Corn:** wallpaper paste, floor wax, hand soap, dusting agents. **Flour:** Fermentation media explosives, gypsum wallboard, paper products, briquettes, label adhesives, edge paste, pharmaceuticals. **Oil:** lecithin, soluble oils, insecticides, linoleum, printing inks, rubber substitutes, textiles. **Wet-milled corn:** antibiotics, chemicals pharmaceuticals. **Starch:** adhesives, candles, ceramics, labels, insecticides, printing inks, fire works, textiles, wallpaper, aspirin, disinfectants. **Glucose:** medicinal syrups, explosives, tobacco products

FUEL

Dry Grind ethanol: fuel ethanol. **Fermentation:** engine fuel, fuel octane enhancers, oxygenate in engine fuels.

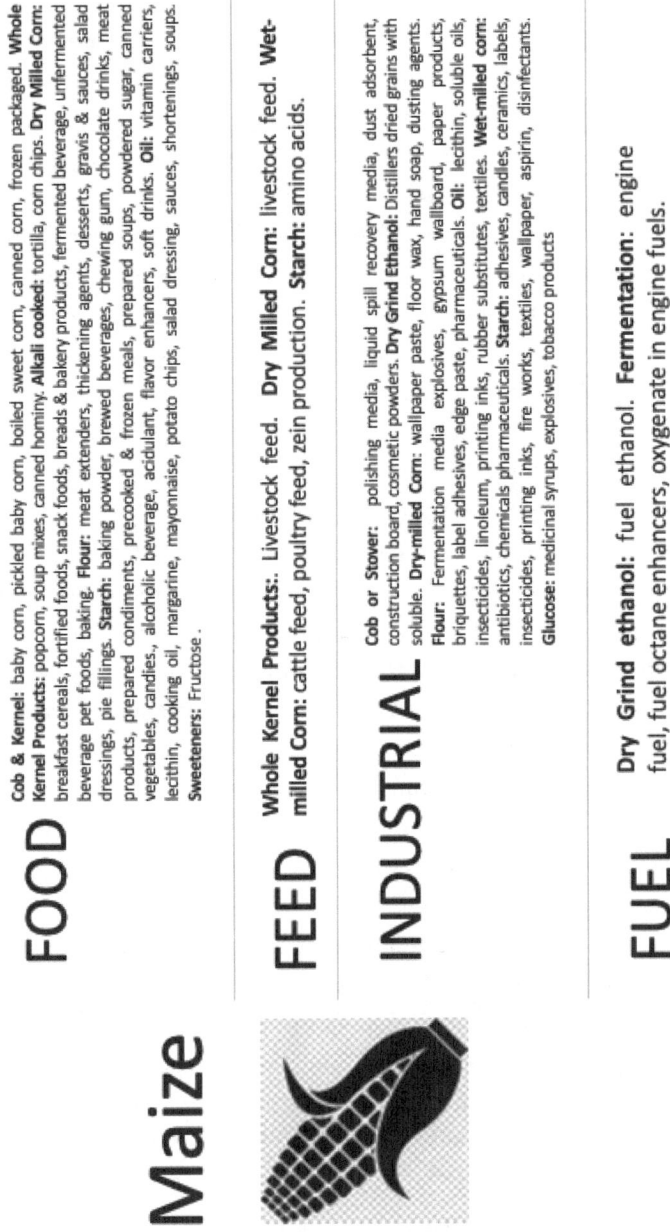

Source: adapted from Center of crop utilization research—Iowa State university

2 The Maize Colonization: from racism to flex crop

Maize is maybe one of the most interesting examples of plant domestication. First, maize does not exist in a wild state, "without human labor to separate and disperse seed, corn would disappear in only a short amount of time" (Warman, 2003, p. 27). Second, it is a plant with a great capacity to adapt to diverse ecological conditions: "it has the broadest cultivated range of all crops, from the south of Chile 408S to Canada 508N, from the Andes, where it can grow at altitudes of 3400 m above the sea level, to Caribbean islands" (Tenaillon & Charcosset, 2011, p. 222). Third, it is extremely diverse: "Hence, two maize inbred lines have on average greater divergence than two hominids separated by 3.5 million years" (Tenaillon & Charcosset, 2011, p. 222). And fourth, maize's high productivity derived from its high photosynthetic efficiency, that is, its great capacity to transform solar energy into living matter (Warman, 2003, p. 16).

These great qualities contained in maize are related to the complex process of adaptation that the plant has undergone over the centuries: "It was a prolonged effort that required the interest and the passion of thousands of anonymous agricultural experimenters over dozens of generations" (Warman, 2003:33). The process of domestication would have occurred around 9000 years ago, starting in the area of Central Valley in Mexico to then go through four routes of continuous adaptation and diversification: 1) a south highland route reaching the Andes; 2) a south lowland route toward the East coast of South America; 3) a northward expansion to southwest USA and northern Canada; 4) and most recently discovered, the Amazon route (Tenaillon & Charcosset, 2011; Kistler et al.,2018).

Its unique botanical characteristics are relevant but not enough to determine and understand the fate of this plant in the world market history. It is possible to identify two dominant and successive trends. First, the modern food revolution that will change how millions of people eat but that also will create food hierarchies and culinary colonialism (Pilcher, 2001; Warman, 2003; Grey and Newman, 2018). And second, the commodification and industrialization of agricultural production, which will have multiple impacts on society and the environment, such as the imposition of new global food consumption and production patterns and the transformations in agrarian relations.

2.1   Conquest, racism, and silent expansion

The universal history of maize begins with the conquest and defeat of Maize's Civilizations. On August 13th, 1521, the great Mexica Empire was defeated by the European conquerors and their indigenous allies. In the following eight decades, it is estimated that nine-tenths of the indigenous population succumbed to war, enslavement, and new diseases: "above the ancient pyramids, Christian cathedrals rose and Old-World crops sprouted in fields where maize once flourished" (Pilcher, 2001, p. 48).

The Maize Civilizations were defeated, mortally wounded, but not wiped out. A process of *food mestizaje* took place, sometimes intentionally but often behind people's backs. However, this just happened in the margins of the "main" food culture. While it was possible and desired to incorporate flavors, colors, and supplements to the staple foods, it was unthinkable to substitute maize for wheat, and vice versa, for its deep civilization meaning (Pilcher, 2001; Pérez, 2014).

Colonizers and colonized considered their civilization plant as superior. The indigenous people rejected wheat, which they identified as "famine food, as dried corn stalks", growing maize again, whenever it was possible, in the areas where the wheat was forcibly introduced (Pilcher, 2001, p. 66). The conquerors rejected maize, which they were forced to consume, due to lack of European supplies. The reasons for this stubborn preference around wheat or maize outweighs the reasons for taste or culinary tradition, including religious and deep identity reasons (wheat for Christianity and maize for Toltecayotl in Mesoamerica) (Pilcher, 2001: 56).

As a result, the triumphant conquerors needed to bring the Old World foodstuff to the conquered lands to continue with their diet (Pérez, 2014, p. 19). This opened the transformation of the American landscape with the successful expansion of wheat and livestock. The success of Europeans on this task was considered as a sign of divine favor (Earle, 2014, p.142). The introduction of cattle and wheat was also an effective way for the colonization process. From the plains of the United States to the incursions of the *Bandeirantes* in Brazil and Paraguay, the advance of cattle was a mechanism for the expropriation of the communitarian indigenous lands (Pilcher, 2001, p. 67). Also, forced work schemes were established for the production of wheat. As argued by Braudel, the success of a plant may also be the success of a culture.

The diffusion of maize in the so-called Old World has had a slow and difficult history of acceptance. Around 1493, maize left the American continent and began a continuous and uninterrupted diffusion in all directions (Warman, 2003, p.37). Spain was the gateway and maize followed a route eastward, with evidence of its arrival in France, Italy, and the Balkans around 1530. The crop arrived in China around 1560 by two possible routes, one maritime carried by the Portuguese merchants, and by land, through the paths of spices and silk controlled by the Ottoman Empire (Warman, 2003, p.42). Around 1540, maize arrived in West Africa, carried also by Portuguese merchants.

In Europe, from the 15th to the 17th century, was the silent diffusion of maize. This plant was first introduced as a garden plant, a botanical curiosity (Warman, 2003, p.101); and later as an agricultural crop in marginal lands, those not suitable to grow wheat or dedicated to other summer crops (Flandrin, 2018a: 539). Its productivity and great ability to adapt favored its cultivation as a reserve grain, displacing other coarse grains, such as sorghum or millet, but never intending to replace wheat. There was some cultural resistance to maize since it was associated with *inferior humans or animals*. As a 16th-century naturalist stated, maize was: "a more convenient food for swine than for men" (Warman, 2003, p. 101).

Carried out by Europeans, maize arrived in West Africa alongside the traffic of enslaved African people: "corn was the principal staple food, the dietary mainstay, for the vast human mobilization brought about by the slave trade" (Warman, 2003, p.60). It remains unclear why the Portuguese chose maize as the common staple food for enslaved people's traffic especially at the expense of local cereals, such as sorghum. In any case, during the 17th-century, maize was widely considered *as the food of enslaved people.*

From the 18th to the first half of the 19th century, maize was promoted as a cheap food between the impoverished peasantry (Levi, 2014, p.112). As related by Levi in northern Italy, a far-reaching alteration in the agrarian contracts and the structure of land ownership lead to a deterioration of living conditions which will finally break maize marginal position to be incorporated as a staple food in peasants' diets (Levi, 2014). The bias against Maize was already entrenched: "(maize and potatoes) these foods would not easily lose their image of *food for the poor*, their absence in celebration menus confirms this status" (Flandrin, 2018b: 712).

Finally, it is interesting to one more episode of maize misfortune in the world's history, and which, possibly, represents the apex of racist stigma against it. The protagonists are not the European conquerors/slavers but the mestizo elite of independent Mexico. By the end of the 19th century, Mexican elite "which at one time set aside maize as simple Indians' fodder, began to attribute a new and sinister meaning to native cereal, considering it as one of the main impediments to national development" (Pilcher, 2001: 118). In 1899, one of the scientists connected to the Mexican dictator Porfirio Diaz, Francisco Bulnes, published an influential book, in which presents the idea that humanity could be divided into three different races: "the wheat race, the maize race, and the rice race" (Bulnes, 1899, p. 5). A prior formulation of Braudel classification.[41] Bulnes' main message was that the wheat race was superior to the rice and maize races due to an alleged nutritional superiority of wheat:

> The peoples that eat wheat as their main or exclusively foodstuff must achieve the highest degree of physical and mental development since they are nourished with its technical element ... These (maize and rice) races were devastated by the lack of food that they civilized, they are not guilty of their inextinguishable barbarism or their natural decline (Bulnes, 1899, p. 11, 13, 17).

For independent Mexico to overcome backwardness, it would be necessary to do what 300 years of colonization had not been able to do or had not

---

41   Braudel refers to a 1943 book from the French geographer Maximilien Sorre as the source of his classification. However, the origin of this classification actually refers to the research carried out by Justus von Liebig in 1845, a pioneer in the chemical analysis of food but with tendencies towards naturalistic sociology.

even dared to do: eradicate maize consumption and substitute it with wheat (Pilcher, 2001, p. 80). Because the Mexican Elite was mestizo, it was not possible to simply reproduce the deterministic race hierarchies of social Darwinism, what was done was the adoption of the idea that civilization, the superior race, could be achieved through the change of daily habits: "It was not necessary to be a European by birth, it was enough to act like a European, dress like a European, eat like a European" (Pilcher, 2001: 130).

Maize acquired a new stigma: *a backward food*. This was a powerful idea that came to influence Mexican public opinion until the first years of the 20th century. Fortunately, this project was interrupted by the Mexican Revolution. Only in 1940 scientific research would show that in nutritional terms there is no substantial difference between maize and wheat. However, this did not mean the end of maize misfortune, as it will be explained in the next section. In the mid-20th century, the Green Revolution science appropriated maize through a racial logic rooted in whiteness (Eddens, 2017).

2.2   Commodification and re-functionalization

In the 20th century, maize was one of the protagonists of the great transformation in agriculture that culminated in the commodification and industrialization of agricultural production on a global scale (Pruitt, 2016; Trometter, 2012; Kloppenburg, 2004). Maize was one of the first seeds to go through the process of hybridization in the first decade of the twentieth century. Also, it was one of the key crops for the Green Revolution in 1950, and finally, one of the first seeds to go through genetic changes with the advent of biotechnology.

Until the 20th century, agriculture around the world was mainly done by using saved seeds, then for the first time, the breeding activity left the hands of farmers to become a commercial activity (Pruitt, 2016; Kloppenburg, 2004). During the second half of the 19th century, the activity of seed commercialization developed more strongly in some parts of the world, especially in the USA and France.

The first attempt of seed hybridization was carried out at Michigan State College in 1875 and it was with maize seeds. The milestone that opened the door to hybridization came with the publication, in 1908 and

1909 respectively, of two articles by George Shull, a geneticist working at Cold Spring Harbor Laboratory. Observing maize fields he noticed and described the heterosis phenomenon (hybrid organisms tend to have increased size and vigor). Although this was already known for centuries, Shull's great innovation at the time was the precise description of procedures for obtaining hybrid maize. Shull's idea to cross inbred lines was implemented over the following decades in several research centers and laboratories in the USA (Crow, 1998). The first commercial sale of this variety took place in 1924. From that time on, maize hybridization gained strength, the areas cultivated with hybrid maize in the US rose rapidly and by 1950, 90 % of maize cultivated in the USA was hybrid (Pruitt, 2016; Kloppenburg, 2004; Crow, 1998).

The advent of hybrid seeds changed the relationships established between the producers and the seeds. Despite these seeds proved to be more productive, they tended to lose vigor after the first generation, so producers became dependent on the market for the next harvest: a market that did not exist before. Thus, the creation of hybrid maize resulted in a reduction in seed storage activity, a common practice for agricultural producers (Kloppenburg, 2004); and it also paved the way to establish the first intellectual property legislation in the area of plants. Companies working with plant breeding and seed production played a central role in creating and expanding intellectual property rights for cultivars (Kloppenburg, 2004). The decade of the 1930s in the United States showed signals of the high profitability of the sector, such as the creation of the US Plant Act and the repeal of seed distribution (Kloppenburg, 2004).

Among all the research carried out in this context, the one conducted by the Rockefeller group was fundamental for the hybrid research and its geographical expansion. In 1943 the Rockefeller Foundation in partnership with the Mexican government started a program to solve an alleged food deficit in Mexico. The idea was to train agricultural researchers to increase the productivity of crops, starting with wheat, and then expanding it to maize (Patel, 2013; Stapleton, 1999, Fitzgerald, 1986). For this purpose, the International Center for the Improvement of Maize and Wheat (CIMMYT for its acronym in Spanish) was created with the support of what is now one of the largest seed companies: Pioneer Hi-Bred Seed. Approximately 850 maize varieties and hybrids were released in developing countries between 1966 and 1990 (Morris & López-Pereira, 1999, p.12). Along with the seeds there was also the so-called Green Revolution technological package, a set of agricultural inputs such as fertilizers, herbicides, insecticides, specific machinery and irrigation techniques that had to be combined with hybrid seeds to ensure effectiveness and the promised results in agricultural production (Howard, 2015;2009; Patel, 2013; Fitzgerald, 1986). As a result, world agricultural production soared.

Along with all its great promises, the Green Revolution imposed a new reality on agricultural production. Eddens (2017) points out that a white-race logic was embedded in the seeds of the Green Revolution. Mexican maize was considered as a repository of "undiscovered" wealth that could be useful for commercial breeding. Then, through the ability to scientifically control nature, in association with modern white civilization, the massive private appropriation of indigenous maize by companies was justified. As Eddens concludes: "It is only when it is possessed by the modern scientist (figured as white, male and American) that maize becomes a modern object" (Eddens, 2017, p. 14). The implications for the rural producer, especially the smaller ones in developing countries, were several, the most important one being that from that moment onwards they became dependent on the purchase of the seeds and agricultural inputs (Patel, 2013).

As these hybrid seeds advanced through the territories and as the seed storage activity lost strength, the market was consolidated and expanded to new cultivars. The 1970s was a major turning point for the seed industry. Due to several process of acquisitions and mergers of companies, plus the entry in the market of bigger companies already consolidated in other sectors such as petrochemical and pharmaceutical, family-owned companies started to close, and the market became more concentrated. Therefore, as Howard (2015) argues, not only did they gain market shares, but these companies also acquired laboratories, trained employees, and gained access to their research bank and germplasm. Just as it happened with the germplasm accumulated and modified by the CIMMYT in Mexico, sponsored by public initiatives but who lost control over the use and destination of the genetic material donated by it to private companies: "CIMMYT materials have been used extensively by private-sector breeders. Although detailed information about the genetic background of proprietary hybrids is not always available we estimate that 75% of all seed sold by private companies in Latin America in 1996 contained CIMMYT-derived germplasm" (Morris & López-Pereira, 1999, p.25)[42]. Maize germplasm material went from community storage and exchange practices, to be the domain of national public scientific research centers, then to be controlled by private and foreign companies.

Another fundamental fact for the consolidation of the seed market and its subsequent concentration was the so-called Biotechnology Revolution. The cornerstone of this revolution was the development of techniques for genetic manipulation after the recombinant DNA technology developed by Boyer and Cohen (Raustiala & Victor, 2004). In the case of plants, this technology allowed gene transfer between living organisms, including those coming from different kingdoms, for example, the introduction of genes from bacteria into plants. The technique took a step beyond that of hybridization already used by the sector: if in the past the transmission of the characteristics depended, essentially, on the reproductive organs of the plant itself, now the process was done from the isolation and transference of genetic information. This was expected to reduce, in general, the timeframe of production and would guarantee a higher control over the results (Sell, 2006).

In 1996, Bt Maize, a GM variety of maize that was genetically modified with the introduction of the bacteria *Bacillus thuringiensis* to increase the resistance against pests, was cultivated in the USA. In the following years, countries such as Canada, Argentina, South Africa, and Spain

---

42   "The primary germplasm distribution channel is the system of international trials, which consists of sets of materials sent to local cooperators for evaluation under controlled levels of management; in return for reporting performance data back to CIMMYT, the cooperators are free to incorporate any material selected out of the trials into their breeding programs. A second germplasm distribution channel consists of seed shipments sent from the Wellhausen-Anderson Plant Genetic Resources Center, a state-of-the-art storage facility in which more than 10,000 maize accessions are permanently maintained" (Morris & López-Pereira, 1999, p. 7).

started to cultivate this variety (James, 2003). In 1998, the United States approved the Roundup Ready™ Maize, a maize genetically modified variety for increased resistance to glyphosate created by Monsanto. Nowadays, in this country, 85% of GM maize patents are owned by the three largest firms in the industry: Syngenta, Monsanto-Bayer, and Dupont (Howard, 2009; Baker, Jayedev & Stiglitz, 2017).

According to ISAAA (International Service for the Acquisition of Agri-biotech Applications), maize is the second-largest genetically modified (GM) crop commercialized globally, preceded only by soybeans. Also, it is the plant with the biggest number of researches conducted to produce genetic variations (Rostoks et al. 2019). Among the GM crops, maize has the highest number of approved events (genetically engineered crop varieties), until the year 2019 it counted 146. This put a clear contrast to wheat, with just one variety, and rice with seven. Wheat has even been called as an orphan, among genetically modified crops, understood as the cereal abandoned by GM (Wulff & Dhugga, 2018).[43]

The vast majority of these GM seeds were developed by just four companies: Monsanto (now Bayer AG), Syngenta (now ChemChina), Dow Agroscience (now Dupont), and Dupont Pioneer Hi-Breed (now Dupont). Most of the modifications are related to herbicide tolerance and insect resistance. Less than 5% of the modifications are related to what they call *modified product quality*: the introduction of genes that enhance bio-ethanol production or introduce minerals/nutrients for animal feed varieties (ISAAA, 2020).

Throughout the 20th century, maize has been the object of countless transformations. It was not only commodified but its characteristics were industrially altered to produce a homogeneous variety, a more stable and productive one, to meet the interests of the capital food system. All these transformations are the counterpart to the wide uses of this plant: maize is a flex-crop, a social-biological product of last century capitalism (Borras et

---

43   In October 2020, Argentina became the first country to approve the commercial grown of GM wheat. And in 2018 in Canada, GM wheat were identified in Alberta, despite the fact that it is not allowed in that country.

al. 2016). Flex-crops have two determining attributes, the multiple-ness and the flexible-ness: those crops that have at least two different uses, namely food, feed, fuel among other uses, and that this destination can be interchanged by another flex crop if necessary. Maize is considered one of the most established flex-crops together with soy, sugarcane, and palm oil. For the market, these crops promote, or increase, some stability in the revenue of those who cultivate them directly and for those who produce intermediate or final goods using them. Sales can be allocated to where it has the highest market value at the time or the lowest production cost. For example, in the event of an increase in demand for animal feed, maize production will be directed to supply this market but nothing ties it to this final market, in the face of a change in prices, demand, etc., it can move towards the best option. The possibility of diversification of investment in a crop makes it more attractive.

However, Borras et al. (2016), warned of a potential reverse trend in the case of maize multiple-ness attribute. When we look at the modifications carried out on maize, which are available in the ISAAA platform, it is possible to observe that most changes regarding modified product quality are either creating a variety that is intended for the production either biofuels or feed, in both cases not suitable for human consumption. An example of this variety exists within the trade name Enogen™, created by the company Syngenta, whose commercial trait is enhancing bioethanol production, or the variety BVLA430101 developed to be used only as animal feed by the Chinese company Origin Agritech.

The two historical stages presented in this section, food racism, and capitalist functional incorporation, are intricately linked. The maize misfortune in early modern times can be considered as the necessary condition to its later full incorporation as a key crop into capitalist agriculture. Successively associated with defeated indigenous civilizations, identified as adequate only to feed animals, regarded as the food of enslaved people, as the food for the poor peasantry and the food for times of hardship or backwardness, was the way maize was prepared to be subsumed under capitalist logic. Only through the disassociation from its civilizing matrix, its food, cultural, religious, and community relevancy, maize became a success in meeting the demands of the capitalist food system not as a plant of civilization but as a cheap and agri-industrial input. From this perspective, the world history of maize is far from confirming the Braudelian thesis. It would be better considered as culinary colonialism. However, it is still necessary to explore other side of maize history.

3   Resistance: the obstinacy of a plant of civilization

As mentioned above, the transformations undergone by maize, from hybridization to transgenics, resulted in a more stable, productive and homogeneous variety with a greater capacity of multiple-ness. However, this versatility seems to be biased. There is a contradictory trend to specialize this plant as a universal input at the expense of its civilizing matrix. It is possible to understand it as the production of a very specific versatility, suitable to the logic of capital and its profit imperatives. Thus, within the great and diverse qualities contained in maize, some have been enhanced and others suppressed. As pointed out, there seems to be a tendency to suppress the qualities of this plant as direct human food. In fact, within the wide variety of maize, yellow maize is the favorite one for feed and starch industries, and therefore hybrid or transgenic seeds are almost exclusive from this type (Morris & López-Pereira, 1999, p.19).

In a very similar sense to that of Braudel, Mexican biologist Victor Toledo proposes the concept of biocultural memory to express the close relationship between biological, genetic, cultural, linguistic, agricultural, and landscape diversity (Toledo & Barrera-Bassols, 2008). For Toledo, this biocultural memory is preserved, not in large laboratories, warehouses, or modern private seed banks, but as a historical community consciousness of traditional rural societies, both indigenous and peasant (Toledo & Barrera-Bassols, 2008, p. 29). Together with the erosion of phylogenetic diversity generated by capitalist agriculture, it is possible to find a communitarian logic of conservation and diversification that persists not because these communities are isolated, untouched by modern capitalism, but as a *mestizaje*/resistance response to it. Two active levels can be identified at which the maize biocultural memory is conserved, reproduced, and reinvented: daily resistance, through the production and consumption of maize great diversity, and the organized resistance against transgenic maize over the last three decades. These experiences, in which maize seems to preserve its civilizing force, are briefly presented below.

3.1   Windows of resistance in Latin America.

"America, from a grain of maize you rose ..." this is how the *Oda al maíz*, written by the Chilean poet Pablo Neruda begins. "Pour out your light, your flour, your hope, the loneliness of America, to hunger your spears are enemy legions" (Neruda, 1957).

Maize: *centli* (Nahuatl), *xiim* (Mayan), *sara* (Kichua), *jank'a* (Aymara), or *avati* (Guarani) (Bravo, Martín, & Rojeab, 2011, p. 10). From the Navajo people in the USA to the Mapuches lands down south, maize grows as a civilization plant in *milpas*, terraces, or even on steep hillsides and slopes far from the large commercial and yellow monocultures: "sowing life, giving birth to communities" (Bravo, Martín, & Rojeab, 2011). In religious ceremonies or everyday food, maize is drunk as a fermented alcoholic beverage; eaten as polenta in South America: the way maize returned from Italy. Maize; present in all meals as *tortillas* (México and Central America) and as *arepas* (Colombia and Andean countries); it is consumed as sweet or salty *tamales*, *hallacas*, or *pamonha* from Mexico to Brazil. As a dessert, in the form of *majarete* (Cuba), *choclo* cake (Chile), or *mazamorra* (Argentina). And even as an important *axe food*, the food offered to the Orixas in the Afro-Brazilian religions. Maize continues to feed stomachs, minds, and spirits across the continent: "the multiple forms, colors, flavors, uses, and cultural expressions that maize presents in Latin America show the strength and power that people and communities have" (Cárcamo et al., 2011).

However, the everyday life of people of maize has not remained unscathed. The maize from capitalism, the transgenic-universal input, yellow maize, is advancing throughout the continent. In 1999 The Network for a Transgenic-free Latin America was born denouncing that the sacred food was being transformed into a business of hunger (Acción Ecologica, 2004). From Mexico to Uruguay, social, peasant, and indigenous organizations have risen up against transgenic maize and the corporations that promote it, sometimes with success and sometimes not. They have asked for legal protection or even destroyed experimental fields. The transgenic maize is not only expanding through its legal promotion, like in Argentina since 1999, but it is also expanding as a silent, invisible, and illegal transgenic pollution, as in Mexico, where the cultivation of transgenic maize is forbidden until today, or Brasil, before it was legalized (Villa et al., 2012; GRAIN, 2014; Aranda, 2020).

We will close this section with the experience of the Zapatista communities and their struggle against transgenic maize, taken from Brandt (2014). When news of the genetic contamination reached the autonomous Zapatista territories in 2001 panic set in. An organization from the USA financed the project Mother Seeds, donating pollution detection kits and seed bank equipment (schoolsforchiapas.org). The tests reassured the communities but the seed bank was not so well received. For the rebellious Mayan Indigenous people, looking to freezer-based 'sleeping' seed bank had no sense: living maize seed (its cultivation, collection, and consumption) is at the heart of community life (Brandt, 2014, p.881). Zapatistas soon left the seed bank and decided instead to create the Zapatista Maize: seeds free of GMOs, produced, cared for, exchanged, planted, and consumed by the autonomous communities. In addition, a "living seed bank" was created. Zapatista Maize seeds, seeds of resistance, travel through their international solidarity networks: "Through its travels, Zapatista corn enacts the biocultural metonymy between the people and their corn, allowing recipients 'to know the Zapatistas' and participate in their resistance" (Brandt, 2014, p.892). The two levels of resistance are finally the same considering the biocultural memory or the plants as plants of civilization.

3.2   Windows of resistance in Africa

A different and more complex experience of resistance is the maize route in Africa. As previously discussed, in the 16th century maize was introduced in Africa. Since then it has been grown under a wide range of ecological and socioeconomic conditions and adopted into diets: "An immigrant crop, maize is today the most widely-grown staple food of Sub-Saharan Africa" (Smale, Byerlee & Jayne, 2011, p.2). In Yoruba culture (West Africa) there are folk tales addressing maize and its reproductive capacity: "All alone, Maize went to the farm, and she came back with two hundred children" (McCann, 2005, p. 32).

Maize-meal receives different names in the continent, Sadza (Zimbabwe), Banku or Kenkey (Ganha), nshima in Zambia, nsima in Malawi, Phutu pap in South Africa and Lesotho, ugali in Kenya. It is also consumed fermented, as Ogi/akamu (Nigeria), Mutwiwa pap (Zimbabwe) or uji, ikii (Kenya). Or even drunk in alcoholic or non-alcoholic beverages as Obiolo (Nigeria), busaa, chang'aa (Kenya), mahewu (South Africa), munkoyo (Zambia, Zaire), among many other dishes (Ekpa et al., 2018). In contrast to the dominant trend in the world, white maize prevails in African. The British Empire promoted this specific variety of maize in its colonies (McCann, 2005). Later, during the liberation struggles in the mid-20th century, white maize was embraced as a staple food. Thus, the plant not only became interesting for external interests but also for the revolutionary nationalist governments (Mccann, 2005).

In Sub-Saharan Africa, the firsts hybrid maize developments started on the eve of independence in Zimbabwe (1960), Kenia (1963), Zambia (1964) and Malawi (1964) (Smale, Byerlee & Jayne, 2011). In the post-independence period, many governments continued with these projects and actively promote the new maize hybrids, in what authors called the African maize revolution (Smale, Byerlee & Jayne, 2011). The breeding programs were based in a mix of local white varieties with landraces from America and were supported by CIMMYT and of International Institute of Tropical Agriculture (IITA-USAID) (Smale, Byerlee & Jayne, 2011).

There is strong international pressure to modernize African agriculture to face problems such as hunger and poverty. In this scenario hybrid and genetically modified seeds are often presented as solutions to many social issues and for local development (Mccann, 2005). In 2006, the Bill and Melinda Gates Foundation and the Rockefeller Foundation launched the Alliance for Green Revolution in Africa (AGRA). A recent balance of the program found little evidence of significant increases in productivity, income, or food security for people. However, this program promotes the removal of national barriers, which allows the introduction of private seeds and makes local producers strongly tied to the interests of agrobusiness firms (Bayer-Monsanto, BASF, Cargill) and monoculture farms. (Mkindi et al., 2020). And even though most of the maize was cultivated by small-holder farmers, there is a growing trend of acquisition of enormous areas of land for the cultivation of yellow maize, phenomenon also known as land grab.

Many farmers resist the introduction of modified maize in several countries on the African continent (GRAIN, 2019; Aheto et al. 2013: Davison, 1993). Although there is, among African populations, a preference for white maize, some projects and studies suggest the adoption of the cultivation of the yellow, most common, cheap and transgenic maize (Ekpa et al., 2018, p.49; Tschirley & Santos, 1995). Behind this rests the idea that a society with hunger and poverty should change its local preferences in direction to cheapest foods. This is yet another case, among so many others, of food racism and of the imposition of external interests on local populations. Despite these efforts, communities in Africa seem to resist, and keep the production of white maize, usually produced with hybrid, open-pollinated or local seeds.

Another example of the clash between different interests is the case of a community in the Yala region in Kenya. There are currently two types of maize production in this region: the use of Nyaluo maize (a local variety) and another that combines this local variety with hybrid maize. As treated by Kimanthi (2019), several reasons make the population resist the cultivation of genetically modified varieties and to continue cultivating and protecting the local variety. The population claims that the local variety is much tastier and suitable for the preparation of dishes that are the basis of the local diet. Moreover, the foods prepared with it would keep the population satiated for longer. Also, regarding the costs and returns on investments, the local population claims to have become dependent on the purchase of inputs to maintain the productivity level. Finally, unlike the modified variety, the local one is adapted to the ecological conditions of the area and the local pests. About this many growers have reported the loss of the crop because the GM variety is not resistant to changes in climate: "Nyaluo maize adapted to the local ecology, became part of the culture of the Luo people and became stable and sustainable" (Kimanthi, 2019, p. 89).

Final considerations

The study of the fate of maize within the capitalist agri-food system was presented, not by chance, through different narratives. In the first part, the optimistic economic view is presented, and the exceptional success of maize in the world market is shown. In the second, the narrative enters the depths of the complex history of food hierarchies established within the project of the universal capitalist diet. Showing the culinary colonialist conditions under which maize is disseminated, the success image is transformed into a history of dominance/appropriation: the misfortune of maize. To continue with the capitalist subsumption of the plant in the 20th century. While wheat maintains its status as the human food par excellence (Fiat Panis, let there be bread, is the FAO motto) and then orphan of transgenic modifications. Maize was transformed into a universal transgenic input, not as a sign of its success but as the crowning achievement of its misfortune. Finally, our narrative seeks in everyday life evidence of maize resistance.

This transit between different ways to approach to maize history seemed to us adequate to present the dialectics of colonial universalism. The success, the domination/appropriation, and the mestizaje/resistance coexist, each re-signifying the other. The view on just one would result in a limited, insufficient, and to some extent, false understanding. As sometimes happens with the denunciation of culinary colonialism, or any other colonialism, that erases the positive germ contained in the universalization of human wealth, as the potential human and even anti-capitalist use of maize along with different societies, in Africa or the living bank seed of the Zapatistas communities. Braudel was right, the plants of civilization are very long-lasting structures that, despite the attacks of capital, survive and conserve the biocultural memory that will help us to build a better humanity.

References

Acción Ecológica, (2004). *Maíz de alimento sagrado a negocio del hambre.* Red por una América Latina libre de Transgénicos. Quito, Ecuador.

Aheto, D. W., Bøhn, T., Breckling, B., van den Berg, J., Ching, L. L., & Wikmark, O. (2013). Implications of GM crops in subsistence-based agricultural systems in Africa. In Breckling B, Verhoeven Reditors. *GM-Crop Cultivation-Ecological Effects on a Landscape Scale.* Frankfurt: Peter Lang, 93–103.

Aranda Dario (comp) Atlas del agronegocio transgénico en el Cono Sur: monocultivos, resistencias y propuestas de los pueblos. 1a ed ilustrada.—Marcos Paz: Acción por la Biodiversidad, 2020.

Baker, Dean; Jayedev, Arjun; Stiglitz, Joseph (2017). *Innovation, Intellectual Property and Development: a better set of approaches for the 21st century.* Durbanville: AccessIBSA.

Borras, S., J. Franco, et al (2016). The rise of flex crops and commodities: implications for research. *Journal of Peasant Studies* 43, no. 1: 9–115.

Brandt, M. (2014). Zapatista corn: A case study in biocultural innovation. *Social Studies of Science,* 44(6), 874–900.

Braudel, F. (1982*). The Structures of Everyday Life: Civilization & Capitalism, 15th-18th Century.* Harper & Row.

Bravo, E., Martín, M. M., & Rojeab, V. (2011). *Hijos del maíz. Maíz patrimonio de la humanidad.* Red por una América Latina Libre de Transgénicos (RALLT) con apoyo de Global Green Fund Miserrior. Manthra Editores.

Bulnes (1899) *El porvenir de las naciones hispanoamericanas ante las conquistas recientes de Europa y los Estados Unidos.* México: imprenta de Mariano Nava.

Cárcamo, M. I., García, M. M. M. I., Manzur, M. I., Montoro, Y., Pengue, W., Salgado, A., & Vélez, G. (2011*). Biodiversidad, erosión y contaminación genética del maíz nativo en América Latina.* Red por una América Latina Libre de Transgénicos. Mas Grafica, Santiago.

Crow, James F (1998). 90 Years Ago: The Beginning of Hybrid Maize. *Genetics,* Rockville, v. 148, n. 3, 923–928, mar.

Earle Rebeca (2014) Diet, Travel, and Colonialism in the Early Modern World IN Aram, B., & Yun-Casalilla, B. (Eds.). (2014). *Global goods and the Spanish Empire, 1492–1824: circulation, resistance and diversity.* Springer.

Eddens Aaron (2017): White science and indigenous maize: the racial logics of the Green Revolution, *The Journal of Peasant Studies,* DOI: 10.1080/03066150. 2017.1395857

Ekpa, O., Palacios-Rojas, N., Kruseman, G., Fogliano, V., & Linnemann, A. R. (2018). Sub-Saharan African maize-based foods: Technological perspectives to increase the food and nutrition security impacts of maize breeding programmes. *Global food security*, 17, 48–56.

Fitzgerald, Deborah (1986). Exporting American Agriculture: The Rockefeller Foundation in Mexico, 1943–53. *Social Studies of Science*, Newbury Park, v. 16, n. 3 p. 457–483, ago.

Flandrin (2018a) Os tempos modernos IN Flandrin Jean-Louis & Montanari Massimo (edit*). História da alimentação*. 9a edição. Rio de Janeiro: Estação liberdade. 2018.

Flandrin (2018b). Os séculos XIX e XX IN Flandrin Jean-Louis & Montanari Massimo (edit). *História da alimentação*. 9a edição. Rio de Janeiro: Estação liberdade. 2018

GRAIN (2019). The real seeds producers: Small-scale farmers save, use, share and enhance the seed diversity of the crops that feed Africa. GRAIN.

GRAIN (2014). *¡No toquen nuestro maíz! El sistema agroalimentario industrial devasta y los pueblos en México resisten.* GRAIN.

Grey Sam & Newman Lenore (2018) Beyond culinary colonialism: indigenous food sovereignty, liberal multiculturalism, and the control of gastronomic capital. *Agriculture and Human Values* (2018) 35:717–730

Grey Sam & Patel Raj. (2015) Food sovereignty as decolonization: some contributions from Indigenous movements to food system and development politics. *Agric Hum Values* (2015) 32:431–444

Howard, Phillip H (2009). Visualizing Consolidation in the Global Seed Industry: 1996–2008. *Sustainability*, Basel, 1, p. 1266–1287.

Howard, Phillip H (2015). Intellectual Property and Consolidation in the Seed Industry. *Crop Science*, Madison, v. 55, nov.

James, Clive (2003). Global Review of Commercialized Transgenic Crops: 2002 Feature: Bt Maize. *ISAAA Briefs* No. 29. ISAAA: Ithaca, NY.

Kimanthi, Hellen (2019). *Peasant maize cultivation as an assemblage Peasant maize cultivation as an assemblage An analysis of socio-cultural dynamics of maize cultivation in western Kenya. 194 p.* PhD thesis, Wageningen University, Wageningen, the Netherlands. DOI: https://doi.org/10.18174/478306.

Kloppenburg, Ralph. *First the Seed: the Political Economy of Plant Biotechnology.* Madison: University of Wisconsin Press, 2004.

Kistler, L., Maezumi, S. Y., De Souza, J. G., Przelomska, N. A., Costa, F. M., Smith, O., ... & Morrison, R. R. (2018). Multiproxy evidence highlights a complex evolutionary legacy of maize in South America. *Science, 362*(6420), 1309–1313.

Levi Giovanni (2014) The Diffusion of Maize in Italy, from resistance to the peasants defeat IN Aram, B., & Yun-Casalilla, B. (Eds.). (2014). *Global goods and the Spanish Empire, 1492–1824: circulation, resistance and diversity.* Springer.

McCann, James (2005). *Maize and grace: Africa's encounter with a New World crop, 1500–2000.* Cambridge, Mass.: Harvard University Press.

Mkindi Abdallah, Maina Anna, Urhahn Jan, Koch Josephine, Bassermann Lena, Goita Mamadou, Kketani Mutinta, Herre Roman, Tanzmann Stig and Wise Timothy (2020). *False Promises: The alliance for a Green Revolution in Africa (AGRA).* BIBA, BROT, FIAN GERMANY, Forum on environment and Development, INKOTA, IRPAD, PELUM, Rosa Luxemburg Stiftung Southern Africa, TABIO, TOAM: Bamako, Berlin, Cologne, Dar es Salaam, Johannesburg, Lusaka, Nairobi, July 2020,

Morris Micheal & López-Pereira Miguel (1999). *Impacts of Maize breeding research in latin America, 1966–1997.* Mexico, D.F: CIMMYT

Murphy, S., Burch, D., & Clapp, J. (2012). *Cereal secrets: the world's largest grain traders and global agriculture.* OXFAM research reports. August 2012.

Neruda, Pablo (1957) Oda al Maiz. *El tercer libro de odas 1955–1957.* Chile. Available: http://centroderecursos.educarchile.cl:80/handle/20.500.12246/53597.

Patel, Raj (2013). The Long Green Revolution. *The Journal of Peasant Studies*, Londres, v. 40, p. 1–63.

Pérez Samper Maria de la Ángeles (2014) The Early Modern Food Revolution A Perspective from the Iberian Atlantic IN Aram, B., & Yun-Casalilla, B. (Eds.). (2014). *Global goods and the Spanish Empire, 1492–1824: circulation, resistance and diversity.* Springer.

Pilcher, J. M. (2001). *Vivan los tamales!: la comida y la construcción de la identidad mexicana.* CIESAS/Ediciones de la reina roja/CONACULTA. Mexico.

Pollan, M. (2002). *When a crop becomes king.* New York Times, 19 July 2002 https://www.nytimes.com/2002/07/19/opinion/when-a-crop-becomes-king.html

Pruitt, Jon Derek (2016). *A Brief History of Corn: Looking Back to Move Forward.* PhD dissertation, The University of Nebraska-Lincoln.

Raustiala, Kal & Victor, David (2004). The Regime Complex for Plant Genetic Resources. *International organization*, Cambridge, v. 58.

Sell, Susan (2006). Books, Drugs and Seeds: The Politics of Access. IN: *Transatlantic Consumer Dialogue, The Politics and Ideology of Intellectual Property*, Mar. 22–26, San Diego.

Smale, M., Byerlee, D., & Jayne, T. (2011). *Maize revolutions in sub-Saharan Africa.* The World Bank.

Stapleton, Darwin H. The past and the future of research in the history of science: medicine and technology at the Rockefeller Archive Center. *História, ciências. saúde-Manguinhos*, Rio de Janeiro, v. 5, n. 3, p. 716–732, Feb. 1999

Tenaillon, M. I., & Charcosset, A. (2011). A European perspective on maize history. *Comptes rendus biologies*, 334(3), 221–228.

Tschirley, D. L., & Santos, A. P. (1995). *Who eats yellow maize? Preliminary results of a survey of consumer maize preferences in Maputo*, MOA/MSU Research Team. Mozambique (No. 1096-2016-88467).

Toledo, Victor & Barrera-Bassols, Narciso. (2008). *La memoria biocultural: la importancia ecológica de las sabidurías tradicionales.* Icaria editorial, México.

Villa, V., Robles, E., Berrueta, J. G., & Herrera, R. V. (2012). *El maíz no es una cosa, es un centro de origen.* Red en defensa del Maiz. México.

Warman Arturo (2003) *Corn and Capitalism How a botanical bastard gres to global dominance.* University of North Carolina Press.

Wulff, B. B., & Dhugga, K. S. (2018). Wheat—the cereal abandoned by GM. *Science*, 361(6401), 451–452.

CHAPTER 7
International Food Aid and Genetically Modified Organisms: the Case of the United States

Thiago Lima (UFPB); Erbenia Lourenço (UFPB); Henrique Zeferino de Menezes (UFPB)

1 Introduction[44]

Food insecurity exists when people do not have access to adequate food in sufficient quantities to enable them to have an active and healthy life. The persistence of food insecurity into the twenty-first century is an outrageous phenomenon, as there is no shortage of material resources to guarantee that everyone can eat properly. In fact, the number of undernourished people in the world fell from 945 million to 820.8 million between 2005 and 2017. However, the most recent figure is still astonishing, particularly if we consider that the undernourished population has actually grown over the last three years. In 2014, 783.7 million people went hungry (FAO, 2018).

Food insecurity has a number of different causes. Although some are primarily the result of natural disasters (earthquakes, hurricanes, droughts, etc.), all food insecurity has a human component. Events such as wars, economic crises or military blockades, among others, may restrict people's access to food. In 2017, of all the hungry people in the world, 489 million were in countries experiencing a violent conflict (WFP, 2017). However, as Amartya Sen (2008) argues, the fact that it is technically possible to feed all of humanity proves that the continued existence of hunger is a human decision. In other words, every acute hunger crisis can be avoided, if there is political will.

44 We thank the National Institute of Science and Technology for Studies on the United States (*Instituto Nacional de Ciência e Tecnologia para Estudos sobre os Estados Unidos—INCT-INEU*) for its financial support of this work. We also thank Pedro Henrique Mota and Solange Reis for their comments on prior versions of this text.

International humanitarian food aid—i.e., donations of food in the event of a disaster or a crisis—is a way to alleviate hunger or even the only way to save lives, in the case of catastrophes. Aid, as the sole intervention, is not intended to solve the problems that cause calamities but, rather, to guarantee a palliative improvement in crisis situations, which can often be completely hopeless. Recognizing the importance of international humanitarian food aid, we seek to address a particular issue: the donation of genetically modified (GM) food. Although this type of food is allowed and widely consumed in countries such as Brazil and the United States, other countries have banned its production and sale. This chapter proposes to reflect on food aid containing genetically modified organisms (GMOs) through the experience of the world's largest food donor: the US.

2 Food aid containing GMOs

Defining food aid is more complex than it may seem at first glance. Basically, it is the distribution of food to people in need. However, this action can occur in many ways. In this chapter, we use the concept of "Emergency Food Aid" from the World Food Program (WFP), which defines it as

> The food that is provided on a short-term basis for victims of natural disasters or political instability. It is freely distributed and is usually provided on a grant basis. Emergency food aid may be channeled bilaterally, multilaterally or through NGOs (PMA, 2012).

An important variation in food aid is the way in which it is provided: tied or untied. In the former, the donor country must buy/obtain the food to be donated—or at least part of it—from its domestic producers. In other words, the aid is tied to the donor's domestic market. Untied aid occurs when the donor is not required to purchase the food on its internal market (BARRETT, 1998).

In this chapter, we broaden the debate by examining one type of food aid that deserves further consideration: the donation of food produced in the US containing GMOs. The issue is important from different angles. From the perspective of human rights, it is important to reflect on whether the donations are safe in terms of human health, and if they are, whether it would be legitimate to refuse to receive them, in order to not jeopardize trade interests. From the perspective of international relations, it is important to ask whether donations have interests that are not humanitarian or interests that cannot be combined with humanitarian ones harmonically.

According to Jennifer Clapp (2012), the debate on food aid was intensified in recent years, and one reason for that has been precisely the inclusion of GMOs in US aid packages. Trade disputes also have become part of that debate.

The first case involved countries in Southern Africa and, indirectly, the European Union, Argentina and Canada (ZERBE, 2004). Southern Africa was on the brink of a serious food crisis in 2002 due to a complex combination of factors, including climate change, the proliferation of the HIV virus and governance issues. That year, however, the countries in the region unexpectedly put up different types of obstacles to the acceptance of food aid. Some of them only accepted ground corn kernels, to ensure that they could not be used as seeds, as was the case with Angola, which amended its legislation to receive aid on those terms in 2004. In a more radical move, Zambia completely rejected US and Canadian donations because the packages destined for the region contained transgenic corn. The main arguments used by the Africans to justify their refusal are related to three factors: first, the effects of transgenic food on organisms that are undernourished or weakened by diseases such as AIDS are still unknown; second, the food, if used as seeds, could contaminate the local production, jeopardizing exports to the EU, which has banned the sale of GMOs and is the primary market of those countries; and third, potential harmful effects on the environment. This sparked a broad debate on biotechnology applied to agriculture and food (ZERBE, 2004; TAHRI, 2005; CLAPP, 2012).

In response to the controversy created by the African countries' refusal to receive food aid containing GMOs, the UN published the *UN statement on the use of GM foods as food aid in Southern Africa*, stating that the decision to receive food should be made by the receiving country. It also stated that Genetically Modified (GM) food poses no risk to human health and that the donor is responsible for ensuring that the food is safe.

While some countries have put up resistance to aid containing GMOs, claiming that there are no assurances about the food's safety in terms of human and animal health or the environment, generating a certain amount of controversy, other donations made by the US were more clearly controversial. These are cases involving food not approved for consumption in the US, such as StarLink corn and LibertyLink rice (TAYLOR, TICK, 2001; BHATTACHARJEE, 2009)[45].

These products were considered harmful to human health or unsuitable for other purposes due to risks of contamination. Even so, between at least 2002 and 2005 they were included in packages sent by the United States Agency for International Development (USAID), the WFP and other agencies to Latin American countries, such as Bolivia, Ecuador, Guatemala and Nicaragua, and West African countries, such as Cameroon, Burkina Faso and Sierra Leone (FOE, 2006; Associated Press, 2005). In the case of rice, particularly noteworthy is the fact that the US legalized the product days after the variety was discovered in Sierra Leone, which generated outrage among different actors in international civil society (CLAPP, 2012).

The debate created around GM food within the context of food aid indicates the need to further discuss institutional and regulatory parameters—domestically and internationally—to guide this important type of

---

45   Michael R. Taylor and Jody S. Tick (2001) explain that StarLink is the name given to corn that has been genetically modified witha Bt toxin called Cry9C, allowing it to become resistant to certain types of insects. However, in 1998, the US Environmental Protection Agency (EPA) approved StarLink only for animal consumption or non-food purposes, based on the finding that the Bt toxin called Cry9C may cause allergies in humans.LibertyLink (LLRICE601), according to Bhattacharjee (2009), is a rice variety that was genetically modified by the German agribusiness company Bayer CropScience, making the plant resistant to the herbicide glufosinate-ammonium, also manufactured by Bayer. When the herbicide was applied, it would thus not kill the field of rice. Bayer decided not to sell LibertyLink and therefore did not submit it for testing to the Food and Drug Administration (FDA) or the United States Department of Agriculture (USDA). After the discovery of contamination in US food crops, however, the company decided to submit this variety of GMOs for approval, but as Clapp (2012) notes, LL601 was not approved for sale in the US and was abandoned by Bayer in 2001. The main companies involved in selling StarLink and LibertyLink are Aventis, Pioneer, Monsanto and Bayer. See Schlessinger and Endres (2015).

humanitarian cooperation. As the US is the primary source of donated food, it is natural to focus on its behavior, although it is important to examine the policy of other donor countries. We will now look briefly at some of the controversies surrounding transgenic food.

3   GM food and some of its controversies

GM food is another critical chapter in the technological revolutions that have occurred in agricultural production. The production, trade and consumption of transgenic food has been controversial since it was first approved for growing in the US in the 1990s. Through the cases reported above, in the early 2000s, food aid became a specific part of this discussion, overlapping debates on international solidarity, human rights, foreign policy and economic interests.

GM food is the axis of at least three controversies. The first is the clearest and deals with the harmfulness of certain varieties to health—as in the case of StarLink corn. The second is more subtle and concerns the potential health risks, i.e., risks that may or may not exist. The third controversy is related to economic losses in countries receiving aid containing transgenic components.

Researchers have noted that many GMOs can be harmful for human and animal consumption, given the lack of sufficient testing to confirm their safety, particularly in regard to long-term risks. It would therefore be prudent to recommend not adopting those types of food until a definitive conclusion about their safety has been reached. Regarding the potential risks to human health, certain first-generation transgenic plants have antibiotic resistant genes, which can be transferred to bacteria that live in humans, making them equally resistant to certain medicines. In terms of agricultural production, plants that are genetically more resistant to pests may end up triggering the emergence of super pests, which can be much more difficult to combat (NODARI, GUERRA, 2003; MURPHY, YANACOPULOS, 2005; CAMARA ET. AL., 2009).

Concerns about the potential harmful effects of GMOs were present in negotiations over the Cartagena Protocol on Biosafety[46], signed in 2000 and in effect since 2003, which adopted the 'principle of precaution' and 'putting information about GMOs on food labels,' not only characterizing them as GM or not but also specifying the type of gene present in the food (NODARI, GUERRA, 2003; MORGAN, GOH, 2004). The aid provided by the US to countries in Southern African in the early 2000s seems to have not respected those principles, at least initially. It is important to note, however, that the US is not part of the Cartagena Protocol on Biosafety, which currently has 170 members[47]. This is particularly relevant given its position as the leading provider of international food aid. That position by the US can be understood through its tendency to adopt the 'principle of substantial equivalence' rather than of precaution.

The principle of substantial equivalence requires significant similarities between transgenic and natural organisms in order to guarantee that the GMO is at least as safe as food derived from conventional crops (ACOSTA, CHAPARRO, 2008). According to this principle, foods that are tested and look similar to natural foods in "color, texture, oil content, composition and amino acid content" are considered equivalent (NODARI, GUERRA, 2003 p. 112). It is important to note that foods considered substantially equivalent by US law do not require specific labeling. The concept has thus been widely criticized by scientists from different countries because of its commercial focus and the imprecision of its tests, as it would not be possible to prove that a GM food is safe solely through a test comparing physical and visual aspects. The principle of precaution, in turn, is related to rejecting GM food until there is scientific evidence that it does not pose any risks. This is the context for the debate between the US and the EU on the production, sale and consumption of GMOs, which took

---

46   The Cartagena Protocol on Biosafety emerged from the Convention on Biological Diversity (CBD). Established in 2000, it was approved by the Brazilian Congress in 2003. The Protocol aims to protect biological diversity in light ofbiotechnology innovations, particularly in the commercial regulation of GMOs. It is considered the first international agreement that seeks to regulate the trade, handling and use of GMOs (Borges, 2006).

47   List of members available at http://bit.ly/1tr58Kr. Accessed on 05/17/2015.

place at the World Trade Organization (WTO) and has reverberated into food aid (MORGAN, GOH, 2004; MURPHY, YANACOPULOS, 2005; CLAPP, 2012)[48].

The potential economic losses resulting from food aid containing GMOs is part of the third controversy that will be highlighted in this section. There are some concerns that the adoption of GM seeds may reduce biodiversity and to lead to a decline in the economic autonomy of agricultural producers. Transgenic seeds have a high degree of standardization, which is desirable for the food and processing industry, as well as being more resistant to production problems, such as pests and adverse weather conditions. Transgenic seeds can also be more productive than conventional seeds. However, replacing conventional seeds with GM seeds may end up significantly decreasing—or eventually eliminating—the economic viability of many varieties, including native varieties. At the same time, transgenic seeds intentionally or unintentionally have a lower reproductive capacity, and some are even sterile. This means that with each new harvest, farmers will have to buy new seeds, putting them at the mercy of a highly concentrated group of companies in the sector (MARTINS, 2010).

With all the questions surrounding transgenic foods and the recommendations against their sale, many authors have therefore argued that the interests of agribusiness companies are now prevailing over public health and the environment (NODARI, GUERRA, 2003; TANSEY, 2008; CAMARA ET AL., 2009; CLAPP, 2012).

One element of this debate is the expansion of intellectual property (IP) rules in the international system, including the possibility of protection for living beings, such as GM plants and animals (TANSEY, 2008; MARTINS, 2010). With the proliferation of GMOs and IP rules—driven

---

48 Since 1998, the EU has invoked the principle of precaution at the WTO to restrict US imports. In contrast, the US, which is the largest producer of GMOs and has applied the principle of substantial equivalence, together with Argentina and Canada, formalized its opposition to the EU at the WTO in 2003. The argument used by the US is that the EU would be contradicting the WTO principles of free trade by blocking GM products. Moreover, the EU's stance would largely affect US exports, generating huge losses, insofar as that attitude would also influence the acceptance of its GM products on the international market (Zerbe, 2004; Clapp, 2005; Clapp, 2012).

largely by the demand for new international agreements by the US—control over seed production and distribution has become more strongly concentrated in a handful of companies. This monopolistic control over more effective varieties has an impact on the environment and affects traditional forms of food production, threatening control over possible foods in the future. The patenting of technological innovations in agriculture may affect traditional producers, as they do not have the financial resources to pay for licensing and find it difficult to access more fertile seeds and technological tools for production, making them less competitive. Recently, negotiated international IP rules have led to profound changes in the laws of countries receiving GMOs, including the requirement to patent plant varieties (which is not required by the Agreement on Trade-Related Aspects of Intellectual Property Rights-TRIPS). This is an important change, as it limits the flexibility that farmers—and particularly small farmers—have in the use, storage and distribution of traditional seeds. Moreover, protecting GMOs through patents also tends to create large monopolizing corporations due to the concentration of power in the patent holders. As it is a pioneer in biotech agriculture and strongly defends IP protection, the US has thus become more powerful and hegemonic in the field of food, through the spread of GMOs (TANSEY, 2008).

It is impossible to ignore, however, that certain authors, such as Paarlberg (2010) and Acosta and Chaparro (2008) advocate for the consumption of transgenic food as a solution to the world's food problems. Advances in genetic interventions would be important to preparing agriculture for future global challenges, such as population growth and climate change. For those authors, actors such as the NGO Friends of the Earth (FOE) and Greenpeace end up influencing the decisions of African governments when they publish studies against GMOs.

However, beyond the scientific questions, the fear of the people who oppose the production of GMOs is associated with a broader spectrum of issues, including the idea that transnational corporations are more interested in increasing their profits than protecting the environment or alleviating hunger.

Furthermore, the possibility that GMOs could invade wild ecosystems and have a detrimental effect on biodiversity, in addition to unfair competition with other agricultural systems, such as agroecology, often results in a lack of trust in the agencies responsible for regulating GM crops.

The controversy surrounding GMOs also divides society in the US. According to the Global Legal Research Center (2014, p.209) at the Law Library of Congress, public opinion polls conducted between 2001 and 2006 indicate that "[s]upport for the introduction of genetically modified foods into the food supply held steady at 26 to 27% [...] while opposition to the introduction of such foods fell from 58 to 46% over the period.". Academic and scientific opinion is also divided. In general, organizations focused on scientific research (ex.: National Research Council, American Association for the Advancement of Science, American Medical Association) are in favor, and environmental, organic production and consumer organizations (ex.: Greenpeace, Organic Seed Growers and Trade Association, Center for Food Safety) are against it (Global Legal Research Center, 2014).

4   Motives of the US

In the midst of the controversy surrounding GMOs, it is important to ask why the US uses those products in its food aid. We believe that the US interests encouraging the donation of GM food are primarily economic (ZERBE, 2004; TANSEY, 2008; CLAPP, 2012). Considering that the country is currently the world's largest producer of GM food and that its market is unable to absorb all the production—and in some cases is not even legally allowed to absorb some production—an outward flow becomes imperative. Traditionally, food aid has been one of the main ways to reduce the domestic grain supply in the US, and in the case of transgenic grain, it seems to be no different (LIMA, DIAS, 2016). Diven (2006), for example, demonstrates that donations are based on surplus stocks of commodities that cannot be absorbed by the markets and are not primarily related to deficiencies in grain production in the receiving countries. Her study, which focuses on the period 1955 to 1991, concludes that aid has a low humanitarian concern and a greater trade motivation, in the sense of off-setting negative variations in US food exports (DIVEN, 2006).

Moreover, according to its history, the development of foreign markets would also be an objective of international food aid. The greater the number of countries that allow GMOs to be grown, consumed and traded, the greater the number of markets that can be reached by the US. In other words, GM food aid could be a way of introducing GMOs indirectly, forcing a situation that leads to permission being granted, opening up economic possibilities in the fields of production, trade and technology. This could have impacts on international regimes, for example, on IP. As the practice of GM food becomes more pervasive and widespread among states, there will be greater support—or less resistance—to stricter IP standards. The inverse would also be true. As more countries become signatories to IP agreements that include patent protection for seeds, they will become more vulnerable to market pressures from companies demanding the sale of GMOs.

These traits—more commercial than humanitarian—result from political relations among interest groups, legislators and actors in the executive branch. Focused more on pursuing private and electoral interests, although not entirely excluding actors concerned with solidarity, the humanitarian emphasis would be relegated to the background.

FOE also points out the economic interests that may be guiding US actions in terms of the preference for donating GM food. The 2015 FOE report finds that internationally, US crops containing GMOs have been blocked by laws and regulations. Moreover, technology related to genetic engineering has been rejected by consumers in certain regions. The government then began to defend actions against regulations restricting the use of GMOs. These include actions to aid countries that are in the process of implementing national biosafety structures (FOE, 2015).

Sustainable Pulse (2016) and Cornish (2018) draw attention to the fact that the Gates Foundation works in partnership with USAID, the UK's Department of International Development and the Japan International Cooperation Agency to spread GMOs in developing countries. This occurs through investments in biotechnology, primarily in African countries, on the grounds of reducing food insecurity by reducing the use of chemicals and reducing plant vulnerabilities during droughts, among other arguments.

The work of USAID, which is influenced by agribusiness, demonstrates the position of the US by promoting GMOs in projects such as the Agricultural Biotechnology Support Project (ABSP) and the Program for Biosafety Systems (PBS). The ABSP and the PBS have budgets totaling close to US$ 28 million and aim to implement pro-US policies for biosecurity, food security, IP rights and technology transfer in Africa and Asia (FOE, 2015).

However, after years of experience on the African continent with the production of GMOs, food security has not been guaranteed. The African Model Law on Safety in Biotechnology is one response to try to protect African countries from the potential negative effects of GMOsand halt the expansion of agribusiness and IP rules that may only benefit large corporations (FOE, 2015).

After 60 years of systematic food aid, however, the US has been attempting to adopt a new position as a result of the critiques and controversies as well as the political strengthening of groups more closely linked to human rights. The Bush and Obama administrations sought to implement untied donation policies in order to reduce food aid costs without losing soft power, demonstrating greater humanitarian concern. Protectionist interests, however, end up severely limiting the possibilities for reform (DIVEN, 2006; LIMA, DIAS, 2016). Having to purchase food for aid on the domestic market—saturated with GM commodities—is, in theory, more difficult than sorting packages with natural food, assuming that was an objective. However, Zerbe (2004) notes that significant stocks of non-GM foods were available, despite government claims to the contrary. The problem was USAID's reluctance to engage in discussions on GMOs and to seek alternatives to tied food aid.

We should not ignore, however, the US arguments for GM food aid. Speaking on the controversy with Southern Africa during the 2002 crisis, the strongest argument from the US was the fact that its own citizens eat those foods[49]. It also used arguments from scientists that GMOs would be a tool against hunger in the future, as this type of food can be manipulated to contain more nutrients and programmed to be more resistant to pests and viruses (ZERBE, 2004; HALEWOOD AND NNADOZIE, 2008). Take, for example, the report from the International Service for the Acquisition of Agri-biotech Applications (ISAAA) (2014):

> Provisional data for 1996 to 2013 showed that biotech crops contributed to Food Security, Sustainability and Climate Change by increasing crop production valued at US$133.3 billion; providing a better environment, by saving ~500 million kg a.i. of pesticides in 1996–2012; in 2013 alone reducing CO_2 emissions by 28 billion kg, equivalent to taking 12.4 million cars off the road for one year; conserving biodiversity in the period 1996–2013 by saving 132 million hectares of land; and helped alleviate poverty by helping 16.5 million small farmers and their families, totaling >65 million people, who are some of the poorest people in the world. Biotech crops can contribute to a "sustainable intensification" strategy favored by many science academies worldwide, which allows productivity/production to be increased only on the current 1.5 billion hectares of global crop land, thereby saving forests and biodiversity. Biotech crops are essential but are not a panacea, and adherence to good farming practices, such as rotations and resistance management, are a must for biotech crops as they are for conventional crops (ISAAA, 2014).

However, the data published by the ISAAA is controversial. FOE, in its 2015 report, criticizes the ISAAA and explains that it helps to spread GMOs. According to FOE (2015), the ISAAA can be considered the most powerful tool created by the US—with assistance from USAID and the private sector—for promoting GMOs, as it seeks to demonstrate the adoption of GMOs around the world as well as the idea that this expansion would be safe. FOE frequently analyzes the data provided by the ISAAA and has found errors that overestimated the volume of GMO crops around the world. The errors include double counting of crops containing more than one engineered trait and rounding the number of hectares planted in a given country up to the nearest million. Nonetheless, the success of GMOs is accepted and reproduced in academia and the media.

---

49   The argument must be taken with caution, as there are different varieties of GMOs, and each must be tested and approved after they are invented. One variety of GMOs consumed in the US may not be the same as the variety present in food aid (Halewood and Nnadozie, 2008).

Following the GMO incident in Africa, as a testament to the safety of GMOs, the Washington Foreign Press Center conducted a study in which Southern African journalists analyzed US policy for agricultural biotechnology. At the end of the study, the reports indicated that the African journalists were convinced of the safety of GMOs and even excited about the possibility that biotechnology could bring development to the African continent. Along the same lines, USAID and the Zambia National Farmers Union (ZNFU) promoted a plan for implementing biotechnology in Zambia. Well aware of the risks to the environment and to biodiversity, USAID and the ZNFU carried out the Zambia Trade and Investment Enhancement Project (ZAMTIE) in June 2002, in the middle of the African crisis, to propose strategies that would offer economic and commercial development to Zambia through biotechnology (GREGORY, SIMWANDA, 2002). However, although the ZAMTIE may demonstrate the benefits of biotechnology—which is one of the primary US arguments for its dissemination—it can also be used as a USAID tool for opening up markets to US biotechnology.

5 The spread of GMOs by international regimes

The emergence of developers of new plant varieties created a large market for seeds, which in turn began to demand private protection for those new products. The protection of new plant varieties originated in US law and became global with the approval of the International Union for the Protection of New Varieties of Plants (UPOV) Convention[50] in 1961. Under the agreement, countries must grant protection to new plant varieties that meet the minimum requirements[51] (Plant Variety Protection, or PVP) and result from improvements through either traditional methods, such as

---

50 The UPOV is a Geneva-based intergovernmental organization established in 1961 and revised by agreements in 1972, 1978 and 1991.

51 In general, in order to be granted protection, the new plant variety must be new to the market, distinct, uniform and stable (Dutfield, 2011).

asexual reproduction, or methods that use genetic engineering, such as GMOs.

The approval of the TRIPS Agreement in 1995 also required countries to grant private protection to new plant varieties but allowed countries to be exempt from the requirement to grant them patents[52]. The TRIPS Agreement thus did not require patents to be granted for plant varieties but established that developers will have some kind of protection over their innovation. However, the agreement did not establish exactly which model of protection should be adopted. The UPOV system was generally preferred by countries when they adapted their domestic systems to the new multilateral rules (YAMAMURA, 2006; BRAHMI, CHAUDHARY, 2011).

A key aspect of the protection system for new plant varieties is the balance between the rights of those who develop them and the users. This balance is expressed in farmers' privilege and breeders' exemption. The former specifies that farmers have the right to store, replant and exchange protected propagation material (flowers, fruits and seeds), whilethe latter establishes the right to access and use protected varieties for research and development purposes (without authorization from the rightsholder), including for the development of new varieties. These two flexibilities, clearly set out in the 1978 UPOV Convention, enable the sustainability of small farming, while authorizing research for the continued improvement of new varieties (CORREA, 2012). Many developing countries, including Brazil, have adopted this regime. However, the 1991 UPOV Convention severely limited these two exceptions. With regard to farmer's privilege, it limited it by extending the inventors' rights to virtually all acts involved in the production and reproduction of plant varieties: storage, replanting and exchange would be allowed with the payment of royalties. In turn, breeders' exemption was limited by considering it illegal to use protected varieties for research purposes without permission from the rightsholder.

---

52   Article 27 sets out the obligation to protect "plant varieties, either through patents, through an effective sui generis system, or through a combination of both."

In its free trade agreements, the US requires its trading partners to grant patents for living beings, including new plant varieties, or to sign the 1991 UPOV Convention, which pulls the protection system closer to the patent mechanism (the kind of protection that gives the most absolute right to the rightsholders). The US has thus been pursuing a growing number of systems to protect plant varieties that are in line with the monopolistic interests of its seed and GMO development companies.

Given these considerations on the advances of IP protection for organisms and plant varieties, it is important to consider the commercial effects of including GM food in US food aid packages. Two cases offer interesting evidence.

One controversial case regarding the protection of inventions related to plant varieties involved Monsanto and a Canadian farmer, Percy Schmeiser. According to Ziff (2005), Schmeiser committed patent infringement when he used Roundup Ready canola seeds from Monsanto on his farm without authorization. In 2001, the corporation sued Schmeiser for using seeds patented by the company. Schmeiser claims that he did not acquire Monsanto biotechnology in any way and that the GM plants may have been the result of contamination through cross-pollination: the seeds may have arrived on his land with the wind or been carried by animals or insects. In this case, the patent was on the gene, rather than on the plant; thus, even if the farmer had a different plant in his field, if seeds with the protected gene somehow made their way onto his farm, that gene could be present in any plant that came into contact with it, automatically making the plant protected. The Supreme Court of Canada ruled in favor of Monsanto, arguing that the patent on the variety was valid and that the farmer had infringed upon the protection granted to Monsanto (KIMBRELL, MENDELSON 2005; SCHUBERT, 2005; ZIFF, 2005).

There are several cases similar to that of Schmeiser (SCHUBERT, 2005). Kimbrell and Mendelson (2005), in a 2005 report for the Center for Food Safety, titled "Monsanto vs US Farmers," note that the corporation has used its IP rights over GM seeds to prosecute farmers who use those seeds without permission. However, many of those farmers complain that their farms have been inadvertently contaminated with GM material from

Monsanto. Tom Wiley, a farmer from the state of North Dakota, expresses his frustration, explaining that "[f]armers are being sued for having GMOs on their property that they did not buy, do not want, will not use and cannot sell" (WILEY apud KIMBRELL AND MENDELSON, 2005).

Kimbrell and Mendelson (2005) cite two other cases similar toSchmeiser, with farmers who were harmed by the multinational in the US: Hartkamp and the Thomason family. In the first case, Hartkamp was sued by Monsanto in 2000 for using Roundup Ready soybeans on his farm without authorization, even though it had occurred inadvertently. The farmer ended up losing millions of dollars in the lawsuit and eventually sold his property for a lower price than when he bought it.

The Thomason family was also sued by Monsanto, this time for the inadvertent use of GM Bt cotton, whose patent belongs to the multinational. The dealer who sold the seeds did not tell Thomason that the seeds were patented, nor did he ask the family to sign any technology agreements. The result was that the Thomason family was sued and had to pay Monsanto over US$ 1 million for growing 4,000 hectares of Bt cotton, even though their lands had been inadvertently contaminated. Many farmers end up going bankrupt due to the cost of the lawsuits and the compensation they are required to pay the corporation for the use of patented GM seeds (KIMBRELL, MENDELSON, 2005).

This has had and may continue to have enormous impacts on small producers or even large producers, as those seeds could be spread around the world and Monsanto would have the right to sue any farm contaminated with its patented genes.

This can also have a major impact on food aid, as small farmers who receive seeds through food aid are restricted from using those seeds. Furthermore, there is a risk that crops will inadvertently be contaminated with GMO seeds. In the case of countries in Southern African, this could subject producers to prosecution under the country's law; but even if there is no risk of prosecution, it could lead to them losing the important European consumer market.

6   Final considerations

After analyzing the US international food aid, specifically the aid containing GM foods, we identified the infiltration of economic interests linked to biotechnology in the country's humanitarian agenda. The existence of large surplus in food production and the possibility of opening up markets seem to be motivations for including GMOs in aid packages, even if these foods are not allowed in the receiving countries. The need to open up the international market encounters at least two obstacles—public health concerns and trade rules—that are intertwined. In the case of the former, the principle of precaution was applied by the EU at the WTO, which vetoed the importation of GM foods due to a lack of sufficient evidence from studies on the safety of consuming those foods. This argument is also used by countries in Southern Africa, which have refused to receive donations of GM food. In turn, there are also trade interests. Specifically, in those African countries, it is a precaution against the loss of the EU import market. While emergency measures are intended to remedy problems in African countries, they also advance US political and economic objectives, without regard for the conception of public health in the receiving countries or their trade interests.

References

ACOSTA, Orlando; CHAPARRO, Alejandro. Genetically Modified Food Crops and Public Health. Acta Biológica Colombiana, v. 13, n. 3, p. 3–26, 2008.

ASSOCIATED PRESS. Group: Banned corn included in food aid. NBC News. Available at: <ttps://goo.gl/FgVZha> Accessed May 8, 2015.

BARRETT, Christopher B. Food aid: is it development assistance, trade promotion, both, or neither? American Journal of Agricultural Economics, p. 566–571, 1998.

BORGES, Izaías de Carvalho et al. Impactos do Protocolo de Cartagena sobre o Comércio de Commodities Agrícolas. Segurança Alimentar e Nutricional. Campinas, 2006.

BRAHMI, Pratibha; CHAUDHARY, Vijaya. Protection of plant varieties: systems across countries. Plant Genetic Resources, v. 9, n. 03, p. 392–403, 2011.

CAMARA, Maria Clara Coelho et al. Transgênicos: avaliação da possível (in)segurança alimentar através da produção científica. Hist. cienc. saude-Manguinhos, Set 2009, vol.16, no.3, p. 669-681.

CAVALLI, Suzi Barletto. Segurança alimentar: a abordagem dos alimentos transgênicos. Rev. Nutr., 2001, vol.14, p. 41-46.

CLAPP, Jennifer. Hunger in The Balance: The new politics of international food aid. Cornell University Press, p. 94-117, 2012.

CLAPP, Jennifer. The political economy of food aid in an era of agricultural biotechnology. Global Governance: A Review of Multilateralism and International Organizations, v. 11, n. 4, p. 467-485, 2005.

CLAPP, Jennifer. The US Food Aid Debate: Major Reform on the Horizon? Available at: <https://goo.gl/gbXHrP>. Accessed November 12, 2013.

CLAPP, Jennifer. Turning the Tied? 2014 Farm Bill and The Future of U.S. Food Aid. Available at: <https://goo.gl/6thPt5>. Accessed January 3, 2014.

CORNISH, Lisa. Who are the donors taking on GMOs? Available at: <https://goo.gl/Zta7xH>, Accessed September 21, 2018.

DIVEN, Polly. A coincidence of interests: The hyperpluralism of US food aid policy. Foreign Policy Analysis, v. 2, n. 4, p. 361-384, 2006.

FAO, IFAD, UNICEF, WFP and WHO. The State of Food Security and Nutrition in the World 2018. Building climate resilience for food security and nutrition. Rome, FAO, 2018.

FRIENDS OF EARTH. Africa Contaminated By Unapproved GM Rice From The United States. Available at: <https://goo.gl/BzLtc5> Accessed May 8, 2015.

GLOBAL LEGAL RESEARCH CENTER. Restrictions on Genetically Modified Organisms. The Law Library of Congress, 2014. Available at <https://goo.gl/QiSzLu>. Accessed July 2, 2015.

GREGORY, Pete; SIMWANDA, Lovemore. Agricultural Biotechnology and Biosafety in Zambia. Zambia National Farmers Union, Zambia Trade and Investment Enhancement Project (ZAMTIE), 2002.

HALEWOOD, Michael; NNADOZIE, Kent. Giving Priority to the Commons: The International Treaty on Plant Genetic Resources for Food and Agriculture. Resources for Food and Agriculture (ITPGRFA). In: The Future Control of Food. Routledge, 2012. p. 137-162.

HATTACHARJEE, Rash Behari. Liberty Link Rice: A True History of Contamination. Malaysia: Pesticide Action Network Asia And The Pacific (PAN AP), 2009.

JAMES, Clive. Global status of commercialized biotech/GM crops: 2014. ISAAA brief, v. 49, 2015.

KIMBRELL, Andrew; MENDELSON, Joseph. Monsanto vs. US farmers. Center for Food Safety, 2005.

LIMA, Thiago; DIAS, Atos. Ajuda alimentar internacional dos EUA: política externa, interesses econômicos e assistências humanitária. Revistas Brasileira de Políticas Públicas e Internacionais, João Pessoa, vol. 1, n. 1, p. 189–211, 2016.

MARTINS, Aline Regina Alves et al. Dependência e monopólio no comércio internacional de sementes transgênicas. 2010.

MORGAN, David; GOH, Gavin. Genetically modified food labelling and the WTO agreements. Review of European Community; International Environmental Law, v. 13, n. 3, p. 306–319, 2004.

MURPHY, Josef e YANACOPULOS Helen. Understanding governance and networks: EU-US interactions and the regulation of genetically modified organisms. Geoforum, n. 36, p. 593–606, 2005.

NODARI, Rubens O. GUERRA, Miguel P. Plantas transgênicas e seus produtos: impactos, riscos e segurança alimentar (Biossegurança de plantas transgênicas). Rev. Nutr., Jan 2003, vol.16, no.1, p.105–116.

ONU. United Nations Statement Regarding the use of GM Foods as Food Aid in Southern Africa. Available at: <https://goo.gl/x3ruSv>, Accessed September 21, 2018.

PAARLBERG, Robert. Food Politics. What everyone needs to know. Oxford University Press, 2010.

SCHLESSINGER, Lisa. ENDRES, A. Bryan. The Missing Link: Farmers' Class Action Against Syngenta May Answer Legal Questions Left After the StarLink and LibertyLink Letigation. *Farmdoc Daily*, 5(35), 2015.

SUSTAINABLE PULSE. Gates Foundation and USAID Spread GMO Industry Control over Traditional African Crops. Available at: <https://goo.gl/Ney Phn>, Accessed September 21, 2018.

TANSEY, Geoff (Ed.). The Future Control of Food: A guide to international negotiations and rules on intellectual property, biodiversity and food security. Routledge, 2008.

TAYLOR, Michael R.; TICK, Jody S. The StarLink case: Issues for the future. Washington DC: Resources for the Future, 2001.

WFP. UN World Food Programme Review of 2017. Available at: <https://goo.gl/zytSH7>, Accessed October 1, 2018.

YAMARURA, S. Planta Transgênicas e Propriedade Intelectual: Ciência. Tecnologia e Inovação no Brasil Frente aos Marcos Regulatórios. 2006. Dissertação de Mestrado do curso de política científica e tecnológica da UNICAMP, 150p.

ZERBE, Noah. Feeding the famine? American food aid and the GMO debate in Southern Africa. Food Policy, v. 29, n. 6, p. 593–608, 2004.

ZIFF, Bruce. Travels with my plant: Monsanto v. Schmeiser revisited. U. Ottawa L. & Tech. J., v. 2, p. 493, 2005.

CHAPTER 8
From Food Insecurity to Food Dependence: Pattern of Land Accumulation and Land Grabbing in Argentina

Agostina Costantino (IIESS, UNS-CONICET)

1 Introduction

Since the late nineteenth century, Argentina has often been called the "world's breadbasket" due to its ability to produce grain and other foods. In the same vein, the media and many political leaders often state that "we can" feed millions of people. However, Argentina's food scenario has worsened in recent years. Objectives related to food security and food sovereignty cannot be achieved simply through a country's ability to produce food, nor can they be achieved through simply the free play of market laws.

Since the late 1970s—and more rapidly since the 1990s—Argentina has experienced a deregulation of markets in general, and food markets in particular, resulting in increased vulnerability for small producers, price liberalization and the complete disappearance of a great deal of the production supplying local markets. This set of measures is part of a new pattern of accumulation oriented towards the production and export of primary and manufactured goods based on natural resources (including food). Beginning in the 2000s, the intensification of this model gave rise to a phenomenon that also began to occur in other dependent countries: land grabbing, understood as the form taken by the historical process of land concentration within the context of the opening of foreign accounts and the free mobility of international capital. This phenomenon led to the expropriation of millions of hectares, which passed into the hands of foreign investors or governments.

This chapter's objective is to demonstrate the effects that this pattern of accumulation has had on food security in Argentina. At the same time, we consider the potential effects of the phenomenon of land grabbing (or *acaparamiento de tierras* in Spanish) on food sovereignty (understood as the ability to decide what food is produced, how and by whom) in the long term.

The chapter is structured as follows: Section 2 presents an overview of the food situation in Argentina; Section 3 discusses the relationship between the pattern of accumulation and food security; and Section 4 shows the potential impacts of land grabbing on food sovereignty. Some conclusions are presented at the end.

2   The food situation in Argentina

According to data on food security from the Food and Agriculture Organization (FAO), in recent years, Argentina has followed the global decline in the proportion of the population experiencing undernourishment and, compared to other countries in the region, has a better infrastructure in terms of access to clean water and other healthcare services. However, as shown in Figure 1, several indicators show worsening in the population's food conditions. For example, the percentage of the adult population with obesity has increased, as has the proportion of women of reproductive age with anemia.

Figure 1.   Selected indicators for the food situation in Argentina I (1999–2017), % of the total population

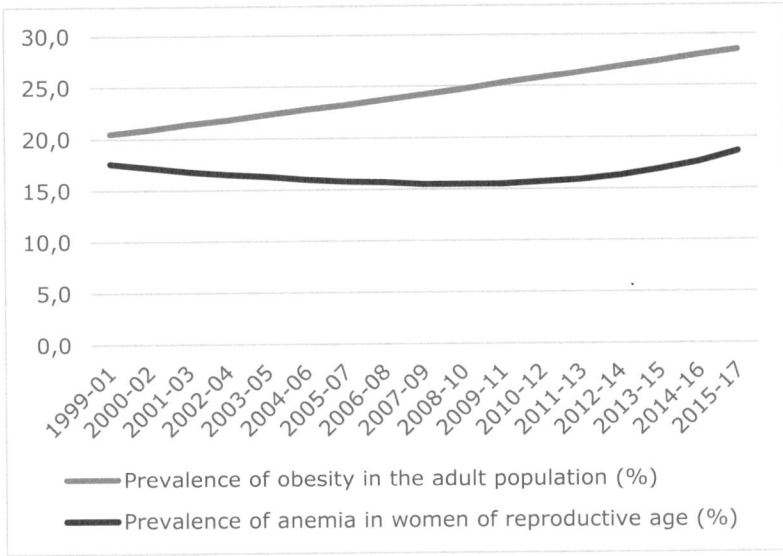

Source: The author, based on the FAO Food Security Indicators.

Moreover, despite the improvement in certain structural food indicators in Argentina over the last few years (the prevalence of malnutrition decreased from 5.3% in 2002–2004 to 3.8% in 2015–2017), a steeper drop in other indicators of malnutrition has begun to be observed more recently. The "adequacy of the average food energy supply" (Figure 2) refers to the supply of food energy as a percentage of each country's energy needs. This indicator, together with the prevalence of malnutrition, makes it possible to analyze whether malnutrition refers primarily to an inadequate supply of food or poor food distribution. In general, Figure 2 shows that these two series have followed opposite trends since the late 1990s, i.e., the prevalence of malnutrition increased as the food supply decreased (until 2002–2004) and vice-versa (beginning in 2002–04).

Figure 2.   **Selected indicators for the food situation in Argentina II (1999–2017)**

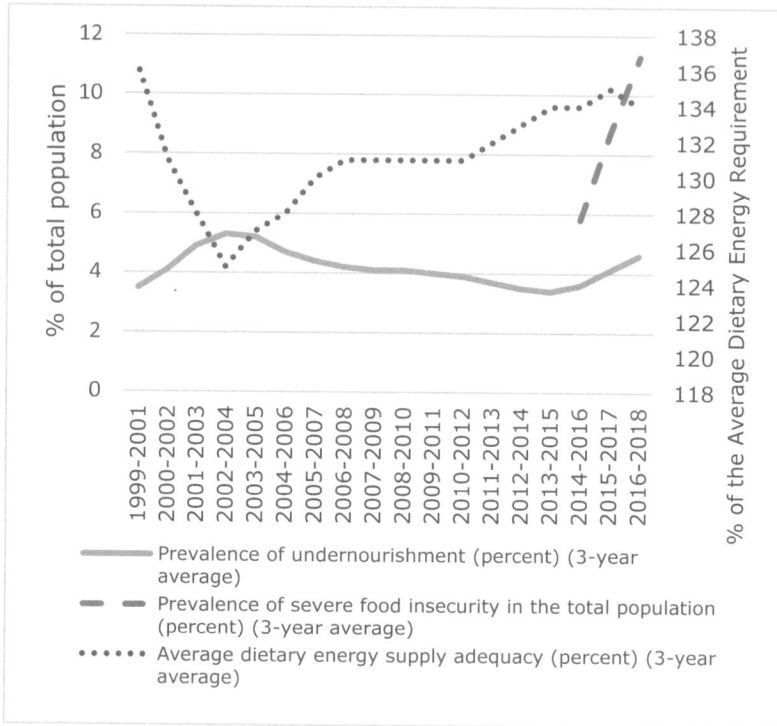

Prevalence of undernourishment (percent) (3-year average)

Prevalence of severe food insecurity in the total population (percent) (3-year average)

Average dietary energy supply adequacy (percent) (3-year average)

Source: The author, based on the FAO Food Security Indicators.

However, this correlation is disrupted beginning in the period 2014–2016, when there is a clear increase in the food supply, at the same time that the percentage of the undernourished population increases. Although it is difficult to draw conclusions from such recent data, it is possible to argue that severe food insecurity in the country has also increased considerably since 2014–2016. According to the FAO indicator, a family is classified as experiencing severe food insecurity when at least one adult reports that they have been exposed—for at least one year—to the most severe experiences described by the "Food Insecurity Experience Scale," which include, for example, having been forced to cut back on food, skip meals, go hungry or

spend an entire day without eating due to a lack of money or other resources. We will now look at the characteristics of the pattern of accumulation that developed in Argentina. By explaining the decline in the current
situation, we will be able discern some of the causes behind the specific
configuration of the food situation in Argentina.

3   The pattern of accumulation and food security

A "pattern of accumulation" refers to the way in which capital is accumulated and reproduced in a particular time and place. The objective of capital is always to expand by making profits, but the way this objective is
achieved changes over time and between countries and has major social
and political consequences.

There is strong evidence that the last major change in the pattern of
accumulation in Argentina occurred during the civil-military dictatorship
in 1976.[53] Since that time, the country's economy has shifted from state-
led industrialization to exploiting comparative advantages and beginning
to apply "structural reforms." The government sought to remove obstacles
to accumulation by lowering wage costs (through direct repression) and
other costs (through trade liberalization). It also sought to solve the credit
crisis (liberalization of capital movements and deregulation of the financial system) and to direct government funds towards the promotion of
business in the most concentrated sector of the bourgeoisie (through state
promotion and procurement and the denationalization of public enterprises). In short, the idea was to discipline both part of capital (through
opening up and increasing competition) and labor (through repression).

---

53 This does not imply that there have been no important political, economic or social
changes since that date. However, the major characteristics of the way capital accumu-
lates (exploitation of comparative advantages for export in the hands of large transnational capital) remain almost unchanged, despite changes in the government. For a
more detailed discussion of the subject, see Schorr (2013).

This process was completed during the 1990s. In 1991, the decree of economic deregulation was sanctioned "with the objectives of consolidating economic stability, preventing distortions in the relative price system and improving the allocation of resources in the domestic economy" (Poder Ejecutivo Nacional, 1991), making use of the police power sanctioned by the state reform law in 1989. Under the idea that state intervention was "incompatible with the spirit of this Decree" (p. 8), it included, among other types of deregulation (Poder Ejecutivo Nacional, 1991):

- the elimination of restrictions on the supply of goods and services throughout the country and all other restrictions that distort market prices, preventing the spontaneous interaction of supply and demand;
- liberalization and deregulation of road freight transport;
- elimination of all restrictions, quotas and other quantitative limitations on the import and export of goods;
- dissolution of the following regulatory agencies and institutions: National Board of Grains, National Board of Meats, National Forestry Institute, National Institute of Equestrian Activity, Yerba Mate Production and Trade Regulation Committee, the national marketplace for yerba mate and the national management of sugar;
- liberation and elimination of quotas for the production and sale of yerba mate, wine, milk and other regional production; and
- elimination of restrictions on working days and hours for operators who provide loading and unloading services, in order to facilitate the uninterrupted operation of ports.

In 2002, a series of policies intended to encourage agriculture and mining started to be implemented. In political terms, one of the core points was the "Participatory and Federal Strategic Plan on Agrifood and Agribusiness 2010–2020," launched in 2010 and signed by the government, national universities, international organizations (the Economic Commission for Latin America and the Caribbean [ECLAC], the FAO, the Inter-

American Institute for Cooperation on Agriculture [IICA], the United Nations Development Program [UNDP)), business groups and representatives of the main value chains. Its primary objectives were to increase the production and, particularly, the export of agricultural products. There were also announcements about the creation of more domestic consumer markets, but there were no details on which types of production would be increased for those markets (as was done with export markets); the increased production of vegetables (not included in the export targets and, therefore, intended for the domestic market) was the lowest objective (see the third item on the list below). The following are some of the plan's specific objectives:

- increase the area for growing grain from 33 million hectares in 2010 to 42 million hectares in 2020 (27%), in particular rice (62%); sunflower (61%); corn (56%), soybean (20%) and wheat (111%);
- increase the area for growing cotton by 126%, from 310,000 to 700,000, increasing production by 235% (from 388,000 to 1.3 million);
- have only 4% of the surface area dedicated to growing vegetables between 2008 and 2020 (food that is effectively for the domestic market);
- increase the productivity of all previous crops;
- increase the conversion of pasture to cropland by 30%; and
- increase the volume of exports by 153%, specifically:
  o primary exports (80%); rice (129%); sunflower (312%); and cotton (242%); among others;
  o agricultural exports (193%): sunflower complex (428%), corn complex (1100%), soybean complex (93%); and
  o soybean-based biofuels (317%).

The government therefore planned to invest in public infrastructure projects "for the full economic and social development of agrifood and agribusiness activities" (p. 119). Moreover, it would promote "the legislation needed for the full and sustainable development of agrifood and agribusiness activities" (p. 139).

What effect did the intensification of this pattern of accumulation have on food security? According to the FAO, food security refers to physical and economic access by all people, at all times, to sufficient, safe and nutritious food that meets their dietary needs, taking into account the cultural context. Also according to the FAO, the best mechanism to achieve this is the market, i.e., increasing the production of food in the country is more efficient for obtaining surpluses and—having exported those surpluses—importing the food that is lacking.

One way to measure this is through the "apparent consumption" indicator, which can be considered a proxy variable for consumption, i.e.:[54]

$$APPARENT\ CONSUMPTION_x$$
$$= Production_x + Imports_x - Exports_x$$
$$\pm\ stock\ variation_x$$

The graphs in Figure 3 show trends in the domestic production and apparent consumption of selected foods in Argentina. The first thing to note is that the production of soybean and corn, both produced with genetic modifications (beginning in the 1990s) and with technological packages belonging to major transnationals, increases exponentially, while the production of other, more traditional goods in Argentina (such as wheat and beef) begins to stagnate. The reforms resulted in land use substitution. In all cases, they are goods for which production was always above consumption, and the surplus was exported.

---

54   This indicator can be understood also as the supply available for internal consumption.

Figure 3.   Foods for which production was always greater than apparent consumption, in millions of tons

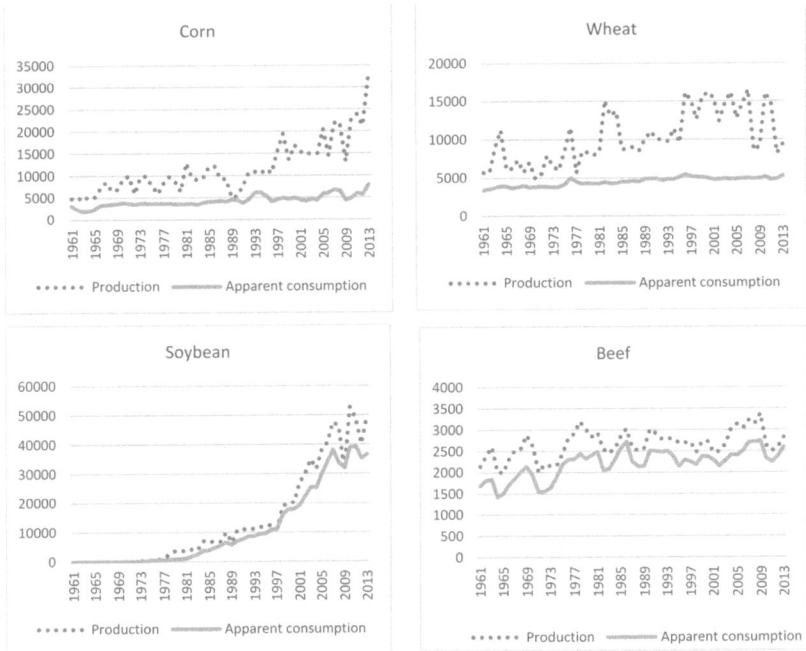

Source: The author, based on FAOSTAT.

The second case shown in Figure 4 is food for which production was equal to domestic consumption, i.e., they were produced to supply the domestic market, until the beginning of the liberalization process. The production of onions, milk and poultry was separated from the domestic consumption in the 1990s (the first two) and the 2000s (poultry). The integration of Brazil and Argentina's markets through the Common Market of the South (*MERCOSUR*) played a key role in increasing Argentina's exports of those foods.

Figure 4.   Foods for which production became greater than apparent consumption, through market deregulation (1961–2013), in millions of tons

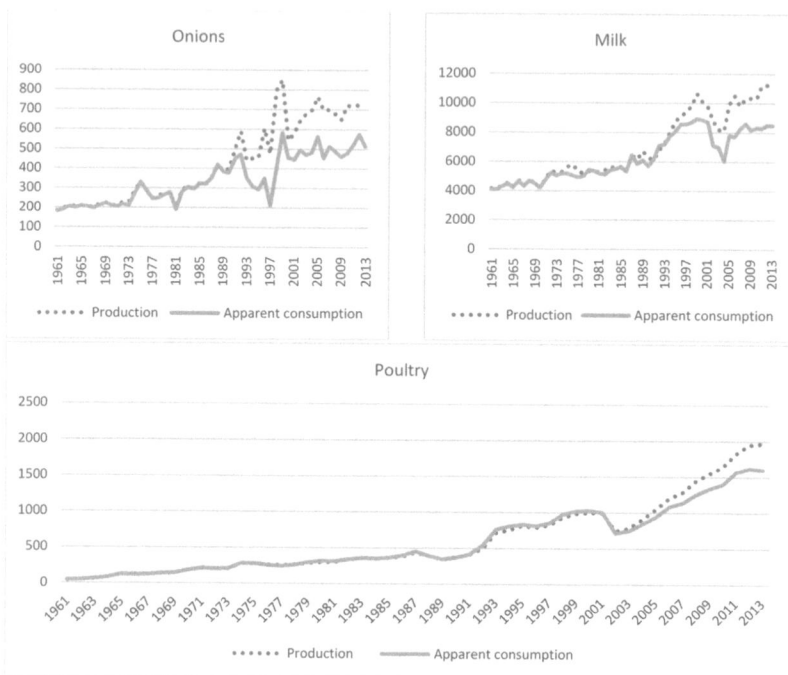

Source: The author, based on FAOSTAT.

The separation between the logic of production and domestic consumption had effects on per capita food availability. Figure 5 shows how per capita domestic consumption of certain key foods in the diet of Argentines, such as meat, wheat, potato, sweet potato and tomato, has systematically declined. In other words, production increased exclusively for export. According to the FAO, this would make it possible for Argentina to purchase products that it produces less efficiently abroad, but in reality, domestic consumption was replaced by external consumption rather than an improvement in food security.

Figure 5.   Per capita apparent consumption of selected foods in Argentina (1961–2013), in millions of tons.

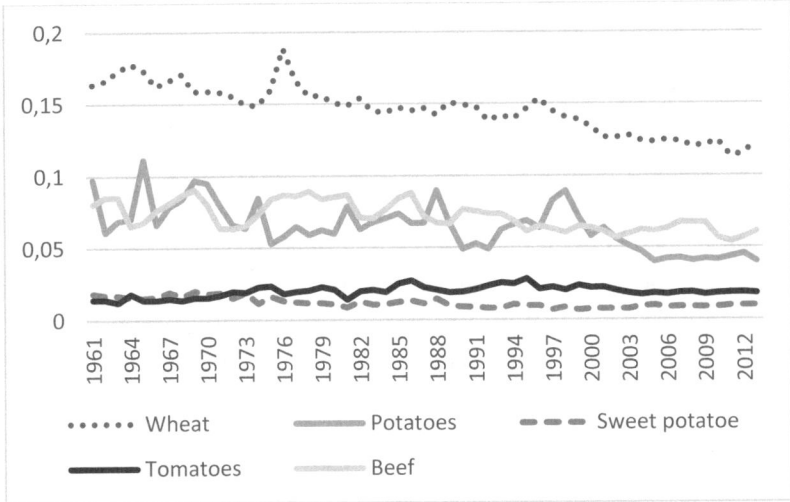

Source: The author, based on FAOSTAT.

Many foods had to be imported, such as tomato and pork, which shows a clear change in the food pattern of Argentines, through market deregulation and economic openness.

Figure 6.   Food for which production is less than domestic consumption (1961–2013)

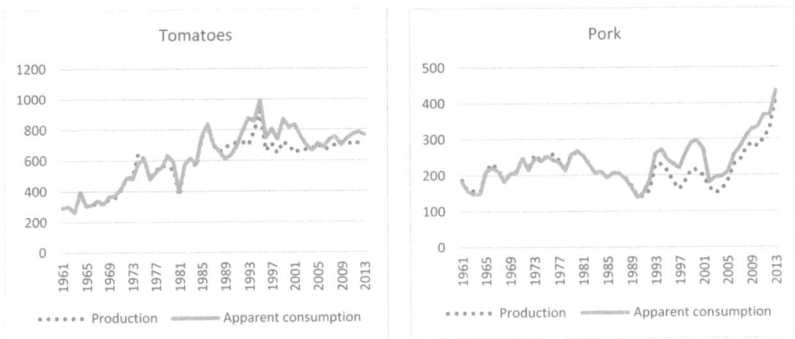

Source: The author, based on FAOSTAT.

What was the performance following the change in government in December 2015? At that time, a new government with a clearly liberal style came to power. The main policy instruments that began to be applied and that defined the map of winners and losers for this stage were (Cantamutto and Schorr 2016): (i) devaluation of the peso; (ii) elimination of export duties (taxes) on wheat, corn, meat, regional products, oil and mining products and a decrease in soybean exports (La Nación 2015; Infobae 2017; Página 12 2016); (iii) increase in the local price of hydrocarbons (as a result of the devaluation but also through direct price regulation) (Infobae 2016); (iv) increase in public utility rates (Cantamutto 2016); (v) deregulation of foreign trade; (vi) elimination of capital controls on foreign currency purchases; and (vii) a contractionary policy by the Central Bank that kept debt interest rates at very high values (Ostera 2016).

These measures explain the decline in the indicator for prevalence of malnutrition shown in the previous section: increased food production, combined with the reduction and elimination of export tariffs (in addition to the dismantling of the price control policy), led to a considerable increase in prices for the domestic market. Part of the population could no longer access those foods through the market.

In short, if we accept the FAO's mechanism of achieving food security through the market—increasing the production of certain foods, exporting their surpluses and importing foods that the country does not efficiently produce with those foreign currencies—we will see that intensifying the pattern of accumulation based on specialization in comparative advantages was a resounding success. There was an increase in the production of all foods with high international prices towards which Argentina's agriculture was oriented, i.e., those favored by technological advances in their production (such as soybeans and corn) and those that benefited from processes of regional integration (such as onions, poultry and milk).

However, if we assess the impact of this mechanism on food security—understood as access to food, taking into account the cultural context—we see that there is a drop in the per capita supply of food crucial to the Argentine diet, such as meat, wheat and potato. All this caused a change in the food basket, which partly explains the poor performance in nutrition observed in Section 1. The question is therefore not about increasing the supply of certain products but about how the population can access them. As the prices of basic commodities are deregulated and begin to depend on the international market, they become fix to the dollar. If this is not accompanied with another policy enabling the people to purchase this food at those prices (for instance, a citizen income policy), production will increasingly depend on foreign markets rather than on domestic demand.

4 Land grabbing and food sovereignty

In recent years, there has been a proliferation of case studies from different countries focused on describing the process of land grabbing, which has intensified around the world. But what do we mean when we talk about "land grabbing"? In this chapter, we understand the term as a new arrangement that results in land concentration, within a context of intensifying global capital flows and a deregulation of the external accounts of countries. Operationally, we will consider the characteristics of the land grabbing process beginning in the 2000s, not because that is when the phenomenon began but because it was when it started to take on particular characteristics (in quantitative terms but also in terms of the investing countries, the objectives and the methods of accumulation).

In this period, a combination of different factors intensified the phenomenon, namely, the crisis in the process of capital accumulation that was occurring in developed countries, manifested in a series of speculative bubbles (the dot-com crisis in 2000, the mortgage crisis in 2008) as well as a rise in the international prices of primary goods during that same period. Both factors led capital to pursue other lucrative investments that would prevent a further fall in profits, such as financial derivatives linked to primary goods, direct production of primary goods and land grabbing.

One of the most important dimensions that characterizes land grabbing in Argentina during the 2000s refers to the investors' objectives.[55]

---

55 For a more detailed analysis of other characteristics of this phenomenon, see: Costantino (2015; 2016; 2017).

This dimension allows us to visualize how the phenomenon may be affecting the country's food sovereignty. The concept of food sovereignty was promoted by La Via Campesina and the Forum for Food Sovereignty and refers to people's right to determine their own food and productive system. It is envisioned as a precondition for achieving food security, i.e., in order for the entire population to have access to a complete and healthy diet, it is necessary to consider who produces what, how it is produced and for whom.

The analysis below is based on a database constructed by the author using the following sources: Landmatrix, the balance sheet reports of the companies listed, interviews with key informants and news reports. Acquisitions of 1,000 hectares or more by foreign investors in the country are considered "land grabbing."[56]

All the land grabbing operations recorded have a general objective: capital accumulation. This means investing capital in different ways and in different circuits but always seeking to increase its value by making profits. However, the way this general objective is pursued may vary between two distinct dynamics, according to two main groups: i) those that produce for the market and will face competitors in the search for buyers; and ii) those that seek to produce to guarantee supply. While the latter are driven by the specific needs of supplying food for consumption and raw materials for the production of goods in a particular economy, the former can be

---

56   In this chapter, we focus only on foreign investors. However, the idea of land grabbing does not refer only to foreign investments but, rather, the way the process of land concentration occurs in many countries, based on the opening of external accounts and the globalization of the planet. This flow of capital had two well-defined directions: one that was typically North-South, in which US and European capital began to acquire land abroad, and another that could be considered South-South, of countries seeking to guarantee their food security or the supply of raw materials for their own industrialization. Examples include capital from China or certain Arab countries. This does not exclude investments between central countries (Lima and Lourenço, 2018), between peripheral countries (ex.: Argentine investments in Paraguay) or intra-country (investments by the Argentine company Cresud in Argentina), which are undoubtedly relevant for explaining the phenomenon in each specific country. However, this capital can never reverse the direction of the flow mentioned above: due to its dependent and peripheral characteristics, it is never able to compete for investments in central countries and plays a very defensive role in local economies.

found in the following segments: primary production, tourism and conservation.

During the 1990s, land grabbing was done for the purpose of production (and within that objective, for larger scale agricultural production), conservation and tourism (particularly during the convertibility crisis, when land prices were lower). Following the currency devaluation in 2002 and the rise of certain countries on the stage of global capitalism beginning in the 1990s (such as China or India), the panorama of land grabbing changed in terms of objectives. It doubled for agricultural production and became more important for mining operations, and there was a new objective: controlling land in order to guarantee the supply of raw materials and food for the investing countries. We will now explain the evolution and key characteristics of each of these objectives.

Table 1. **Objectives of foreign land investments in Argentina, 1992–2001 and 2002–2013**

Objectives			1992–2001		2002–2013	
Demand	Specific objective	Sector	Hectares	%	Hectares	%
For the market	Primary production	Production for the market—total	624,736	48.4	1,469,608	56.1
		Agricultural sector	48,209	[77.0]	846,079	[57.6]
		Mining sector	2,000	[4.3]	433,469	[29.5]
		Forestry sector	116,527	[18.7]	190,060	[12.9]
	Tourism		354,000	27.4	264,567	10.1
	Conservation		311,017	24.1	50,649	1.9
Assured demand	Guarantee supply		–	0	837,006	31.9
Total			1,289,753	100	2,621,830	100

Source: The author, based on the database constructed.

4.1   Primary production for the market

This objective refers to land grabbing with the explicit aim of making a profit, not only through primary production but also through the valorization of land acquired for capital gains. The primary investments with this objective, in both the 1990s and 2000s, are made by the United States (through companies based in Argentina, Luxembourg and the US), Canadian mining companies and German agrifood companies.

There are two different types of investments with this objective: land grabbing by agrifood companies that explicitly include the objective of land valorization and acquisitions by large transnational mining companies. In the case of the former, investments by Adecoagro and Cresud play a dominant role. In both companies' reports for the Securities and Exchange Commission (SEC), the core business is agricultural production and "land transformation." As far as agricultural production is concerned, they produce grain, oilseeds and livestock that will be sold to major traders and industrial companies, which end up exporting it.

It is important to examine what these companies are calling "land transformation." They use this term to refer to the acquisition of land that they define as "underdeveloped" (savannas and natural pastures) and "undermanaged" or "underused" (poorly managed pastures or agriculture), which become suitable for more profitable productive uses through the implementation of state-of-the-art production technology and agricultural best practices.

In other words, the companies' objectives are not only productive but also real estate-based and speculative, acquiring land at low prices and subsequently selling it at a higher price (either because the price of the land has risen as a result of rising commodities prices or because it has risen as a result of investments made) (Adecoagro SA 2013; Cresud S. A. 2010). Between 2006 and 2013, Adecoagro sold over 53,000 hectares of land, generating capital gains of approximately US$ 160 million. According to the company, those capital gains were made as a result of (i) the acquisition of land at prices below market value; (ii) the land transformation process implemented by the company; and (iii) land valorization as a result of rising commodities prices (Adecoagro SA 2010).

There have also been large land acquisitions by mining companies that seem to have a solely productive aim (rather than being real estate-based, like those in the agrifood sector). In this case, the Canadian Pan American Silver Corporation is particularly noteworthy, as it has over 235,000 hectares across Patagonia for gold, silver and lead exploration and extraction.

4.2   Conservation and tourism

In this section, we will present the objectives related to tourism and conservation alongside each other, as they are closely related and, in many cases, even have the same investors. The literature has characterized this type of acquisition as "green grabbing," i.e., the acquisition of land and resources for environmental purposes (Fairhead, Leach, and Scoones 2012). This phenomenon is generally presented as a consequence of the commodification of nature, i.e., as a way of creating new investment opportunities, particularly in the neoliberal stage. "Nature" has become a commercial asset that generates income through the "environmental services" it provides (emission of oxygen, clean water, beautiful scenery, pest control, etc.). The owners of the resources that provide those services raise funds (government or international organizations) for conservation, earn income from ecotourism, sell organic and sustainable products, etc. This has resulted in the spread of "languages of valuation" (Martínez Alier 2009) (through academia, the press, civil society organizations, etc.), such as endangered biodiversity and the need for biofuels, among others. Regardless of their veracity or falsity, they justify reserves of natural areas to prevent extinction, offset greenhouse gas emissions in other regions and facilitate the emergence of a market for "environmental goods" (now converted into commodities) (Kelly 2011). Argentine Patagonia is a paradigmatic case around the world in terms of land grabbing in the name of protecting nature and the environment, particularly during the 1990s (Zoomers 2010).

Most of those acquisitions were made in the 1990s and 2000s, taking advantage of the exceptionally low land prices: in the first stage, 97.9% of the land for tourism and conservation was acquired between 1997 and 2001, i.e., during the recessive period of the convertibility cycle, when land prices steadily fell, while in the second stage, 87% of the land for this purpose was purchased between 2002 and 2003, i.e., when the economy was still in a recession following the crisis in the previous decade and land prices were only just beginning to recover (although they were still below the 1999 prices).

One of the major investors is Douglas Tompkins, through his foundation "Tompkins Conservation." This investor follows two distinct mechanisms for his acquisitions, following a philosophy of "deep ecology," i.e., nature without human intervention, which transforms the land in order to leave it as "virgin" and wild as possible. On the one hand, acquires big farms that recover introducing endangered species and rehabilitating the landscape, flora and fauna. Part of this farms are leased for sustainable production and green activities (i.e., following certain organic and resource management laws), and the other ones are intended for luxury ecotourism. As we saw in the case of productive companies that transformed land in order to increase its value, Tompkins has sold thousands of "restored" hectares in Argentina in recent years, obtaining significant profits (Tompkins Conservation 2014; 2013). A study by García (2004) also showed that this company (associated with domestic environmental foundations, such as Fundación Vida Silvestre) temporarily turns the land over to the government (national or provincial), imposing a series of conditions that are very difficult to comply with (for example, establishing "marine parks"—parks with more water surface than land—in less than 3 years). If they are not carried out within a certain period of time, the agreement allows Tompkins to reclaim that land.

In addition to Tompkins, there are other major tycoons who have acquired land in order to exploit the landscapes of Argentine Patagonia through luxury "ecotourism" mega-projects, accessible only to high-income tourists. This is the case of Ted Turner, Joseph Lewis and the Dutchman Hubert Gosse. The case involving Joseph Lewis has been extremely contentious, as the property he purchased from the government contains Lago Escondido (which is public, according to Argentine law), and the businessman fenced off the public entrances in order to prevent free access to that natural landscape (a single day at the Lewis complex costs more than US$ 1,700). In all three cases, these are large areas (many of which are acquired from the provincial governments) with large freshwater reservoirs and other strategic resources.

Although there is still no a carbon credit market in Argentina, in 2013, the government sent a proposal to the United Nations for REDD + (Reducing Emissions from Deforestation and Forest Degradation), which is a program that provides funding to states and landowners that meet certain standards of afforestation. Furthermore, the Forestry Law passed in 2007 also allocates funds to landowners in exchange for environmental services provided by forests. All of these incentives are combined with profits from tourism and other funds from international organizations, which can be used by landowners for conservation. It is therefore an investment with the purpose of producing goods and services for the market. In other words, despite the personal definitions that these types of investors have about themselves and their investments, there seems to be little philanthropy in green grabbing.

Many of these cases refer to the fencing off of government and communal lands that were previously used by peasants or indigenous peoples with precarious ownership over the land, i.e., with no titles. All these cases thus involve investments that produce a drastic change in land use, in many cases replacing production for the local food supply with businesses in the "green markets" sector and ecological tourism for high-income consumers.

4.3   Guaranteeing the supply of raw materials for their countries of origin

One of the new elements of land grabbing by foreigners in the 2000s is acquisition to guarantee supply carried out by certain countries, particularly countries that have been experiencing strong growth and industrialization in recent years, demanding a constant supply of raw materials to sustain those rates.

Table 2. Countries that purchase land in Argentina to guarantee the supply of raw materials, hectares in %, 2002–2013

Country	China	India	Saudi Arabia	South Korea	Japan	Total
Hectares	320,000	273,700	212,306	20,000	11,000	837,006
Percentage	38.2	32.7	25.4	2.4	1.3	100

Source: The author, based on the database constructed.

In first place is China, which began making major land grabs in the country in 2011. Since 2010, China has begun investing in Argentina in multiple strategic sectors in order to supply the raw materials needed for its process of capital accumulation. It invested in the energy sector (it bought 50% of the Argentine oil company Bridas from Carlos Bulgheroni as well as stakes in the Argentine subsidiary of Occidental Petroleum, Exxon Mobil and Electroingeniería), the financial sector (the Chinese bank ICBC purchased 80% of Standard Bank Argentina SA), the transport sector (railways and a joint venture with the automotive company SOCMA), the agricultural sector (a joint venture with CRESUD) and the chemical sector (The Heritage Foundation 2014).

In 2010, the Chinese state-owned company Heilongjiang Beidahuang signed a cooperation agreement with the Argentine province of Río Negro for an agrifood project that involved Chinese investors investing in an irrigation infrastructure system for more than 300,000 hectares across five valleys bordering the Río Negro (Black river). In return, they would receive multiple government incentives and "free" use of the San Antonio Este port for 50 years (automatically renewed) (Gobierno de la provincia de Rio Negro 2010).

The agreement involved the following: the company would invest in the irrigation system, which would be considered a loan to the producers who benefited from that system. The producers would continue to produce on their own land, but in return for the loan, they were required to produce only what the Chinese company was requesting and sell them the entire production. If the producers were unwilling to do so, they could sell or rent their land, provided that the buyer or renter agreed to produce the goods requested by the Chinese company; otherwise, the land could be expropriated by the government. Moreover, the producers had to hand over 30% of their land as collateral for the Chinese investment and pay the debt for that investment for 20 years (if they did not want to or could not do so, they would be able to surrender the land that had been offered as collateral).

This means that although the Chinese company did not take possession of 100% of that land, it had absolute control over production. The original landowners would become third-party producers who produce for China (going from independent producers to "outsourced employees" of the company). According to the particular characteristics of this agreement, it thus appears that China's main objective—in addition to getting a return on the investment in the irrigation system—is to guarantee the supply of raw materials necessary for its own process of capital accumulation. China's urbanization and industrialization has increased the need for raw materials and food, through both a growth in demand to supply industrial processes and increased consumption resulting from better income levels for part of the population as well as increased pressure on the arable land in the country's interior. At the same time, it is increasingly necessary for the economy to find new investment opportunities for what has accumulated through structural market reforms and the superexploitation of the labor force (wages below the capital labor force value and high labor intensity). Along those lines, foreign investments in land grabbing for the production of raw materials serves those two needs: it assures the supply of the necessary raw materials and offers a profitable investment opportunity for the expansion of Chinese capital.

Something similar has occurred with Arab and Indian investments in land in Argentina, but unlike in the case of China, where it is carried out by state-owned companies, these are private equity investments with government support. In 2011, the Arab Sheik Mohammed Al-Khorayef signed an agreement with the government of Chaco Province to use 200,000 hectares in the *Bosque Impenetrable* region to produce and export grain to Arab countries, committing to invest in irrigation infrastructure. The project of the Arab investors is part of a national policy called "King Abdullah's National Food Security Initiative," which involves providing funds, credit and logistics from the government to Saudi private investors in order to invest in foreign agriculture. The objective is to form a strategic reserve of food raw materials to meet food needs and prevent future food crises (particularly because they have no control over the international price of food). This policy emerges through the elimination of the subsidy policy for Saudi producers, which increased food import needs. In other words, once again, as in the case of China, land grabbing in Argentina responded to factors related to processes of accumulation in the investors' countries.

Finally, in the case of India, the main investor group is Walbrook, which acquired land during the Argentine crisis in 2002, when it was very undervalued. Backed by the Indian government, private investors began purchasing land in Argentina in order to produce potato and goats to supply India and support the accelerated urbanization taking place in that country.

In all three cases, the Argentine territory and its use are subject to the accumulation and geostrategic needs of other countries, reaffirming Argentina's dependent position. It is important to note that the three cases mentioned above do not involve countries that are currently considered hegemonic centers of the world but, rather, countries that are on the rise. Argentina is subject to both types of countries.

We therefore believe that the phenomenon of land grabbing in Argentina during the 2000s responds to three different objectives: (i) to take advantage of rising prices and the global demand for food and minerals and profit from "environmental services"; (ii) capital accumulation in real estate, which implies an increase in land prices, through both food prices inflation and infrastructure investment (either for food production or conservation); and (iii) to guarantee the supply of food and raw materials that will support processes of capital accumulation in the investors' countries of origin. These three objectives respond to decisions beyond the scope of a country such as Argentina (although it is facilitated by the incentive policies that are applied here) and involve the external transfer of value produced internally (in terms of land profits and rent). Similarly, the three objectives reinforce Argentina's role as a reservoir of natural resources and a supplier of raw materials, which is a clearly subordinate position in the world order.

5 Final comments

As shown in this chapter, just because a country increases food production does not mean that all people will have access to it, as the producers' objective is not always to provide food but, rather, to accumulate and reproduce their capital. The structural reforms that have been implemented in Argentina since the late 1970s—and accelerated beginning in the 1990s—considerably increased the production of many agricultural products that were highly profitable internationally (such as soybean and corn) and decreased the production of other foods that were part of the population's diet (such as meat, wheat and certain vegetables). The process of liberalization and deregulation was completed by the rise to power of a clearly liberal political force in December 2015. That government eliminated export taxes and left its prices at the mercy of international markets while dismantling the entire policy for controlling commodities prices that had been developed during the Kirchner administrations.

All this caused a change of the food basket in Argentina, which partly explains the poor performance of certain nutritional indicators. The question is therefore not about how to increase the food supply but, rather, how the population can have access to it. If the price of domestically produced food is pegged to the dollar and there is no income policy enabling people to keep up with those prices, then production decisions will increasingly depend on external demand rather than on domestic consumers.

With regard to the discussion on food sovereignty, the widespread phenomenon of land grabbing in the 2000s is increasingly leaving food production policy in the hands of large agrifood corporations and certain foreign governments. As we have shown, the primary objective of those investments is to produce goods intended exclusively for export, according to the investors' own parameters, with less and less interference from the local government in determining the characteristics of agrifood policy. Land grabbing thus reinforces the loss of food sovereignty, adding food dependence to the existing problem of food insecurity.

References

Adecoagro SA. 2010. *United States Securities and Exchange Commission Form 20-F*. Vol. 12. 1. Washington, D.C.: United States Securities and Exchange Commission.

———. 2013. *United States Securities and Exchange Commission Form 20-F*. Washington, D.C.: United States Securities and Exchange Commission.

Cantamutto, Francisco J. 2016. *El tarifazo: breve estudio sobre el caso del gas*. Buenos Aires: Fundación Friedrich Ebert en Argentina.

Cantamutto, Francisco J, and Martín Schorr. 2016. 'Timba Agroexportadora'. *Marcha*, 17 November 2016. http://www.rebelion.org/noticia.php?id=219278.

Costantino, Agostina. 2015. '¿Quiénes Son y Para Qué? El Proceso de Extranjerización de La Tierra En Argentina a Partir Del 2002'. *Ambiente y Sostenibilidad* 5 (1): 43–56.

———. 2016. 'El Capital Extranjero y El Acaparamiento de Tierras: Conflictos Sociales y Acumulación Por Desposesión En Argentina'. *Revista de Estudios Sociales*, no. 55: 137–149.

———. 2017. 'La extranjerización de la tierra en Argentina. Continuidades y cambios entre el macrismo y el kirchnerismo'. *Estudos internacionais: revista de relações internacionais da PUC Minas* 5 (2): 103. https://doi.org/10.5752/P.2317-773X.2017v5n2p103.

Cresud S. A. 2010. *United States Securities and Exchange Commission Form 20-F*. Washington, D.C.: United States Securities and Exchange Commission.

Fairhead, James, Melissa Leach, and Ian Scoones. 2012. 'Green Grabbing: A New Appropriation of Nature?' *Journal of Peasant Studies* 39 (2): 237–261. https://doi.org/10.1080/03066150.2012.671770.

Gobierno de la provincia de Rio Negro. 2010. *Acuerdo de Cooperación Para El Proyecto de Inversión Agroalimenticio Entre Heilongjiang Beidahuang State Farm Business Trade Group Co. y El Gobierno de La Provincia de Río Negro, Argentina*.

Infobae. 2016. 'Argentina, Donde Suben Las Naftas Mientras Baja El Petróleo—Infobae'. 12 January 2016. http://www.infobae.com/2016/01/12/1782623-argentina-donde-suben-las-naftas-mientras-baja-el-petroleo.

_____. 2017. 'El Gobierno Eliminó Las Retenciones a La Exportación de Petróleo'. Infobae. 9 January 2017. http://www.infobae.com/economia/2017/01/09/el-gobierno-elimino-las-retenciones-a-la-exportacion-de-petroleo/.

Kelly, Alice B. 2011. 'Conservation Practice as Primitive Accumulation'. *Journal of Peasant Studies* 38 (4): 683–701. https://doi.org/10.1080/03066150.2011.607695.

La Nación. 2015. 'El Gobierno Oficializó La Eliminación a Las Retenciones al Agro, Salvo a La Soja'. 17 December 2015. http://www.lanacion.com.ar/1854990-el-gobierno-oficializo-la-eliminacion-a-las-retenciones-al-agro-salvo-a-la-soja.

Martínez Alier, Joan. 2009. 'Lenguajes de Valoración'. *El Viejo Topo*, no. 253: 95–103.

Ostera, Ignacio. 2016. 'Anuario 2016: Un Año de Cambiemos: Ganadores y Perdedores de La Macroeconomía Macrista'. *Bae Negocios*, 25 December 2016. http://diariobae.com.

Página 12. 2016. 'Página/12 :: Economía :: La Eliminación de Retenciones Mineras'. 7 March 2016. https://www.pagina12.com.ar/diario/economia/2-293979-2016-03-07.html.

Poder Ejecutivo Nacional. 1991. *Desregulación Económica. Nº 2284*. Buenos Aires: Poder Ejecutivo Nacional. http://www.infoleg.gov.ar/infolegInternet/anexos/5000-9999/7539/texact.htm.

Schorr, Martín. 2013. 'Nuevo Patrón Sobre Un Viejo Modelo: El Problema de La Concentración'. *Publicación de Ciencias Sociales Que Lleva Adelante La Carrera de Trabajo Social de La Facultad de Ciencias Sociales de La Universidad de Buenos Aires, Con El Objetivo de Generar Un Espacio de Debate y Difusión de Conocimiento Social.*, 47.

The Heritage Foundation. 2014. *China Global Investment Tracker*. http://www.heritage.org/research/projects/china-global-investment-tracker-interactive-map.

Tompkins Conservation. 2013. *Tompkins Conservation*. http://www.tompkinsconservation.org/home.htm.

_____. 2014. *The Conservation Land Trust*. http://www.theconservationlandtrust.org/esp/our_mission.htm.

Zoomers, Annelies. 2010. 'Globalisation and the Foreignisation of Space: Seven Processes Driving the Current Global Land Grab'. *Journal of Peasant Studies* 37 (2): 429–447. https://doi.org/10.1080/03066151003595325.

CHAPTER 9
China's Food Security and Land Grabbing. The Case of Argentina.

Sol Mora (EPyG-UNSAM, CONICET)

Introduction

The explosion in primary products demand that accompanied the transformation of the People's Republic of China into the second world economy deepened its historical concern over food security. One of the power greatest achievements is its increase in agricultural production that enabled it to feed one-fifth of the world's population, thereby achieving self-sufficiency while leaving behind the recurrent episodes of food shortages and famine experienced in the past (Zha & Zhang, 2013). However, industrialization, rapid urbanization, and increased population incomes only deepened the gap between food supply and demand.

Under the assumption that domestic and global food security are inseparable (State Council of the People's Republic of China, 2019), the Chinese government explored various modalities to respond to its population food challenges. This resulted, in the first place, in an extraordinary grow in agricultural products external purchases, which made China the world's second largest importer, after the European Union (Ministry of Agriculture and Rural Affairs of the People's Republic of China, 2017). However, since the 2008 global food crisis, China gave prominence to investments in foreign agriculture, especially operations aimed to control agricultural land in other States.

Consequently, China acquired a central role in the global land grabbing (Borras et. al, 2012). Despite this transactions pursue a variety of purposes including speculation, energy security and conservationism, the maintenance of food security has been the main motive behind States involvement in the process (Toulmin et. al, 2011). Conversely, this raised concerns about the negative impact that these operations could have on host countries food security (De Schutter, 2009; FAO, 2012).

This chapter analyses the contribution of investments associated with land grabbing to China's domestic food security and that of the host countries. It is worth mentioning that at the same time China was classified as a land grabber state (Borras et. al, 2012), due to its active search for agricultural land (Hofman & Ho, 2012), Chinese investments began to enter to Argentina. These flows concentrated in primary-extractive sectors and the infrastructure linked to raw materials exportation (Laufer, 2019). Between then, two projects closely linked to land grabbing can be distinguished: the Beidahuang Group agri-food project in the province of Río Negro and the construction of the La Paz-Estacas aqueduct and the irrigation in Mandisoví Chico in the Entre Ríos province. After an intense social resistance to their impacts in land access and use, both were interrupted.

By the study of these initiatives from a neogramscian International Political Economy approach, the paper argues that land grabbing deepens asymmetries in the achievement of the parties' food security. While it facilitates China's access to the natural goods needed to meet its domestic food demand, local populations have to face the loss of their lands, pollution and overexploitation of natural resources, which seriously compromises their food supply.

The first section exposes the links between land grabbing and food security from a neogramscian approach. This is followed by a description of China's food security challenges. Subsequently, will be characterize its land investments strategy. The fourth section analyses the China projects in Argentina selected.

Land grabbing and food security

To analyze the relations between China's land grabbing and food security, it is necessary to refer to Robert Cox's category of hegemony and its links with the agricultural production model. This notion designates the set of values and understandings that permeate society to the point of becoming unquestionable and perceived as the natural order for most actors (Cox,

1993). Whereas these meanings can be supported by coercion, ideological factors are decisive for hegemony (Cox, 1992). In addition, hegemony is not only interstate, but simultaneously a social, economic and political structure, which is expressed in norms, institutions and behaviors that affect states and civil society and that sustain the dominant production mode (Cox, 1993).

In this sense, based on the view that reduces nature to raw materials that serve as productive inputs (Leff, 2004), the current agricultural production model is characterized by the predominance of corporate interests in the global food system organization (McMichael, 2009). Thus, it is articulated in the accumulation logic known as agribusiness, whose pillars are large-scale production, biotechnologies, the connection with financial capital, new forms of productive organization and land grabbing (Gras y Cáceres, 2017).

It should be noted that the global food crisis of 2007–2008, caused by the increase in international commodity prices to their highest level in 30 years, was widely identified as the key factor in land grabbing (Cotula et.al, 2009; Deininger et.al, 2011; De Schutter, 2009; FAO, 2012). This is because States highly dependent on primary products imports, with limited land and water to cover their needs, were seriously affected by skyrocketing food prices, and especially by exports restrictions implemented by certain cereal producers to keep domestic prices under control.

In this context, a high consensus emerged among various States in land grabbing as an appropriate mechanism to guarantee domestic food security. Due to the difficulties in commodities access, grain importers concluded that they should reduce their dependence on international markets, perceived as unstable and volatile. Land investments appeared to be the best way to achieve this goal, as they allow the outsourcing and offshoring of food production, bypassing the markets to ensure supply stability for investors. This entails a strengthening of investors' control from the place of production to the final consumer (De Schutter, 2011).

The central feature of land grabbing is that it involves the "control of relatively vast tracts of land" (Borras et. al, 2012:851). That is, it implies the domain over land access and use, as well as the other natural resources, by large scale capitals. Complementarily, it is associated with modifications in land use. In general terms, these consist in the transformation of lands for domestic food production or occupied by forests towards food or bio-fuels production for exportation (Borras & Franco, 2012). The phenomenon is also characterized by the underlying interests, linked to capital accumulation dynamics in response to the food, energy, climate and financial crises of 2008 and the need for resources of various actors.

The acceptance of these investments was reinforced by the discourse that presents them as an opportunity to improve host countries food security (Deininger et al., 2009), which hides the particular interests that guide these operations. However, following Cox (1992), this article adopts the assumption that China's land grabbing and its impacts on food security can only be understood within the structure of the world order in which they exist. This implies that this process must be analyzed simultaneously as a form of reproduction of the existing order, but also as a sphere of interactions to modify that order.

Since Cox (2002) interprets that social relations of production are the starting point for analyzing the world order, this paper focuses on the interaction between China's land investments and its effects on civil society groups in Argentina. This is because it is considered that there is a co-determination between Chinese investments and its implications for food security so that the nature of the former is explained by the conflicts between subordinate and dominant forces (Saguier, 2010).

Challenges for China's food security

China has understood food security in a particular way. This notion has been equated with grains supply security, which in turn has self-sufficiency as its cornerstone (Zha & Zhang, 2013). In 1996, this approach was condensed in the national food security strategy, which established that 95% of China's food needs must be satisfied by domestic sources, while for cereals such as maize, rice and wheat, self-sufficiency must reach 100% (Zhang and Cheng, 2016). As a result, domestic agricultural production, which grew by 87.4 % between 1978 and 2011 (Zha & Zhang, 2013), became the source of food and raw materials for the power 1.3 billion inhabitants. However, self-sufficiency is being challenged by rising food demand and natural resources depletion (Cheng and Zhang, 2014).

On the one hand, China is facing a surge in food demand as a result of increasing population incomes, which led to a middle class nutritional transition. The change in diet is reflected in the expanding consumption of proteins and processed foods, which is accompanied by a greater interest in food quality and safety. Example of this is the expansion, between 1996 and 2018, of per capita consumption of dairy products by 333.3%, fruits by 176.5%, vegetables by 104.2%, aquatic products by 72.5% and pork, beef and mutton, by 55.5% (State Council of People's Republic of China, 2019).Another indicator of the move towards a more western diet is the rise of fresh vegetable production, as well as maize for animal feed, while the traditional crops production, such as rice, has stabilized (Finnin, 2016).

This trend will be intensified by the country's middle class growth from over 50 million in 2005 to approximately 1 billion in 2030. Thus, in the next decade, is projected a 20% increase in per capita consumption of sugar and poultry and sheep meat; as well as a between a 10% and 20% increment in fish, vegetable oils, fruits, vegetables, milk and beef demand. On the contrary, per capita consumption of staple crops is going to decrease (OECD, CEPAL y CAF, 2015).

On the other hand, this scenario poses a dilemma for China because it has only 8.5 % of the world's arable land and 6.5% of the world's water reserves to feed 21% of the world's population (Hofman & Ho, 2012). This is equivalent to a land availability of 0.1 hectare per capita, less than half of the world's average, while per capita water resources constitute only a quarter of the world's average (Ministry of Agriculture and Rural Affairs, 2017).

Although productive limitations did not impede the multiplication of grain production, this took place at the expense of soil deterioration due to intensive agriculture, the expansion of irrigation and the adoption of high-yield seeds. In addition, China consumes around 30% of the world's fertilizers and pesticides (Zhan & Chen, 2016). It should be added that industrialization and urbanization not only caused the degradation of about 37% of its territory and the pollution of 10% of the arable land (FAO & MOA, 2012), but also the occupation of most of the latter for housing or agricultural production. This forced China to use double cropping, which deteriorates soil nutrients and requires large amounts of fertilizers (Finnin, 2016).The pressures on agricultural activity are exacerbated by water crisis, caused by drought, desertification and main rivers pollution.

As a consequence, the gap between food supply and demand became more pronounced, triggering an increase in external purchases. It is worth noting that importations rise was consequence of a change in domestic production, in which is given priority to high-value and labor-intensive crops, such as meat, vegetables and fruits. Low-value, land-intensive products, whose paradigm is soybean, are acquired in the markets (Zhang, 2019).

Specifically, soybean concentrates China's external purchases. Despite being a net exporter during the 1990s, the power became the world's largest importer of this commodity in following decade. Since then, the country area planted with oilseeds decreased. (Hairong, Yiyuan & Bun, 2015). Currently, China imports 80% of its oilseed annual consumption (Cheng and Zhang, 2014), which is used as oil and feed. In 2017, China imported 96 million tons of soybeans, which represented 64% of global imports, while domestic production was around 13 million tons (OECD & FAO, 2018).

Similar increases are visible in priority crops such as rice and wheat, whose imports grew by 800% between 2004 and 2014 (Zhang and Cheng, 2016). Accordingly, in 2017 China produced 212 million tons of rice, but imported 4.3 million tons (National Bureau of Statistics of China, 2018). China is the world's largest importer of rice and is expected to maintain that position over the next decade (OECD & FAO, 2018). Similarly, wheat production stood at 134 million tons and corn at 259 million tons, but imported 4.4 and 2.83 million tons respectively (National Bureau of Statistics of China, 2018).

The above transformed China into a net importer of agricultural products, which led to an acute deficit in agricultural trade. In response, the central government modified the food security strategy. In 2013, it stipulated that it would be ensured through absolute self-sufficiency in basic goods such as rice and wheat, as well as through moderate agricultural imports of other commodities (Zhang & Cheng, 2016).

Nevertheless, it is worth mentioning that one of the reasons why China chose self-sufficiency is its distrust of food markets. This originated, firstly, on markets limited capacity to regulate grain supplies in order to meet Chinese needs. Worldwide, 250 million tons of grains are traded annually, which is less than a half of China's total production (Zhang & Cheng, 2016). Second, in the commodity prices volatility, particularly since the record levels of 2008. A rise in global commodity prices would lead to domestic inflation, which carries the risk of political and social instability.

Finally, Chinese suspicions are strengthened by the strict control over corn, wheat and soybean trade of the United States and other developed countries through the agri-food transnationals that integrate the ABCD group: ADM, Bunge, Cargill and Louis Dreyfus. While the aim of the international grain trade regime has been the opening of markets to the main exporting countries, it have not restricted neither regulated the latters behavior, which threatens importing countries food security (Zha & Zhang, 2013). This is exemplified by the food producers' restriction of exports during the food crisis.

Concerns about food markets prompted China to project its domestic natural resources shortage overseas through foreign investment in the agricultural sector. In this context, investment in large tracts of land to secure commodity supplies appeared as an appropriate alternative to ensure food security.

Land investments strategy

China's land investments are consistent with the Go Out strategy, designed to encourage the internationalization and global expansion of Chinese companies. It is noteworthy that, after the world food crisis, agriculture became central in Go Out, as evidenced by various governmental programs. Among them is the National Medium and Long Term Food Security Plan (2008–2020), which linked agricultural investments and food security. Furthermore, the expansion of these investments was encouraged by the reformulated food security strategy of 2013. This was reiterated in the guidelines for foreign investment promulgated by the State Council in 2017 (Gooch & Gale, 2018), whereas the 2019 White Paper on Food Security emphasized the support for the going global of Chinese grain enterprises (State Council of the People's Republic of China, 2019).

These documents demonstrate the how significant the access to agricultural raw materials overseas became to China. In conjunction with this, its consolidation as the world's second largest foreign investor, as well as its capital reserves, explains the attention to China during land grabbing acceleration. This motivated a wave of press, NGOs and academia reports warning about this process (GRAIN, 2008; Hofman & Ho, 2012; The Economist, 2009; Vidal, 2010).

Despite data limitations, various studies have shown that while China is not the only protagonist or the biggest land grabber, it has played a prominent role in land grabbing. For example, Anseeuw et al., (2012) reported 86 Chinese projects covering 8.3 million hectares in developing countries. Smaller, Wei and Yalan (2012) confirmed the existence of 54 of them, involving 4.8 million hectares. Meanwhile, GRAIN (2016) identified 490 land deals that were not cancelled in 78 countries. Chinese investors are present in 53 of these initiatives.

Following LANDMATRIX database, Nolte, Chamberlain & Giger (2016) ranks China as the third largest land investor in the world in terms of the number of agricultural agreements concluded, behind Great Britain and Malaysia. Considering the hectares affected by these deals, China is the ninth largest global investor. Updated information from LANDMATRIX (2020) confirms China's involvement in 363 out of 2141 transnational land deals registered in the world, which together cover 18.638.847 hectares. Asia is the main target of the agreements, followed by Eastern Europe, albeit those positions are reversed when considering the number of hectares involved. Africa and Latin America are in third and fourth position according to both criteria.

As argued by Hofman & Ho (2012), these operations are part of a state-facilitated process of outsourcing or off-shoring of agricultural production. These transactions represent a way of avoiding market intervention in food supply, which in turn is a guarantee against price fluctuations and imports disruptions. That is why they were perceived by China as an effective and secure method to guarantee its supply of raw materials.

China's land grabbing in Argentina

Agriculture has been the basis for the accelerated strengthening of relations between Argentina and China. One of its expressions is the unprecedented dynamism of trade, as manifested by the tenfold increase in Argentine exports to the power between 2002 and 2010 (Laufer, 2017). In spite of that, soybeans and soybean oil are the backbone of bilateral trade, since they represented respectively 54% and 17% of Argentine sales to that market in 2012 (Oviedo, 2015). Therefore, it repeats not only the classic model in which raw materials are exchanged for manufactures, but Argentina has also developed a dependence on soybean exports to China, which buys 88% of all Argentine soybeans, as well as 30% of seeds, 64% of meat, 34% of chicken and 12% of fish (Laufer, 2019).

Because of its potential in food production and availability of natural resources, Argentina also became a key destination for Chinese investments. These were mostly directed to primary-extractive sectors, such as oil, minerals and infrastructure linked to raw materials transport. Interest in land was also present. The agri-food project in Rio Negro and the La Paz-Estacas aqueduct and irrigation in Mandisoví Chico in Entre Rios are among China's most ambitious initiatives in the country, both in terms of objectives and size of financing. They were also closely linked to China's effort to control lands for food production.

The agri-food project of Beidahuang Group

The China initiative in the Rio Negro province, in the Argentinean Patagonia, originated in two agreements signed by the provincial governor, Miguel Saiz, with the authorities of Beidahuang Group, a state-owned company from the Chinese province of Heilongjiang. The aim of the deals were to provide 1.5 billion dollars in financing (Aranea y otros, 2011) for the construction, by the Chinese company, of irrigation systems from the Negro river, one of the five largest in the country, to increase grain production. They also included the construction of a port terminal. Therefore, the areas designated for the project were the private lands of two valleys along the watercourse, Valle Medio and Valle Inferior.

The distinctive feature of these agreements is that they did not detail the technical aspects and activities that would be involved. Instead, they explicitly transferred the effective domain of large extensions of irrigable valleys to Beidahuang. As the deals states, the company was going to be provided with 20,000 hectares of unexploited farmland for 20 years lease. Additionally, the government was going to made available all the information for a future investment in the exploitation of 234,500 hectares in Valle Medio. It also offered Beidahuang 3,000 hectares without charge to develop an experimental plantation of high-yield crops and further high-technology agricultural techniques (Beidahuang Group y Gobierno de Río Negro, 2010c, art. 4). Besides, for the port terminal construction, the province put at the company's disposal 5 hectares during a period of 50 years with automatic renovation (Beidahuang Group y Gobierno de Río Negro, 2010c, art.5). Taken together, these land transfers represented 257,505 hectares.

From China's viewpoint, this project was relevant because the control of 257,505 hectares by Beidahuang would allow it to produce in that extension the crops of its own decision. In this case, the predominant interest was the introduction of soybean cultivation in Rio Negro, which was limited by climatic conditions. It should be stressed that oilseeds have been a priority in Chinese investments abroad and this concerns particularly Heilongjiang since its oilseed planting area reduced by 42% in 2013 Hairong, Yiyuan & Bun, 2015).

At the same time, the importance of soybeans arises from the same participation of Beidahuang, the largest agribusiness group in China, specialized in opening new areas for intensive cultivation on a large scale (Brautigam, 2015). It should be mention that the project would include the planting of wheat and maize as well (Río Negro, 2011a). Despite its emphasis on self-sufficiency, Chinese imports of these grains increased, though as they are controlled through quotas, their level is significantly lower than that of soybeans (Gale, Jansen & Hewinson, 2015).

Consequently, regardless the commodities centrality in bilateral trade, the initiative in Rio Negro allowed Heilongjiang to secure its direct supply of oilseeds and grains, in order to reduce its dependence on markets and avoid prices volatility. In fact, the company's desire, according to the governor of Rio Negro, was to prevent Argentina from failing to comply with the orders and to skip negotiations with sowing pools and traders (Iprofesional, 2010). The construction of the port terminal was key to meeting that goal. That would be located in the overseas port of San Antonio Este, where, in addition, an oil factory would be installed.

The benefits of this project for China's food access contrasted sharply with the risks it brings to food security in Rio Negro. This emerges, firstly, from land loss by small and medium-sized farmers, the majority of the Valle Medio and Inferior population, in two ways. On the one hand, according to provincial authorities, after irrigation was installed, the farm owners had to put the land into production; but alternatively, they could lease their land to Beidahuang for the production for 20 years (Rio Negro, 2011b). On the other hand, the threat of expulsion was also made clear in a governor statement to the press, regarding that the farmers should paid back between 20% and 30% of that investment over a period of 20 years, but that they could also sell the lands to China (Premici, 2011).

The difficulties experienced by small producers, such as the lack of credit and the low production price, made leasing or selling the land highly feasible as an alternative to the activity pressures, as well as the impossibility to face irrigation costs. Land loss would impede agricultural activities of this group, whether for household or local consumption, leading to migration to urban areas and a foreseeable increase in unemployment and poverty (Teubal, 2006). It is worth noting that rural exodus and the small farmers disappearance could also be consequence of the installation of an industrial monoculture model in the valleys based on the production of transgenic soybean pursued by the project (Cooperativa de San Javier, 2010). This would obstruct the traditional horticultural, fruit, fodder and livestock production in the valleys, seriously limiting access to healthy and nutritious food.

In this regard, it is important to mention that Beidahuang's activities would transform land use into the production of commodities to export to China. This means that the agri-food project would not only harm the productive activities for domestic consumption, but also over native valleys, which would be exposed to degradation due to the agricultural frontier expansion (Cooperativa de San Javier, 2010).

An element that exacerbates the deterioration of local food security provoked by the project is that, according to the governor, each farmer should sign a contract with the company for the agricultural production commercialization to the Asian giant for 20 years (Premici, 2011). The monopoly on Rio Negro soybeans granted to China is a clear demonstration that local food supply was completely excluded from the project. Furthermore, this indicates that the project itself would mean some loss of local capacity to autonomously define what and how to produce through the sustainable management of their natural resources, that is, the food sovereignty (García Guerreiro y Wahren, 2016).

The damage to adequate food access in Rio Negro would be heightened, secondly, by the project's environmental consequences. Despite the fact that no environmental impact studies were carried out, assemblies of neighbors, environmental and farmers' organizations warned that intensive agricultural exploitation in large scale and long temporary duration would deteriorate the valleys' soil to the point of making them unproductive. In addition, they raised alarm about the soil nutrients that would be exported with the soybean and the ecological degradation that would result from agrochemicals use (Cooperativa de San Javier, 2010).

Another area of concern was the impact of irrigation on river flow and biodiversity. According to the assemblies, it was impossible to irrigate that vast area without compromising the downstream population consumption (Fundación Uñopatún, 2011). These fears were synthesized in a statement by Fundación para la Defensa del Ambiente (FUNAM, 2010), claiming that China intends to absorb the production of 320,000 hectares but leaving in Argentina deteriorated soils, less water and pesticide residues that would contaminate the Negro and Colorado rivers.

In brief, the project's greatest impact on local food security come to light by considering that it would seriously compromise the valleys, the only productive space in the province. For this reason, the assemblies concluded that Rio Negro could never have its own food plan with the devastated lands and the waters contaminated by intensive production for 20 years for China's supply (Vecinos autoconvocados, organizaciones sociales, y alumnos y exalumnos de la ESFA, s.f.).

La Paz-Estacas aqueduct and the irrigation in Mansoví Chico

The La Paz-Estacas Aqueduct and the Irrigation in Mandisoví Chico, in the north of Entre Ríos, was one of the agreements signed during President Xi Jinping's visit to Argentina in 2014. Its purpose was the execution of two projects by the Chinese State Construction and Engineering Corporation (CSCEC). On the one hand, the construction of an open-air aqueduct with water from Paraná River to irrigate La Paz department. On the other hand, the implementation of a collective irrigation system through the Uruguay River, located in the basin of the Mandisoví stream in Federation department. Both would operate from a main channel where water would be taken, pumping stations and distribution channels to the plots to be irrigated (Cámara de Diputados de la provincia de Entre Ríos, 2015). The project received 430 million dollars financing by the Industrial and Commercial Bank of China (ICBC).

However, the initiative would lead to land control by CSCEC. This is because the irrigation system installation allowed the company to obtain the domain and decision-making ability over 24,000 hectares in La Paz and

30,000 in Mandisoví Chico, with an influence over 90,000 and 150,000 hectares respectively (Cámara de Diputados de la provincia de Entre Ríos, 2015). It should be highlighted that in this case there was no explicit land transfers from the government or any other actor to CSCEC. Rather, this control was acquired indirectly, through the imposition of a top-down project, since it was formulated not only excluding the farmers and neighbor's opinions, but also the agreement was not published, so its technical details are unknown.

It is worth emphasizing that the control over 54,000 hectares acquired by CSCEC, which could be extended to the 240,000 hectares of the influence, was of primary importance for China's domestic food security. As noted, the goal of the initiative was the irrigation establishment to increase the production and cultivated area of certain crops. This would enable a transformation in land use towards China's food needs. In this regard, the CSCEC project was specifically aimed at facilitating the production of rice and citrus in Federation and soybeans in La Paz (PROSAP, 2010).

Over the last 20 years, Chinese population has doubled its rice consumption, although consumption in higher-income households has declined because of dietary change. Even though China is the world's largest producer and consumer of rice, its imports climbed from 575 000 tons to a record 3.3 million tons between 2011 and 2014 (United States Department of Agriculture, 2014). Among the causes of this import boom are logistical difficulties, health concerns, and the high domestic prices set by the government, which make it profitable to buy rice abroad for sale on local markets (Cui, 2013). Thus, China overtook Nigeria as the world's largest importer in 2013, generating severe governmental concerns (China Economic Review, 2014).

In addition, the nutritional transition prompted Chinese population, especially from urban areas, to increase their consumption of citrus fruits, which became part of the daily diet. In turn, demand for better quality fruit grew due to health concerns. The limited variety of fruits in China, the price and off-season demand promoted imports (USDA Foreign Agricultural Service, 2015).

Consequently, the initiative was consistent with China's investment strategy to ensure food security, because it allowed CSCEC to control land in Entre Rios for soybean, rice and citrus production. In this way, domestic supply would be guaranteed by avoiding market instability. For this purpose, as in Rio Negro, China gave a key role to production transport. A proof of this is the agreement signed by the province with Chinese investors in 2015 to reactivate Puerto Ibicuy and turn it into a multipurpose port. The works would be carried out by CSCEC. This is the deepest natural port in Entre Ríos, but it is inactive since its collapse in 2011. The province also agreed a Chinese investment in 200 hectares near the port to create an agro-industrial park (Assef, 2015).

The impact on local population food access differs widely from the benefits obtained by China. To begin with, this initiative would lead to the expulsion of La Paz small and medium-sized farmers from their lands in two ways. On the one hand, it would be a result of the difficulties in paying the aqueduct fee, the cost of water and other taxes because of the declining profitability of livestock farming, the main economic local activity. Moreover, as the department is characterized by the presence of slopes, to take water from the canal and spread it in the lands is require the installation of pumping stations, which represents an additional cost, as well as a high energy consumption (AIM, 2014). The payment pressure could lead small and medium scale rural economies to bankruptcy, and a foreseeable selling of lands (M'Biguá y otros, 2015: 68). What makes this forecast more feasible is that the project did not contemplate any financing to facilitate farmers' access to irrigation.

Land dispossession could also be a consequence of expropriations demanded to install irrigation (Ley 10.352, 2010). In particular, because after losing the economic unit, the small farmers would be forced to sell the rest of their plot (Multisectorial en defensa del patrimonio de los Entrerrianos, 2015b). In fact, official documents (PROSAP, 2009) acknowledge that La Paz aqueduct's canals were designed to run along the road shoulders, yet some sections are going to occupy private lands. In addition, agricultural land should be incorporated for the canals partial location, although the areas to be expropriated are unknown.

The land access loss by La Paz farmers undermines their right to food, since it restricts or even totally impedes the agricultural activities on which their livelihoods depends (De Schutter, 2009). Paradoxically, small and mid-sized holders were more vulnerable to this outcome. This is shown by the fact that only 28 producers of over 500 hectares were considered beneficiaries of the aqueduct (Concordia7, 2014), precisely those who had the financial capability to cover the irrigation cost. Meanwhile, the project neither guaranteed that benefits would reach small farmers, nor did it increase agricultural production and cultivated area (M'Biguá y otros, 2015). That's why the investment threatened the land and productive activities of 166 farmers who possess between 10 and 100 hectares and 64 producers between the 100 and 500 hectares scale, mostly dedicated to family farming. As in Rio Negro, this could force an exodus to the cities, increasing poverty and inequality.

It is important to note that indigenous peoples and environmental organizations pointed out that irrigation in Mandisoví Chico would lead to involuntary resettlements and population displacements. However, these claims had a lesser impact because, in addition to 56 large rice producers, who concentrate 130,500 of the hectares to be irrigated, 74 small citrus producers were included as beneficiaries of the project (PROSAP, 2011).

The damage to food security would be worsened by land use change. Although the government stressed that the project would boost agriculture in inactive and unproductive areas (Gobierno de Entre Ríos, 2014), this did not mean that the land was uninhabited, since a significant number of small and medium-size farmers lived there. Even without losing their lands, the activities of this sector would be displaced as a result of the conversion of land to soybean, rice and citrus production for export. The latter would affect specially to La Paz farmers dedicated to livestock and the production of soybeans, corn, flax, wheat, sunflower, sorghum and cotton for domestic consumption (PROSAP, 2010).

The local capacity to access food would also be undermined by the project environmental consequences. First, the advancement of agricultural production would affect the native forests that cover the irrigation area. This was extremely delicate in La Paz, where the last native provincial forest alternate with farmlands. For that reason, according to neighbors and social organizations, turning these lands into soybean production would require clearing, what would lead to a loss of biodiversity. They also warned that irrigation would deteriorate the soils, that are very susceptible to erosion (Laferriere, 2015), and the pollution caused for agrochemicals use. Similar impacts were observed in the Mandisoví Chico initiative. The organizations alerted on the scarce knowledge regarding the consequences of the provincial main water basins modification (Báez, 2017). An additional risk is that irrigation could compromise the minimum water flow needed by urban areas (Orduña, 2017).

In conclusion, CSCEC's land control seriously compromised the sustainability of the resources indispensable for food production in Entre Ríos, such as the soil, water resources, forests and biodiversity. It should be added that the stronger evidence that this plan only responded to China's food interests is that rains frequency and soil type made irrigation unnecessary (M'Biguá y otros, 2015).

Conclusion

Food security, defined in terms of self-sufficiency, is a top priority for the Chinese government. Nevertheless, this article showed that the combination of natural resource scarcity and depletion with rising food demand became a serious obstacle to its fulfillment. After the global food crisis of 2008, China was forced to invest in land abroad to secure its food supply, hence it actively participated in the global land grabbing.

The two Chinese initiatives in Argentina studied clearly show that land investments were directly aimed at strengthening the power's food security. In the first place, the execution of the projects would enabled Chinese companies to acquire control over vast areas of agricultural lands close to major rivers, in order to transform its use towards the production of first concern crops for China. Thus, as it was exposed, 257,505 hectares of Rio Negro valleys transferred to Beidahuang would be destined to the cultivation of soybeans. Similarly, the 54,000 hectares in Entre Ríos controlled by CSCEC, once irrigation was incorporated, would be transformed into rice, citrus and soybean production. The importance that in both cases was assigned to port infrastructure improvement only confirms that China would be the final destination of these commodities.

Consequently, the cases highlights that land grabbing do not represent a direct contradiction to the goal of self-sufficiency that guides China's food security strategy. This is because the offshoring of domestic agricultural production to controlled lands overseas provides China a stable access to food while staying away from market intermediation. Although it now depends on foreign lands, the food of its population is not exposed to price fluctuations or the commodity producers and global traders' decisions.

In this regard, Cox's perspective brings to light that despite China's initiatives reproduce the consensus around land investments as the most appropriate mechanism to guarantee food security, which strengthens the hegemonic agricultural model, they simultaneously open a possibility for transformation. This is the result of social reactions and resistances, which revealed the widening asymmetries in food security between China and the provinces, thereby contributing to the erosion of local support for the projects. In both cases, small and mid-size holders were exposed to the eviction from lands essential as a source of livelihood. In addition, the shift in land use towards commodity production would displace traditional crops production. In short, by impeding the continuity of agricultural activities, both initiatives would seriously restricted local population access to healthy and nutritious food.

This situation would be exacerbated by the environmental impacts associated with large-scale intensive production over a long period of time to meet China's food demand. These includes deforestation and biodiversity loss due to the agricultural frontier expansion, soil deterioration, excessive water consumption and pollution caused for agrochemicals use. As a result, the projects would seriously compromise the natural resources indispensable for agricultural production, which could profoundly and irreversibly damage local food security. This would also undermine the local population ability to decide on their own food programs and strategies.

References

AIM (2014, march 24). Acueductos: una mirada crítica sobre las prioridades de La Paz.

Anseeuw, W; Boche, M; Breu, T.; Giger, M.; Lay, J.; Messerli, P.; & Nolte, K. (2012). Transnational Land Deals for Agriculture in the Global South. *Analytical Report based on the Land Matrix Database.* Bern/Montpellier/Hamburg: CDE/CIRAD/GIGA.

Aranea, H. y otros (2011). *Acción de Amparo.* Superior Tribunal de Justicia de Río Negro.

Asseff, A. (2015). Pedido de informes al Poder Ejecutivo sobre diversas cuestiones asociadas al Puerto multipropósito de Ibicuy-Entre Ríos-y diversas cuestiones conexas. Cámara de Diputados de la Nación.

Baéz, J (2017, july 19). *Rechazan el acueducto Mandisoví Chico.* La nota digital. 2017-07-19. Retrieved june 15, 2020 from https://lanotadigital.com.ar/2017/07/19/rechazan-el-aceducto-mandisovi-chico/.

Beidahuang Group & Gobierno de Río Negro (2010a). Acuerdo de Cooperación para el Proyecto de Inversión Agro Alimenticio entre Heilongjiang Beidahuang State Farms Business Trade Group CO., LTD y el Gobierno de la Provincia de Rio Negro. Harbin, Heilongjiang, 15 de Octubre.

Beidahuang Group, & Gobierno de Río Negro (2010b). Convenio de Cooperación para la presentación de una propuesta de inversión para la instalación de una nueva terminal portuaria en el área del Puerto de San Antonio Este. Harbin, Heilongjiang, 15 de Octubre.

Beidahuang Group, & Gobierno de Río Negro (2010c). Anexo del convenio N° 101016 (2010). Harbin, Heilongjiang, 16 de Octubre.

Borras, S. & Franco, J. (2012). Global Land Grabbing and Trajectories of Agrarian Change: A Preliminary Analysis. *Journal of Agrarian Change, 12* (1), 34–59.

Borras, S., Franco, J., Gomez, S., Kay, C. y Spoor, M. (2012). Land grabbing in Latin America and the Caribbean. *The Journal of Peasant Studies, 39*(3–4), 845–872.

Brautigam, D. (2015). *Will Africa feed China?* New York: Oxford University Press.

Cámara de Diputados de la provincia de Entre Ríos (2015). Versión taquigráfica. 2° sesión de prórroga, 20 de enero de 2015.

Cheng G. & Zhang H. (2014). China's global agricultural strategy: an open system to safeguard the country's food security. S. Rajaratnam School of International Studies, Singapur. Working Paper N°282.

China Economic Review (2014, January 15). Beijing has rice to go around, but that might not be enough. Retrieved march 10, 2020 from http://www.chinaeco nomicreview.com/china-grain-policy-rice-imports-self-sufficiency.

Concordia 7 (2014). Acueductos, de 92 a 300 millones. Retrieved october 7, 2018 from http://concordia7.com/acueductos-de-92-a-300-millones.

Cooperativa de San Javier (2010, december 15). *Mega Proyecto de desarrollo en Potenciales Áreas bajo riego.*

Cotula, L.; Vermeulen, S.; Leonard, R. & Keely, J. (2009*). Land grab or development opportunity? Agricultural Investment and International Land Deals in Africa.* Londres/Roma: IIED/FAO/IFAD.

Cox, R. (2002). Civil society at the turn of the millennium: prospects for an alternative world order. In R. Cox, & M. Schechter, *Political economy of a plural world: Critical reflections on power, morals and civilization* (pp. 96–117). London: Routledge.

Cox, R. (1993). Gramsci, hegemony and international relations: an essay in method. In S. Gill, *Gramsci Historical Materialism and International Relations* (pp. 49–66). New York: Cambridge University Press.

Cox, R. (1992). Multilateralism and World Order. *Review of International Studies, 18*(2), 161–180.

Cui, C. (2013, january 11). Las importaciones de China sacuden el mercado del arroz. *The Wall Street Journal.*

De Schutter, O. (2011). How not to think of land-grabbing: three critiques of large-scale investments in farmland. *The Journal of Peasant Studies, 38*(2): 249–279.

De Schutter, O. (2009). *El derecho a la alimentación.* Informe especial del Relator sobre el Derecho a la alimentación. Consejo de Derechos Humanos. Asamblea General de Naciones Unidas. 13° período de sesiones.

Deininger, K.; Byerlee, D.; Lindsay, J.; Norton, A.; Selod, H.; Sticker, M. (2011). *Rising global interest in farmland. Can it yield sustainable and equitable benefits?* Washington D.C.: The World Bank.

FAO (2012). *Dinámicas del mercado de la tierra en América Latina y el Caribe: concentración y extranjerización.* Roma: FAO.

FAO & MOA (2012). *Country Programming Framework 2012–2015 for People's Republic of China.* Beijing: FAO y MOA.

Finnin, M. (2016). *Food Security in India, China, and the World*. Institute for Defense Analyses. IDA Document D-5823.

FUNAM. (2010). Soja. China y Rio Negro hacen acuerdo ilegal. *Gacetilla de Prensa*.

Fundación Uñopatun. (2011). *Informe para la Prensa*.12 de septiembre.

Gale, F., Hansen, J., & Jewison, M. (2015). *China's Growing Demand for Agricultural Imports*. Economic Information Bulletin. N° 136.

García Guerrero, L. y Wahren, J. (2016). Seguridad Alimentaria vs. Soberanía Alimentaria: La cuestión Alimentaria y el modelo del agronegocio en la Argentina. *Trabajo y Sociedad, (26)*: 327–340.

Gobierno de Entre Ríos (2014, april 1). Una delegación de China State visitó el lugar de los emplazamientos de los acueductos entrerrianos. Secretaría de Prensa y Comunicación.

Gooch, E. y Gale, F. (2018). China's Foreign Agriculture Investments, EIB-192, US Department of Agriculture, Economic Research Service.

GRAIN (2008). Se adueñan de la tierra! El proceso de acaparamiento agrario por seguridad alimentaria y de negocios en 2008. *Documentos de Análisis*. Retrieved from http://www.grain.org/briefings/?id=214.

GRAIN. (2016). Annexe 1. Land deals 2016. In *The farmland grab in 2016: how big? how bad?* Retrieved from https://www.grain.org/article/entries/5492-the-global-farmland-grab-in-2016-how-big-how-bad.

Gras C. y Cáceres, D. (2017). El acaparamiento de tierras como proceso dinámico. Las estrategias de los actores en contextos de estancamiento económico. *Población & Sociedad, 24* (2):163–194.

Hairong, Y., Yiyuan, C., & Bun, K. H. (2016). China's soybean crisis: the logic of modernization and its discontents. *The Journal of Peasant Studies, 43*(2).

Hofman, I., & Ho, P. (2012). China's "Developmental Outsourcing": A critical examination of Chinese global "land grabs" discourse. *Journal of Peasant Studies, 39*(1), 1–48.

IProfesional (2010, october 25). China invierte u$s20 M en Río Negro para asegurarse alimentos. Retrieved from www.iprofesional.com/notas/106268-China-invierte-us20-M-en-Rio-Negro-para-asegurarse-alimentos---para.

Laferriere, L. (2015). Acueductos ¿otra gran estafa al pueblo entrerriano?. *Programa de Extensión Por Una Nueva Economía. Universidad Nacional de Entre Ríos*.

LANDMATRIX (2020). Retrieved june 15, 2020 from https://landmatrix.org/en/get-the-idea/web-transnational-deals/.

Laufer, R. (2019). La asociación estratégica Argentina-China y la política de Beijing hacia América Latina. *Cuadernos del CEL*, 4(7): 74–108.

Laufer, R. (2017). Argentina y su asociación estratégica con China en la era Kirchner. *Análisis y Pensamiento Iberoamericano sobre China. Observatorio de Política China*, (22): 4–24.

Leff, E. (2004). *Racionalidad ambiental: la apropiación social de la naturaleza.* México: Siglo XXI Editores.

Ley 10.352 de la provincia de Entre Ríos. B.O. N° 25.625-018/15, Paraná, 28 de enero de 2015.

M'Biguá y otros (2015), *Demanda presentada ante el Superior Tribunal de Justicia de Entre Ríos.*

McMichael P. (2009). A food regime genealogy. *The Journal of Peasant Studies*, 36(1), 139–169.

Ministry of Agriculture and Rural Affairs of the People's Republic of China (2017). Agriculture in China I. Retrieved June 15, 2020 from http://english.agri. gov.cn/overview/201703/t20170301_247341.htm.

Multisectorial en defensa del patrimonio de los Entrerrianos (2015). La Multisectorial La Paz, marchará a Paraná contra los acueductos. Retrieved june 15, 2020 from http://www.elojomiradordelapaz.com.ar/2015/04/la-multisector ial-la-paz-marchara.html.

National Bureau of Statistics of China (2018). *China Statistical Yearbook 2018.* Beijing: China Statistics Press.

Nolte, K.; Chamberlain, W.; Giger, M. (2016). *International Land Deals for Agriculture. Fresh insights from the Land Matrix: Analytical Report II.* LAND-MATRIX. CDE/CIRAD/GIGA/University of Pretoria.

OCDE & FAO. (2018). *OECD-FAO Agricultural Outlook 2018–2027.* Rome/Paris: OECD Publishing/FAO.

OCDE, CEPAL y CAF (2015). *Perspectivas económicas de América Latina 2016: Hacia una nueva asociación con China.* Paris: OECD Publishing.

Orduña, H. (2017, September 11). Severo cuestionamiento al proyecto de canal Mandisoví. Retrieved from http://www.fundavida.org.ar/web2.0/severo-cuestionamiento-al-proyecto-del-canal-mandisovi/.

Premici, S. (2011, august 25). *China desembarca en Río Negro.* Página 12. Retrieved from http://www.pagina12.com.ar/diario/economia/2-175267-2011-08-25. html.

PROSAP (2011). *Proyecto de sistematización y distribución de agua para riego Mandisoví Chico.* Documento de factibilidad.

PROSAP (2010). *Acueducto La Paz—Estacas, Provincia de Entre Ríos*. Componente Ambiental. Informe de Avance.

PROSAP (2009). *Formulario perfil del proyecto. Estudio de Acueducto del Norte Entrerriano-Acueducto La Paz-Estacas*. Paraná.

Río Negro (2011a, may 22). Chinos empezarán con trigo en Río Negro. Retrieved from http://www.rionegro.com.ar/portada/chinos-empezaran-con-trigo-en-rio-negro-NVRN_628126.

Río Negro (2011, august 25). Incidentes en la presentación de convenio con China. Retrieved from http://www.rionegro.com.ar/portada/incidentes-en-present acion-de-convenio-con-china-JFRN_692568.

Saguier, M. (2010). En el banquillo de los acusados: Empresas transnacionales y violaciones de derechos humanos en América Latina. *Revista de Negocios internacionales, 3*(3), 116–153.

Smaller, C; Wei, Q & Yalan, L. (2012). Farmland and Water: China invests abroad. *IISD Report*. Manitoba, Canada: International Institute for Sustainable Development.

State Council of the People's Republic of China (2019). Food Security in China.

Teubal, M. (2006). Soja transgénica y la crisis del modelo agroalimentario argentino. *Realidad Económica* (220):71–96.

The Economist (2009, may 21). Buying farmland abroad: Outsourcing's third wave. Retrieved from http://www.economist.com/node/13692889.

Toulmin, C; Brindraban, P; Borras, S.; Mwangi, E.; Sauer, S. (2011). *Tenencia de la tierra e inversiones internacionales en agricultura. Informe del grupo de expertos de alto nivel sobre seguridad alimentaria y nutrición del Comité de Seguridad Alimentaria Mundial*. Roma.

United States Department of Agriculture (2014). *Rice Yearbook 2014*. Economic Research Service.

USDA Foreing Agricultural Service, (2015), 2015 Citrus Annual Report. People's Republic of China.

Vecinos autoconvocados organizaciones sociales, & alumnos y exalumnos de la ESFA. (s.f.). *Sí a la soberanía territorial y alimentaria. Sí a la vida y sí a la biodiversidad.*

Vidal, J. (2012, march 7). *How food and water are driving a 21st-century african land grab*. Retrieved from https://www.theguardian.com/environment/2010/mar/07/food-water-africa-land-grab.

Zha, D. & Zhang, H. (2013). Food in China's international relations. *The Pacific Review* 5 (26): 455–479.

Zhang, J. (2019). Beyond the 'hidden agricultural revolution' and 'China's overseas land investment': Main trends in China's agriculture and food sector. *Journal of Contemporary China, 28*(119), 746–762.

Zhang, H. y Cheng, G. (2016). China's Food Security Strategy Reform: An emerging global agricultural policy. In F. Wu y H. Zhang (Eds), *China's Global Quest for Resources. Energy, Food and Water* (pp. 23–41). Londres: Routledge.

Editora
UFPB

ibidem.eu